GREEN SHIPPING CONTRACTS

This book applies a contract-governance theory to the implementation of decarbonisation objectives in the international maritime sector.

In doing so, it provides an overview of how the network of contractual relationships that characterise commercial shipping can become effective sites of collaboration between shipping actors to improve upon energy efficiency and CO_2 reduction.

To achieve this aim, the book investigates and develops a set of contractual tools that can enable private actors to strengthen their commitments to net-zero targets (whether state-mandated or voluntary) and develop cooperative norms to guide decision-making and contractual interpretation. These mechanisms include contractual clauses and drafting considerations which can secure a desired outcome for contractual performance, thereby managing climate risks and providing adequate remedy where such risks materialise.

In a transnational sector such as shipping, where contracts can exert greater influence on corporate decarbonisation efforts than international regulation, the book challenges the traditional limitations of contract law and calls for a deeper integration of green principles into private relationships.

Green Shipping Contracts

A Contract Governance Approach to Achieving Decarbonisation in the Shipping Sector

Pia Rebelo

•HART•

OXFORD • LONDON • NEW YORK • NEW DELHI • SYDNEY

HART PUBLISHING

Bloomsbury Publishing Plc

Kemp House, Chawley Park, Cumnor Hill, Oxford, OX2 9PH, UK

1385 Broadway, New York, NY 10018, USA

29 Earlsfort Terrace, Dublin 2, Ireland

HART PUBLISHING, the Hart/Stag logo, BLOOMSBURY and the Diana logo are trademarks of Bloomsbury Publishing Plc

First published in Great Britain 2024

A catalogue record for this book is available from the British Library.

Library of Congress Cataloging-in-Publication data

Names: Rebelo, Pia, author.

Title: Green shipping contracts : a contract governance approach to achieving decarbonisation in the shipping sector / Pia Rebelo.

Description: Oxford ; New York : Hart Publishing, 2024. | Includes bibliographical references and index. | Summary: "This book evaluates the ways in which maritime transactions can achieve global decarbonisation targets in accordance with contract governance theory. The chapters cover a wide spectrum of considerations and external influences on shipping contracts to enhance the effectiveness of green terms. In a transnational sector such as shipping, where contracts can exert greater influence on corporate decarbonisation efforts than international regulation, the book challenges the traditional limitations of contract law and calls for deeper integration of green principles into private relationships"—Provided by publisher.

Identifiers: LCCN 2024014210 (print) | LCCN 2024014211 (ebook) | ISBN 9781509967926 (hardback) | ISBN 9781509967964 (paperback) | ISBN 9781509967933 (epub) | ISBN 9781509967940 (ebook)

Subjects: LCSH: Maritime law. | Contracts, Maritime. | Charter-parties. | Carbon dioxide mitigation—Law and legislation. | Carbon sequestration—Law and legislation. | Greenhouse gas mitigation—Law and legislation. | Bills of lading. | Freight and freightage. | Shipping.

Classification: LCC K1155 .R425 2024 (print) | LCC K1155 (ebook) | DDC 343.09/68—dc23/eng/20240402

LC record available at https://lccn.loc.gov/2024014210

LC ebook record available at https://lccn.loc.gov/2024014211

ISBN: HB: 978-1-50996-792-6
ePDF: 978-1-50996-794-0
ePub: 978-1-50996-793-3

Typeset by Compuscript Ltd, Shannon

To find out more about our authors and books visit www.hartpublishing.co.uk. Here you will find extracts, author information, details of forthcoming events and the option to sign up for our newsletters.

CONTENTS

ABBREVIATIONS

AfDB	African Development Bank
ADB	Asian Development Bank
AER	annual efficiency ratio
ASI	Avoid-Shift-Improve
BAF	bunker adjustment factor
BIMCO	Baltic and International Maritime Council
BRI	Belt and Road Initiative (China)
BWM	Ballast Water Management
CBI	Climate Bonds Initiative
CFA	Charter of Fundamental Rights (EU)
CLC	International Convention on Civil liability for Oil Pollution Damages
CoA	Contract of Affreightment
COP	Conference of the Parties
CISG	Convention on Contracts for the International Sale of Goods
CO	carbon monoxide
CO_2	carbon dioxide
CSR	corporate social responsibility
ECA	emission control area
EEISS	Energy Efficiency Investment Sharing Scheme
EIB	European Investment Bank
EOL	end of life
EP	Equator Principle
EPFIs	Equator Principles Financial Institutions
ESG	Environmental and Social Governance

ETC	Energy Transitions Commission (UK)
EU	European Union
EU ETS	European Union Emission Trading Scheme
EU SSR	EU Ship Recycling Regulation
FCA	Financial Conduct Authority
FONAR	Fuel Oil Non-Availability Report
GAFTA	Grain and Feed Trade Association
GBP	Green Bond Principles
gCO_2/dwt-nm	grams of CO_2 per deadweight ton-nautical mile
GHG	greenhouse gas emissions
GPCC	General Provisions of the Civil Law of the People's Republic of China
GTAG	Green Technical Advisory Group
GSIA	Global Sustainable Investment Alliance
H&M	hull and machinery
HSFO	high sulphur fuel oil
ICMA	International Capital Market Association
ICS	International Chamber of Shipping
IDFC	International Finance Development Finance Club
IHM	inventory of hazardous materials
ILO	International Labour Organization
IMCO	Inter-Governmental Maritime Consultative Organization
IMO	International Maritime Organization
IMRB/F	International Maritime Research Fund
IWG	Industry Working Group (CBI)
INTERCARGO	International Association of Dry Cargo Shipowners
INTERTANKO	International Association of Independent Tanker Owners
IPIECA	International Petroleum Industry Environmental Conservation Association IPIECA
ISO	International Organization for Standardization Specifications

ITC	International Trade Centre
LDCs	least developed countries
LLMC	Convention for Limitation of Maritime Claims
LOT	load on top
MARPOL 73/78	The International Convention for the Prevention of Pollution from Ships, 1973 as modified by the Protocol of 1978
MDBs	multilateral development banks
MIA	Marine Insurance Act 1906
MoS	motorways of the sea
MSC	Maritime Safety Committee (IMO)
MSC	Mediterranean Shipping Company
NOx	nitrous oxides
OCIMF	Oil Companies International Marine Forum
ODS	ozone depleting substances
OECD	Organisation for Economic Co-operation and Development
OILPOL	Convention for the Prevention of Pollution of the Sea by Oil 1954
PRoC	People's Republic of China
PM	particulate matter
PFOS	perfluorooctane sulfonic acid
PPFI	Poseidon Principles for Financial Institutions
PPMI	Poseidon Principles for Marine Insurance
P&I	protection and indemnity
RSRS	Responsible Ship Recycling Standards
SAYS	Save as You Sail
SBG	Sustainability Bond Guidelines
SBP	Social Bond Principles
SCC	standardised covenant clauses
SCMP	Subcommittee on Marine Pollution
SD	sustainable development
SDGs	sustainable development goals

SECAs	Sulphur Emission Control Areas
SFFSM	self-financing fuel-saving mechanism
SIDs	Small Island Developing States
SLL	sustainability linked loan
SMTS	Sustainable Maritime Transport System
SOLAS	International Convention for the Safety of Life at Sea
SOx	sulphur oxides
SPT	Sustainability Performance Target
SSI	Sustainable Shipping Initiative
TAC	Type Approval Certificate
TCDF	Task Force on Climate-related Financial Disclosures (UK)
TCL	total constructive loss
TEG	Technical Working Group on Sustainable Finance (EU)
TEN-T	Trans-European Transport Network
TFEU	Treaty on the Functioning of the European Union
TWG	Shipping Technical Working Group (CBI)
UCC	Uniform Commercial Code (US)
UCTA	Unfair Contract Terms Act 1977
UK	United Kingdom
UMAS	University Maritime Advisory Services
UN	United Nations
UNCLOS	United Nations Law of the Sea Convention
UNCTAD	United Nations Conference on Trade and Development
UNEP	United Nations Environment Programme
UNFCC	The United Nations Framework Convention on Climate Change
UNGC	United Nations Global Compact
USA	United States of America
VOC	volatile organic compounds
WHO	World Health Organization
WSC	World Shipping Council

TABLE OF CASES

English Cases

International Cases

INTERNATIONAL MARITIME ORGANIZATION DOCUMENTS

Assembly Resolutions

MEPC Resolutions

IMO Submissions and Reports

INTERNATIONAL TREATIES AND INSTRUMENTS

UK LEGISLATION

INTERNATIONAL STATUTES

EUROPEAN UNION LAW

Treaties and Protocol

Directives

Regulations

1

Contract Governance and Sustainable Shipping

Shipping remains the world's most sustainable method of transport and is far more energy-efficient than road, rail, or air. Yet, if the international maritime industry continues on its present trajectory, it will hamper the objectives of the Paris Agreement.[1] This statement may seem unfair given that shipping and aviation were largely exempted from the Paris Agreement, being considered domains requiring their own international instruments.[2] Yet despite these exemptions, work in the aviation sector has progressed far more rapidly, whilst shipping only started to pay attention to carbon emissions in 2011.[3] Due to increasing trade flows and predicted growth in the maritime transport sector, shipping's impact on the environment has become increasingly scrutinised, with criticism of the International Maritime Organization (IMO) mounting for not effectively regulating on greenhouse gases.[4]

The IMO's latest 2023 Strategy on Reduction of Greenhouse Gas (GHG) Emissions from Ships ('2023 GHG Strategy') sets new targets aiming for a 20 per cent reduction in emissions by 2030, a 70 per cent reduction by 2040 (compared to 2008 levels), and ultimately net-zero by 2050.[5] These targets reflect progress, but there are still concerns that present short-term measures and candidate mid-term measures may not achieve the below 1.5°C temperature goal. Although the regulatory agenda is a necessary impetus for driving a green shipping transition, the IMO itself has recognised that achieving a sustainable maritime transport system will require the enrolment of various actors – state and non-state – for pluralistic governance solutions.[6] These actors include a number of stakeholders: investors, banks,

[1] *Fourth IMO Greenhouse Gas Study Full Report* (MEPC 75/7/15) 2020; Erik Rosaeg, 'The Aviation and Shipping Exemptions in the Paris Agreement on Climate Change' (2021) 27 *Journal of International Maritime Law* 55.

[2] Rosaeg (n 1) 56.

[3] The First IMO GHG Study was conducted in 2000, yet the first energy-efficiency measures were enforced in 2013, with transitional periods and limited application to certain vessels.

[4] Bernd Hackmann, 'Analysis of the Governance Architecture to Regulate GHG Emissions from InternationalShipping' (2012) 12 *International Environmental Agreements: Politics, Law and Economics* 85.

[5] Resolution MEPC.377(80).

[6] IMO, *Concept of a Sustainable Maritime Transport System* (Symposium on Sustainable Maritime Transportation System, World Maritime Day on 26 September 2013).

shipowners, shipbuilders, charterers, bunker suppliers, classification societies, marine insurers and even consumers. A number of private governance initiatives have emerged from these various stakeholder groups fuelled by corporate social responsibility (CSR) commitments and accompanying risk management strategies. Significant industry innovations and efforts are being employed to supplement and support the IMO's regulatory framework, and this culmination of efforts is bridging the public/private divide to converge economic and environmental interests.

However, one key regulatory tool has been left out of the sustainable development discussion more generally, and is even more noticeably absent from the green shipping package of solutions: *contractual measures*. Commercial contracts and the contribution of contract governance approaches to implementing both public and private sustainability initiatives have been largely neglected as areas for research and intervention. Yet the effectiveness of both state-led and private measures are highly dependent on contractual implementation for governing the behaviour of shipping actors and for enforcing a set of green standards.

The primary aim of this book is to address this research gap by applying a contract governance approach to achieving a green transition in the shipping sector. Contract governance as a theory is explored more fully below in section II; in brief, it asserts the notion that contracts *are governed* and contracts *can govern*. Maritime contracts are notoriously traditional and are not ordinarily used to achieve non-commercial objectives. However, commercial objectives are becoming more difficult to separate from climate objectives as all actors are having to both mitigate and adapt to the 'super wicked' problem of climate change.[7] It is also becoming increasingly clear that the principles of English common law, the dominant regime for maritime transactions, is not always well suited to pursuing environmental sustainability and climate objectives.

This book is therefore contextualised within a greater debate about contractual formalism versus the modernisation of contract law to achieve sustainable development. This includes conversations on whether contract law should be used for the attainment of environmental justice and its more niche subset, climate justice; while related debates involve contracting for social justice and the protection and realisation of human rights. Within this wider contract law research agenda, this book specifically evaluates existing maritime contracts to investigate and develop mechanisms to overcome the problems associated with contracting for climate change mitigation – ie GHG emissions reduction and net-zero. This is done within the context of ship finance (chapter two), shipbuilding and ship sales (chapter three), chartering (chapter four), and more briefly, other maritime transactions which are soon to be 'greened' and how technology can enable progress in this regard (chapter five).

[7] 'Super wicked' problems arise out of complex socio-economic, political and environmental factors such as climate change, which poses a grave threat for human rights. See Iain D. Cross and Alina Congreve, 'Teaching (super) wicked problems: authentic learning about climate change' (2021) 45 *Journal of Geography in Higher Education* 491, 491.

This first chapter is concerned with contextualising the purpose of this book within the greater milieu of global GHG regulation, pluralistic governance solutions, and contract law theories. It starts by addressing the public law mandate for decarbonising shipping on an international scale and also looks at noteworthy regional efforts such as those seen at the European Union (section I). This is done with a view to illustrating why pluralistic forms of governance are required to achieve the objectives of the regulatory framework and how commercial contracts comprise a key tool for climate governance (section II). Finally, this chapter outlines its key premise that permeates all subsequent discussions: the promotion of a normative green agenda in shipping contracts that bridges the public/private regulatory divide for climate governance through contract law (section III).

These discussions inform the overall purpose of this book: to identify how contractual mechanisms can *facilitate* a desired outcome – namely achieving a green transition in shipping. It looks at the major commercial phases of a vessel's life span and assesses the dominant *agreements* and *forms* used to negotiate and implement a set of net-zero objectives. It then sets out to analyse a range of contractual techniques, both those currently employed and those which should be introduced, to achieve a behavioural shift in how private actors perform their contractual obligations. The purpose here is two-fold: 1) to create a principled change in mind-set and a convergence of objects centred on 'green' or 'climate' norms;[8] and 2) to present tangible legal remedies for accountability. Private law can provide a bottom-up set of contractual strategies which can work within the public regulatory landscape to offer actors a greater set of protections and control over their green transitions – especially where the public law regime presents enforcement gaps and exposes private actors to increased risk.

I. The Decarbonisation Mandate in Shipping

Rather than promote a purely contractual approach, contract governance can more holistically consider a synergistic and pluralistic approach to climate governance in the shipping sector. This book recognises the role of state-led regulation, particularly as a source of legitimate norms and targets, *as well as* the contribution of a myriad of non-state actors who make decarbonisation decisions in everyday *market transactions*. Academic scholarship on environmental governance of the shipping sector has heavily criticised the IMO as 'no longer fit for the task as they reflect a national domination of jurisdictional integrity that is inappropriate for an increasingly global shipping industry'.[9] In 2015, Lister, Poulsen and Pont

[8] 'Green' refers to the broader agenda of environmental sustainability, while 'climate' is focused on climate change mitigation and GHG reductions.

[9] Michael Roe, 'Maritime Governance and Policy-Making: The Need for Process Rather than Form' (2013) 29 *The Asian Journal of Shipping and Logistics* 167, 170.

contended that, 'with the exception of oil spills, regulatory development has stalled with respect to all of the major issue areas including CO_2 and other emissions, and invasive species'.[10] Even after the IMO's recent decarbonisation work, similar frustrations were communicated from environmental interests regarding the IMO's latest 2023 GHG Strategy as not going far enough.[11]

This chapter argues that despite the IMO's expanding environmental governance mandate, it cannot be practically tasked with the sole responsibility for a sectoral energy transition that must employ a number of governance tools.[12] In order for it to operate as such, it would have to be something that it is not: a super-state structure like the European Union, which can mandate a number of controls over all aspects of its regional market whilst being able to allocate funds accordingly.[13] The effectiveness of the IMO's environmental protection efforts are not only dependent on the outcome of meaningful negotiation, but the willingness and capacity of both states and industry actors alike to take up the environmental mandate.

On the other hand, 'the industry' perspective of environmental governance has been largely portrayed as a unified non-progressive voice in opposition to the green shift.[14] The number of private initiatives and innovations aimed at achieving net-zero, as expounded upon in upcoming chapters (from green finance to industry-led platforms), provides contrary evidence for such a polarised view and notes that this view is an oversimplification of the green shipping narrative. From a *contract governance* perspective, the nuances of the IMO's decarbonisation mandate and the implementation of its strategies can serve to identify gaps in effective climate governance.

This book does not assert that decarbonisation of international shipping is ungovernable from a public law perspective; rather, that top-down law making should be *supplemented* by private law mechanisms to manage a set of competing interests and effectively implement solutions. This section looks at the international

[10] Jane Lister, René Taudal Poulsen and Stefano Ponte, 'Orchestrating Transnational Environmental Governance in Maritime Shipping' (2015) 34 *Global Environmental Change* 185. One exception is Md Saiful Karim, who argues that the IMO 'has not only promoted the adoption of numerous international marine environmental legal instruments, but also gradually established well-functioning institutional structures for marine environmental protection'; furthermore, many of its shortcomings are not due to deficiencies in the work processes of the organisation, but are 'related to broad international politics underpinning relations between States'; see Md Saiful Karim, *Prevention of Pollution of the Marine Environment from Vessels: The Potential and Limits of the International Maritime Organisation* (Springer, 2015) 152–53. See also Transparency International, 'Governance at the International Maritime Organization: The case for Reform (Report, July 2018), www.transparency.org/en/publications/governance-international-maritime-organisation.

[11] For example, Clean Artic Alliance, 'MEPC 80: IMO Becoming a Serial Procrastinator on Black Carbon Emissions' (7 July 2023, Press Release), cleanarctic.org/2023/07/07/mepc-80-imo-becoming-a-serial-procrastinator-on-black-emissions.

[12] Something which the IMO's critics rather ironically argue it should do, despite noting its failure in public law governance; see Lister, Taudal Poulsen and Ponte (n 10) 193.

[13] Various initiatives of the EU are addressed in forthcoming sections as examples of comprehensive public–private law making.

[14] See InfluenceMap, 'Corporate Capture of the IMO: How shipping lobbies to stay out of the Paris Agreement on climate' (October 2017), influencemap.org/site/data/000/302/Shipping_Report_October_2017.pdf.

law impetus for decarbonising the sector, whilst section II identifies pluralistic forms of governance to illustrate how contract governance approaches can assist with issues of implementation and enforcement.

A. International Regime: International Maritime Organization

Nowadays, there is a strong *legal basis* for the protection of the marine environment. Article 192 of the United Nations Law of the Sea Convention (UNCLOS)[15] places a general obligation on states to protect and preserve the marine environment. States are also obligated to adopt all measures consistent with UNCLOS that are 'necessary to prevent, reduce and control pollution of the marine environment from any source, using for this purpose the best practicable means at their disposal and in accordance with their capabilities'.[16] Article 211 of UNCLOS specifically deals with vessel-source pollution and provides that states, through the IMO, 'shall establish international rules and standards to prevent, reduce and control pollution of the marine environment from vessels', as well as adopt appropriate routeing systems to minimise and prevent accidents which might cause pollution to the marine environment and coastline, or damage to related interests. There is thus a strong international environmental law foundation for a vessel-source pollution law framework which is bolstered by a number of normative principles such as the 'polluter pays', the 'precautionary approach',[17] and 'sustainable development'.[18] Increased environmental regulation in all major industry sectors is occurring quite rapidly, and the IMO is under increasing pressure from environmental lobbyists to strengthen its hard law approach to reduce environmental threats from shipping.[19]

In April 2018, the IMO's Marine Environmental Protection Committee (MEPC) confirmed its vision to reduce GHG emissions from shipping in adopting an initial strategy to phase out GHG emissions this century.[20] In this Initial IMO Strategy on Reduction of GHG Emissions From Ships, the MEPC outlined levels of ambition and guiding principles which it considers a 'first milestone' in developing a comprehensive Strategy or 'Roadmap' on reduction of GHG emissions from the sector.[21] Under identified 'levels of ambition', the IMO's initial strategy was

[15] UN General Assembly, *Convention on the Law of the Sea* (10 December 1982) 1833 UNTS 399 (UNCLOS).

[16] Art 194, Convention of the Law of the Sea.

[17] For a formulation of the precautionary approach see Principle 15 of the 1992 Rio Declaration on Environment and Development.

[18] Sustainable Development is defined by the ICJ in *GabCikovo-Nagymaros Project (HungarylSlovakia)*, Judgment, ICJ Reports 1997, 7.

[19] Harilaos N Psaraftis and Christos A Kontovas, 'Influence and transparency at the IMO: the name of the game' (2020) 22 *Maritime Economics & Logistics* 151.

[20] IMO, 'Cutting GHG emissions from shipping – 10 years of mandatory rules', (2021), www.imo.org/en/MediaCentre/PressBriefings/pages/DecadeOfGHGAction.aspx.

[21] Resolution MEPC.304(72) (adopted on 13 April 2018). The Roadmap for developing a comprehensive IMO Strategy on reduction of GHG emissions from ships (the Roadmap) was approved at MEPC 70.

for GHG emissions to peak as soon as possible and to then reduce total annual GHG emissions from the sector by at least 50 per cent by 2050 in comparison with 2008, whilst still driving strong efforts to phase them out completely. This Initial Strategy also included working towards an improvement to the existing energy efficiency regulatory requirements to be agreed upon and implemented between 2018 and 2023. At the time, the IMO's technical measure was the Energy Efficiency Design Index (EEDI), which became mandatory for new ships in 2011, whilst the Ship Energy Efficiency Management Plan (SEEMP) was made mandatory for all ships at MEPC 62 (July 2011).[22] This regulation was the first legally binding climate change treaty to be adopted since the Kyoto Protocol and the first GHG standard for shipping. The EEDI is a performance-based mechanism aimed at reducing carbon emissions from fuel usage and leaves the choice of technologies and specific ship design to the industry. Granted that the energy efficiency level is attained, ship designers and builders had free reign in sourcing and using the most cost-efficient solutions in order to comply with the regulations.

The IMO's Fourth Greenhouse Gas Study, published in August 2020, showed that shipping's share of global anthropogenic emissions increased from 2.76 per cent in 2012 to 2.89 per cent in 2018.[23] This sparked renewed impetus to build upon the mandatory energy efficiency requirements to further reduce greenhouse gas emissions from shipping by agreeing to new draft mandatory measures. The amendments were developed by the seventh session of the Intersessional Working Group on Reduction of GHG Emissions from Ships held on 19–23 October 2020. The MEPC approved the amendments at its 75th session in November 2020 and forwarded the draft amendments for assessment of their impact on IMO Member States at the MEPC's 76th session in 2021.[24] The MEPC also agreed the terms of reference for assessing the possible impacts on states, with a particular focus on the needs of developing countries, small island developing states (SIDs) and least developed countries (LDCs).

MEPC 76, held online in June of 2021, was a key moment in the IMO's decarbonisation work. Decisions were made regarding short-term measures and medium-term measures for achieving the GHG contributions of the sector. In respect of short-term measures, the MEPC adopted amendments to MARPOL Annex VI, introducing mandatory goal-based technical and operational measures to reduce carbon intensity of international shipping. These include the Energy Efficiency Existing Ship Index (EEXI),[25] the enhanced Ship Energy Efficiency Management Plan (SEEMP)[26] and an operational Carbon Intensity Indicator (CII)

[22] Along with the adoption of amendments to Protocol to the International Convention for the Prevention of Pollution from Ships (MARPOL) (entered into force 2 October 1983) 1341 UNTS 3, 17 ILM 546, Annex VI (resolution MEPC.203(62)), by Parties to MARPOL Annex VI.

[23] MEPC 75/7/15: 'Reduction of GHG Emissions from ships' (2020) *Fourth IMO GHG Study Final Report.*

[24] MEPC 76/1 Provisional Agenda.

[25] Applicable from the first annual, intermediate or renewal IAPP survey after 1 January 2023.

[26] Approved SEEMP needs to be kept onboard from 1 January 2023.

rating scheme, which took effect from 1 January 2023. These technical and operational measures combined are to affect both how a ship is retrofitted and equipped and how the ship operates. Whilst the former EEDI was only applied to new ships, the EEXI applies to all ships of 400 gross tonnage or more.[27] Regulating the global fleet through the EEDI would not have had a significant enough impact given the slow rate of global fleet renewal, ie prevalence of newbuilds.

A ship's EEXI indicates its energy efficiency compared to a baseline. Existing ships are required to assess their 'attained' EEXI by their first annual, intermediate or renewal International Air Pollution Prevention (IAPP) survey of 2023.[28] This attained EEXI will then be compared to a 'required' EEXI which is based on a reduction factor expressed as a percentage relative to an EEDI baseline set in accordance with different values for various ship types and size categories.[29] The ship's EEXI value must be below the required EEXI in order to meet minimum energy efficiency standards. This is a once-off regulatory requirement and, unlike the CII, is not an operational measure. It is ultimately a design measure that looks at an engine's energy efficiency capacity and its mechanical power, it does not measure actual emissions. The IMO foresees that most vessels will comply with the EEXI standard through: 1) Overridable Shaft Power Limitation (SHaPoLi), meaning a verified and approved system for the limitation of the maximum shaft power; and 2) Overridable Engine Power Limitation (EPL), meaning a verified and approved system for the limitation of the maximum engine power by technical means.[30] The EEXI is therefore a standard which looks to the theoretical fuel use of a ship for propulsion as opposed to its actual fuel use. On the other hand, the CII is based on what the ship actually bunkers or emits. The EEXI is therefore aimed at ship design efficiency whilst the CII is aimed at reducing operational emissions.

The CII is essentially a reporting requirement that will be included in a ship's SEEMP for vessels 5,000 gross tonnage and above. The CII measures energy efficiency in grams of CO_2 emitted per cargo-carrying capacity and nautical mile to determine a ship's annual rating ranging from A to E.[31] The attained annual operational CII will be reported and verified against a required annual operational CII by the administration or authorised organisation to determine this carbon intensity rating: A, B, C, D or E, indicating a major superior, minor superior, moderate, minor inferior, or inferior performance level.[32] Ships rated D for three consecutive years,

[27] Regulation 23 of MEPC 76/15/Add.1.

[28] Reg 5 of MEPC 76/15/Add.1 (page 13). Also refer to the 2014 Guidelines on survey and certification of the Energy Efficiency Design Index (resolution MEPC.254(67), as amended by resolutions MEPC.261(68) and MEPC.309(73)); consolidated text: MEPC.1/Circ.855/Rev.2, as may be further amended.

[29] Regs 23 and 24 of MEPC 76/15/Add.1.

[30] MEPC 76/15/Add.2 Annex 9 (adopted 17 June 2021) 2021 Guidelines on The Shaft / Engine Power Limitation System To Comply With The EEXI Requirements and use of a Power Reserve.

[31] MEPC.339(76), 2021 Guidelines on the Operational Carbon Intensity Rating of Ships (CII Rating Guidelines, G4).

[32] Reg 28 of MEPC 76/15/Add.1.

or rated at E for one year, will have to submit a corrective action plan outlining how they will attain the required C rating.[33] Administrations, port authorities and other stakeholders should provide incentives to those ships with an A or B rating.[34]

The initial problem with measuring carbon intensity for a CII rating was pointed out by Psaraftis (2021) following the adoption of MEPC76.[35] At the time, it was unclear whether emissions for 'transport work' would be calculated in accordance with a Annual Efficiency Ratio (AER), known as the 'supply-based' measure, or the Energy Efficiency Operational Indicator (EEOI), known as the 'demand-based' measure. Both measure CO_2 emissions yet the denominator differs for each calculation.[36] AER divides emissions by a denominator of the ship's deadweight (ie cargo-carrying capacity) multiplied by its distance sailed in a year; while the EEOI would divide emissions by the actual tonne-miles of cargo carried by a ship in a year. The two would clearly proffer different results with a requirement of only 11 per cent reductions for EEOI and a 22 per cent reduction for AER. This resulted in developing states advocating for the demand-based EEOI in accordance with the principle of CBDR-RC (common but differentiated responsibilities and respective capabilities) and states with greater decarbonisation ambitions advocating for the supply-based AER.[37] As pointed out by Psaraftis, the advocation of the EEOI metric seemed 'paradoxical' as it requires the input of sensitive data pertaining to cargo that is not required by the IMO Data Collection System (DCS).[38]

In 2022, the IMO adopted Guidelines that state that the supply-based AER is to be used for CII calculations.[39] However, Psaraftis's other concern – that the CII standard entails no sanctions nor repercussions if not complied with – still remains.[40] As stated above, ships with D or E ratings should merely submit a corrective action plan with no further details provided in the event that a ship fails to do so or act in accordance with such a plan. It is clear that the IMO's CII standard envisions an incentivisation scheme bolstered by relevant stakeholders and industry actors. Although there is no regulatory sanction, commercial repercussions could carry severe consequences if a CII rating of D or E holds relevance for banks, insurers, cargo owners, and port authorities. The CII as a rating system therefore depends quite heavily on private actors to implement a set of outcomes for a ship's attained CII. This is fully aligned with the IMO's 2013 Vision for a Sustainable Maritime Transport which solicits the enrolment of a wide spectrum of actors for pluralistic governance solutions.[41]

[33] Reg 28.7.

[34] Reg 28.10.

[35] Harilaos N Psaraftis, 'Shipping decarbonization in the aftermath of MEPC 76' (2021) 1 *Cleaner Logistics and Supply Chain* 100008.

[36] ibid 1.

[37] MEPC.352(78) (adopted on 10 June 2022) explains the difference, but was only adopted after the commentary by Psaraftis.

[38] Psaraftis (n 35) 2.

[39] IMO resolutions MEPC.352(78), MEPC.353(78) and MEPC.354(78).

[40] Psaraftis (n 35) 2.

[41] IMO (n 6).

In 2023, environmental interests were keenly awaiting the IMO's decision on medium-term measures and renewed short-term measures in its 2023 GHG Strategy. Parallel action was being taken by the European Union as part of its comprehensive legislative package to reduce GHG emissions from ships, and stakeholders were anticipating similar action to be announced at MEPC80 (the July 2023 session). In adopting the 2023 Strategy, it was decided that a review of short-term measures would be initiated in respect of the EEXI, CII and SEEMP, yet a working group will only meet in late 2024 and in 2025 to work on such reviews while implementation of any amendments will only take place in 2026. Only a 'basket' of candidate mid-term measures were put forward comprising of both:[42]

1. a technical element, namely a goal-based marine fuel standard regulating the phased reduction of the marine fuel's GHG intensity; and
2. an economic element, on the basis of a maritime GHG emissions pricing mechanism.

An interim report on the impact assessment of these measures will only be delivered at MEPC 81 (Spring 2024), with a final report to be delivered at MEPC 82 (Autumn 2024). The market-based mechanism proposed, ie the GHG pricing mechanism, has been controversial since it was first put on the table in 2011.[43] The problem that the IMO faces is the potential for disproportionate adverse effects on LDCs coupled with the interests of SIDs. Advocates of the CBDR-RC remain sceptical of MBMs, whilst SIDs have a more obvious and urgent interest in GHG reduction from shipping.[44] There is also much uncertainty as to what sort of MBM would achieve the best result.[45] Options include variations of a bunker levy or a GHG tax, whilst the EU has already decided on the inclusion of shipping in its EU Emissions Trading Scheme (discussed in more detail in section B below).

The concerns around the enforcement of the CII standard and the debates on implementing a suitable MBM are reflective of the wider problems in the public regulation of carbon emissions. The global regulation of carbon emissions is at a impasse due to the differing economic and development needs of states, inconsistent political priorities and inherently contradictory enforcement regimes. Unfortunately, shipping is not an exception amongst other economic sectors that are struggling to reach agreement on sustainable solutions for radical

[42] MEPC.377(80) (adopted on 7 July 2023) 2023 IMO Strategy on Reduction of GHG Emissions from Ships.

[43] Harilaos N Psaraftis, 'Market-based measures for greenhouse gas emissions from ships: a review' (2012) 11 *WMU Journal of Maritime Affairs* 211.

[44] Serhan Cevik, 'Waiting for Godot? The case for climate change adaptation and mitigation in small island states (2022) 11 *Journal of Environmental Economics and Policy* 420. Peter Nuttal, 'Small islands with a strong voice: Why Pacific Islands are playing a critical role in the current shipping decarbonization debate', Article No 46 [UNCTAD Transport and Trade Facilitation Newsletter N° 85 – First Quarter 2020].

[45] Harilaos N Psaraftis, Thalis Zis and Sotiria Lagouvardou, 'A comparative evaluation of market based measures for shipping decarbonization' (2021) 2 *Maritime Transport Research* 100019.

transformations of existing socio-techno regimes. The IMO's latest response to GHG emissions at MEPC 80 was met with much criticism as being 'detached' from the Paris Agreement,[46] 'vague and non-committal'[47] and 'watered-down'.[48] This reflects the sentiment that IMO instruments are failing to meet global expectations.

However, the IMO decarbonisation measures simply reflect the broader limitations of international efforts for GHG reductions. Airbourne emissions are a relatively new regulatory area for the IMO, which derived its initial mandate predominantly from Article 1 of its Convention,[49] suggesting that its mission is confined to marine pollution from ships – ie oil pollution and other discharges into the marine environment. An expansion of its work is seemingly supported by UNCLOS in that it places a duty on states to achieve cooperation for the protection and preservation of the marine environment which broadly incorporates climate change. Yet, in reality, the IMO cannot take exclusive responsibility for decarbonising the maritime sector as its structure and competency is designed merely to respond to issues 'concerning the effect of shipping on the marine environment' referred to it by other United Nations organs and agencies.[50] It not only relies on states to implement its regulations and policies, but private actors who it deems necessary to achieve its goal of SMTS. This has been recognised by the IMO for some time now as it envisions an enrolment of private actors for achieving a sectoral transition. The emphasis placed on IMO standards by global media and environmental campaigners also reflects the preference for a 'one-size-fits-all' model to seeking out collective action solutions.

B. EU Legislative Package for Decarbonising Shipping: Fit for 55

In 2015, the EU adopted the Monitoring, Reporting and Verification (MRV) Regulation requiring ships above 5,000 gross tonnage to monitor and report their carbon emissions, fuel consumption, and transport work on all voyages to, from, and between EU ports.[51] In respect of implementing other measures, the

[46] Ian Taylor, 'MEPC 80: IMO 'Detached' From The 'Urgent Reality' Of Climate Change, Says Environmental NGO' (Bunkerspot, 6 July 2023), www.bunkerspot.com/global/59454-mepc-80-imo-detached-from-the-urgent-reality-of-climate-change-says-environmental-ngo.

[47] Sam Chambers, '"Vague and non-committal": MEPC green targets text comes in for fierce criticism' (Splash247.com, 7 July 2023), splash247.com/vague-and-non-committal-mepc-green-targets-text-comes-in-for-fierce-criticism.

[48] Khaled Diab, 'International shipping's new climate plan provokes storm of protest' (Carbon Market Watch, 7 July 2023), carbonmarketwatch.org/2023/07/07/international-shippings-new-climate-plan-provokes-storm-of-protest.

[49] The Convention on the International Maritime Organization (adopted 6 March 1948, entered into force 17 March 1958) 289 UNTS 3 ('IMO Convention').

[50] IMO Convention, Art 1(d).

[51] Regulation (EU) 2015/757 of the European Parliament and of the Council of 29 April 2015 on the monitoring, reporting and verification of carbon dioxide emissions from maritime transport, and amending Directive 2009/16/EC.

EU maintained that the IMO was the most appropriate forum to regulate emissions from shipping, but adopted the position that shipping would be included in the EU Emission Trading System (EU-ETS) in 2023 if no comparable system was introduced by the IMO.[52] Following the Green Deal in 2019, the EU accelerated its impetus for decarbonisation efforts with an aim for Europe to be the first carbon neutral continent. In July 2021, the EU released its package of proposals to reform climate legislation, entitled 'Fit for 55', which aims to ensure that shipping is aligned with its target to reduce GHG emissions by at least 55 per cent by 2030 in comparison to the 1990 level.[53] This package of measures is aimed at implementing the European Green Deal and was written into law as the 'Climate Law', which sets an ultimate ambition for Europe's economy to be carbon neutral by 2050.[54] For shipping, 'Fit for 55' includes FuelEU Maritime,[55] a proposal to drive the demand for clean fuels coupled with an obligation to use on-shore power,[56] and will also see shipping included in the EU Emissions Trading Scheme.[57]

The subsections below briefly set out these two main proposals. However, it is also important to note that the revision of the Energy Taxation Directive,[58] and the Alternative Fuels Infrastructure (AFI)[59] initiative will also impact shipping. The former comprises a proposal to remove tax exemptions on marine fuels for use within the European Economic Area (EEA). The latter sets requirements for Trans-European Transport Network (TEN-T) maritime ports to ensure that infrastructure is available for liquefied natural gas (LNG) bunkering infrastructure by 2025, and to install shoreside power supply to serve the demand of at least 90 per cent of container and passenger ships calling at that port.[60] The EU has also

[52] Jørgen Wettestad and Lars H Gulbrandsen, 'On the Process of Including Shipping in EU Emissions Trading: Multi-Level Reinforcement Revisited' (2022) 10 *Politics and Governance* 246, 249.

[53] Communication from the Commission to the European Parliament, the Council, the European Economic and Social Committee And The Committee Of The Regions 'Fit for 55': delivering the EU's 2030 Climate Target on the way to climate neutrality (COM/2021/550) final.

[54] Regulation (EU) 2021/1119 of the European Parliament and of the Council of 30 June 2021 establishing the framework for achieving climate neutrality and amending Regulations (EC) No 401/2009 and (EU) 2018/1999 ('European Climate Law').

[55] Proposal for a Regulation of the European Parliament and of the Council on the use of renewable and low-carbon fuels in maritime transport and amending Directive 2009/16/EC (COM/2021/562) final.

[56] The FuelEU maritime proposal used the European Parliament resolution of 27 April 2021 on technical and operational measures for more efficient and cleaner maritime transport (2019/2193(INI)) as a starting point.

[57] Proposal for a Directive of the European Parliament and of the Council amending Directive 2003/87/EC establishing a system for greenhouse gas emission allowance trading within the Union, Decision (EU) 2015/1814 concerning the establishment and operation of a market stability reserve for the Union greenhouse gas emission trading scheme and Regulation (EU) 2015/757 (COM/2021/551) final.

[58] Council Directive 2003/96/EC of 27 October 2003 restructuring the Community framework for the taxation of energy products and electricity. For a legal analysis of the 'greenness' of the intended revisions, see Marina Bisogno, 'Tax In History: Twenty Years After the Adoption of the Energy Taxation Directive, Is Its Reform in a Greener Sense Just an Illusion?' (2023) 51 *Intertax* 679.

[59] Directive 2014/94/EU of the European Parliament and of the Council of 22 October 2014 on the deployment of alternative fuels infrastructure.

[60] Proposal for a Regulation of the European Parliament and of the Council on the deployment of alternative fuels infrastructure, and repealing Directive 2014/94/EU (COM/2021/559) final.

included shipping in its Taxonomy Regulation for sustainable activities, which is discussed in further detail in chapter two.[61]

i. EU's Emission Trading System (EU-ETS)

The EU-ETS works using a 'cap-and-trade' principle, whereby a cap (limit) is set on the total amount of greenhouse gas emissions that can be emitted by entities. Parties are required to hand in allowances equal to their CO_2 emissions (1 allowance = 1 ton CO_2) at the end of each year.[62] Within the cap, the different entities buy allowances which they can trade between themselves. Companies are incentivised to emit less carbon as this will mean that they have spare allowances which can be traded or 'saved' for future needs.[63] As part of the Fit for 55 package announced in 2021, the Commission proposed to amend the EU-ETS Directive to extend the EU-ETS to shipping in manner centred on ship voyages.[64] In 2023, amendments to the EU-ETS Directive (2003/87/EC) for the inclusion of maritime transport activities in the EU-ETS were adopted,[65] as well as amendments to the MRV Regulation for updated changes to supporting reporting rules.[66] From January 2024, the EU-ETS covers emissions from large ships (5,000 gross tonnage and above) and from 1 January 2025, the EU-ETS will also apply to general cargo ships below 5,000 gross tonnage but not below 400 gross tonnage, as well as offshore ships above 400 gross tonnage.

To facilitate a smooth introduction, EU legislators will allow for a phase-in period for the surrender of allowances by shipping companies as follows:[67]

(i) for 2024, 40% of verified regulated GHG emissions;
(ii) for 2025, 70% of verified regulated GHG emissions; and
(iii) for 2026 onwards, 100% of verified regulated GHG emissions.

'Shipping company' means 'shipowner or any other organisation or person, such as the manager or the bareboat charterer, which has assumed the responsibility for the operation of the ship from the shipowner'.[68] The EU-ETS will initially apply to

[61] Regulation (EU) 2020/852 of the European Parliament and of the Council of 18 June 2020 on the establishment of a framework to facilitate sustainable investment, and amending Regulation (EU) 2019/2088.

[62] The price per allowance is not fixed as this will depend on market demand.

[63] European Commission, 'Questions and Answers – Emissions Trading – Putting a Price on carbon' (Press Release, 14 July 2021), ec.europa.eu/commission/presscorner/detail/en/qanda_21_3542.

[64] COM/2021/551 final (n 57).

[65] Directive (EU) 2023/959 of the European Parliament and of the Council of 10 May 2023 amending Directive 2003/87/EC establishing a system for greenhouse gas emission allowance trading within the Union and Decision (EU) 2015/1814 concerning the establishment and operation of a market stability reserve for the Union greenhouse gas emission trading system.

[66] Regulation (EU) 2023/957 of the European Parliament and of the Council of 10 May 2023 amending Regulation (EU) 2015/757 in order to provide for the inclusion of maritime transport activities in the EU Emissions Trading System and for the monitoring, reporting and verification of emissions of additional greenhouse gases and emissions from additional ship types.

[67] Art 3(gb) of Directive (EU) 2023/959 (n 65).

[68] Art 3(d) of Regulation (EU) 2015/757 as amended by Reg (EU) 2023/957.

CO_2 emissions, but allowances for methane (CH_4) and nitrous oxide (N_2O) also need to be surrendered from 1 January 2024.

ii. FeulEU Maritime

In September 2023, the FuelEU Maritime Initiative was adopted to impose uniform rules for:[69]

(a) a limit on the greenhouse gas (GHG) intensity of energy used on board by a ship arriving at, staying within or departing from ports under the jurisdiction of a Member State; and
(b) an obligation to use on-shore power supply (OPS) or zero-emission technology in ports under the jurisdiction of a Member State.

It will apply from 1 January 2025 to all ships, regardless of their flag state and with commercial purpose (ie passenger or cargo), over 5,000 gross tonnes visiting a port within the EU. It sets restrictions on the energy used by the vessel during their stay within the port of a Member State, the energy used on voyages between Member State ports, and 50 per cent of the emissions for voyages between Member State ports and ports in outermost regions or third countries.[70] FuelEU Maritime will gradually increase its restrictions on the GHG intensity of marine fuels and sets reductions targets of: two per cent by 2025, six per cent by 2030, 13 per cent by 2035, 26 per cent by 2040, 59 per cent by 2045, and 75 per cent by 2050.[71] In addition to these targets, the FuelEU Regulation introduces a net-zero emission requirement for ships moored at berth. From 1 January 2030, commercial ships over 5,000 gross tonnage (containerships and passenger ships) not otherwise exempted, where moored at berth in an EU port for longer that two hours, shall be required to connect to an on-shore-power supply or use alternative approved zero-emission technology.[72]

Responsibility for compliance rests once again with the 'shipping company' which is the same responsible entity under the EU-ETS Directive and MRV Regulation for surrendering allowances and reporting emissions respectively. From 31 August 2024, shipping companies must submit a monitoring plan for its ships which provides, among other things, the amount and type of energy/fuel used onboard each ship (during voyage and at berth), the connection to on-shore-power, information on type and amount of substituted sources of energy for onboard or on-shore power, and the chosen methodology for reporting. The monitoring plan is to then be submitted to an independent third-party verifier appointed by the MRV Regulation. Shipping companies will need to start recording such information from January 2025 and submit their reports by

[69] Art 1 of Regulation (EU) 2023/1805 of the European Parliament and of the Council of 13 September 2023 on the use of renewable and low-carbon fuels in maritime transport, and amending Directive 2009/16/EC.
[70] Regulation (EU) 2023/1805, Art 2.
[71] Art 4.
[72] Art 6.

30 March of each annual reporting period.[73] The FuelEU Regulation also allows for voluntary 'pooling' of vessels in a fleet so that the overperformance of one vessel may be offset against the underperformance of another.[74] The pooled vessels do not need to share a common shipowner, but it is important that a ship's compliance balance is not included in more than one pool during the same reporting period.

Non-compliance with the limits on the yearly average GHG intensity of the energy used on board a vessel will attract a 'FuelEU penalty' with dissuasive effect and proportionate to the removal of any economic advantage of non-compliance.[75] A FuelEU penalty should also be imposed by Member States for each non-compliant port call by Member States. These financial penalties shall be calculated in accordance with Part B of Annex IV of the Regulation. Furthermore, if a ship fails to comply with the obligations of the Regulation, it will not be issued with a FuelEU document of compliance. If it fails to obtain such a compliance document for two consecutive reporting periods, a Member State administration can impose serious consequences, such as a detention order.[76]

In view of the parallel systems of an IMO regulatory framework and the EU's comprehensive legislative package, the question has been posed as to whether a 'Brussels effect' will have an impact on global governance of decarbonisation in shipping.[77] Will the IMO be pressured by EU action to endorse a ETS or will it opt for a carbon levy? Eftestøl and Yliheljo posit that there is no 'pure Brussels effect', yet the EU is playing a significant role in speeding up international efforts. Although the EU provides a noteworthy example of progressive legislative measures, the European Maritime Safety Agency reports that EU Member State-flagged vessels account for nearly a fifth of the world's vessels by gross tonnage.[78] Although this is a significant share of the global fleet, coupled with port state control of third country vessels calling at EU ports, it is still not enough to posit a global solution. The EU's work will largely be in vain if the rest of the world continues to increase its GHG emissions from shipping.

II. A Contract Governance Approach to Decarbonisation

This book requires a theoretical framework that offers a holistic approach to contract theory: one that recognises both internal and external factors that impact upon private actor behaviour and the instruments employed to facilitate their

[73] Art 16.
[74] Art 21.
[75] Preamble, para (60).
[76] Art 25.
[77] Ellen Eftestøl and Emilie Yliheljo, 'International Shipping: Who Levels the Playing Field?' in Abhinayan Basu Bal et al (eds), *Regulation of Risk Transport, Trade and Environment in Perspective* (Brill | Nijhoff, 2022) 282–314, 303.
[78] EMSA, 'The EU Maritime Profile – the maritime cluster in the EU' (2023), www.emsa.europa.eu/eumaritimeprofile/section-2-the-eu-maritime-cluster.html.

interests, ie contracts. This section considers the approach of 'contract governance' to contract theory in order to address diverse issues of governance in contract law.[79] Unlike private governance theories, contract governance is yet to be explored in relation to sustainability issues as contracts are often overlooked in the climate change regulatory tool package.[80] This is because moralistic reasoning in contract law is met with suspicion,[81] and freedom of contract is said to prevail so that parties will always opt to contract out of default rules that will increase their costs.[82] This section argues against classical assumptions of autonomy, individualism and objectivity in contracts, as propounded by traditionalist notions of the common law thus 'crowding out alternative normative standards based on contractual justice, collective action and responsibility'.[83] It sets out to illustrate why contract governance provides a suitable theoretical framework for studying how contracts *govern* and how they *are governed* in achieving climate mitigation and green energy transitions. This is a particularly important question in the maritime sector that has thus far failed to align itself with the Paris Agreement. The following subsections justify the chosen theoretical framework of this study by: 1) asserting that pluralistic governance solutions are needed for transitioning the shipping sector to net-zero; 2) investigating why contracts have been left out of the governance discussion thus far; and 3) highlighting the aspects of contract governance that allow it to recognise and effectively implement pluralistic solutions.

A. Pluralistic Governance Solutions

The problem of climate change is still considered, to a large extent, a public governance issue to be solved by states through multilateral treaties and a commitment to their implementation on a domestic level.[84] Hence, in the context of global shipping, all 'eggs' are generally placed in the IMO 'basket'. However, corporate and private governance theories have recognised that an exclusive focus on government action fails to consider that many private institutions operate as semi-autonomous rule-makers and not mere participants in existing state-controlled governance systems.[85] The juxtaposition of 'public governance' with 'private governance' is

[79] Stefan Grundmann, Florian Möslein and Karl Riesenhuber, 'Contract Governance: Dimensions in Law and Interdisciplinary Research' in *Contract Governance: Dimensions in Law and Interdisciplinary Research* (Oxford University Press, 2015) ch 1.

[80] Kateřina Peterková Mitkidis, 'Using Private Contracts for Climate Change Mitigation' (2018) 2 *Journal of International Law* 54.

[81] Jean Braucher, 'Contract versus contractarianism: The regulatory role of contract law' (1990) 47 *Washington and Lee Law Review* 697, 701, 702.

[82] Jonathan Morgan, 'Against regulation through contract law' in *Contract Law Minimalism: A Formalist Restatement of Commercial Contract Law* (Cambridge University Press, 2013) 114–57, 117.

[83] Catherine Mitchell, 'Vanishing Contract Law' in *Vanishing Contract Law: Common Law in the Age of Contracts* (Cambridge University Press, 2022).

[84] Michael Vandenbergh and Jonathan Gilligan, 'The Governance Challenge' in *Beyond Politics: The Private Governance Response to Climate Change* (Cambridge University Press, 2017) 64–116.

[85] ibid 89.

reinforced by the classical division of public and private law. This conceptual divide is not well-adapted to the reality that the private law, in particular contract law, is also an instrument for the obtainment of collective objectives and the pursuit of public policy goals.[86] In the context of climate mitigation, collective solutions are generally met with the primary question of: 'What can governments do?'.[87] This unduly narrow question significantly limits the number of solutions whilst creating a number of biases. Vandenbergh and Gilligan note that these biases presume that the goal of research and advocacy is to promote one optimal solution which rules out all second-best options and is often met with political unfeasibility, thus delaying implementation.[88] This bias culminates in Ostrom's notion of the 'Panacea problem', which illustrates a preference for one comprehensive solution even when it is less feasible than smaller fragmented solutions.[89] Moving beyond the panacea problem requires a number of institutional responses and polycentric governance to reach net-zero ambitions. Ostrom's work identified that:[90]

> [I]ndividuals facing [collective action] problems do not always need an external authority to extract them from their tragedy. When they have arenas in which they can engage with one another, can learn to trust one another, can draw on sources of reliable data, can ensure monitoring of their decisions, can create new instrumentalities, and can adapt over time, they are frequently, though by no means always, able to extract themselves from these challenging dilemmas.

Indeed, corporate governance theories have recognised that companies do not require external sources of authority. Corporate governance literature embodies a number of research theories including managerial theory, agency theory, stakeholder theory, stewardship theory and socio-emotional wealth.[91] All of these theories seek out legitimacy for the sources of company power through investigating the systems that establish how this power is to be exercised and held accountable. There is also an established sentiment that companies can contribute to better climate governance as there are mutual benefits for the company's long-term sustainability and business goals.[92] Companies can act as 'orchestrators' for the coordination of national governments for climate policy through assisting with research exchange and developing multi-actor international initiatives.[93]

[86] Olha O Cherednychenko, 'Contract Governance in the EU: Conceptualising the Relationship between Investor Protection Regulation and Private Law' (2015) 21 *European Law Journal* 500.

[87] Vandenbergh and Gilligan (n 84) 88.

[88] ibid 89.

[89] Elinor Ostrom, Marco Janssen and John Anderies, 'Going beyond Panaceas' (2007) 104 *Proceedings of the National Academy of Sciences of the United States of America* 15176; see also Elinor Ostrom and Michael Cox, 'Moving beyond panaceas: A multi-tiered diagnostic approach for social-ecological analysis' (2010) 37 *Environmental Conservation* 451.

[90] Elinor Ostrom, 'A long Polycentric Journey' (2010) 13 *Annual Review of Political Science* 1, 6.

[91] Salvatore Principale, 'Corporate Governance and Strategic Management' in *Fostering Sustainability in Corporate Governance* (Springer, 2023) 1–17.

[92] Lisa Benjamin and Stelios Andreadakis, 'Corporate Governance and Climate Change: Smoothing Temporal Dissonance to a Phased Approach' (2019) 40 *Business Law Review* 146, 158.

[93] United Nations Environment Programme. The Emissions Gap Report (Nairobi, 2018) xix–xx.

This is an optimistic way to view the role of the corporation in climate governance and has placed trust in managerial decisions to consider climate risks so that the company is not exposed to negative impacts on the corporation value.[94] As such, much climate activism has focused on directors' fiduciary duties in aligning decision-making with climate mitigation efforts and to be more ambitious than governments in setting targets.[95] However, critics of a corporate climate governance system note that this approach of 'boardroom ambitions' has been heavily influenced by the notion that climate change is a market failure, meaning that excess CO_2 emissions are a negative externality that needs to be priced in the market.[96] This has the result that pollution is commodified, with the practical reality that the responsibility for emissions is simply shifted downstream or passed on through offsetting.[97] GHG reporting still largely focuses on scope one and scope two emissions, whilst offsetting is often criticised (with good reason) for being a monumental greenwashing scam.[98] GHG commodification presents, yet again, a dominant 'panacea problem' solution with some dubious implementation issues and outcomes.

An alternative corporate governance approach to market-based measures that commodify GHG emissions is soft law policy on the alignment of company behaviour with global sustainable development goals. The world's largest corporate sustainability initiative is the UN Global Compact (UNGC), which requests that its participants conduct business in the way that promotes the SDGs by incorporating Ten Principles of the UN Global Compact widely into their strategies and operations.[99] The UN Protect, Respect and Remedy Framework also provides businesses with five key ways in which they can 'work to promote and protect corporate respect for human rights and prevent corporate abuses of human rights'.[100] To implement the Protect, Respect and Remedy Framework, the Guiding Principles on Business and Human Rights was unanimously endorsed in 2011 by the Human Rights Council.[101] Based on these Guiding Principles, the Organisation for Economic Co-operation and Development (OECD) published its own Guidelines on Multinational Enterprises on Responsible Business Conduct to provide non-binding principles for businesses based on the shared values of

[94] Principale (n 91) 12.

[95] *Abrahams v Commonwealth Bank of Australia* NSD864/2021; *Client Earth v Shell Board of Directors* [2023] EWHC 1897 (Ch).

[96] Jayme Walenta, 'The Limits to Private-sector Climate Change Action: The Geographies of Corporate Climate Governance' (2018) 94 *Economic Geography* 461.

[97] This view is also largely attributable to the Kyoto Protocol to the United Nations Framework Convention on Climate Change, 10 December 1997, 37 ILM 22 (1998); 2303 UNTS 148; UN Doc FCCC/CP/1997/7/Add.1.

[98] Robert Watt, 'The fantasy of carbon offsetting' (2021) 30 *Environmental Politics* 1069.

[99] UN Global Compact, unglobalcompact.org/what-is-gc.

[100] John Ruggie, 'Protect, Respect & Remedy: A Framework for Business and Human Rights' (2008) 3 *Innovations: Technology, Governance, Globalization* 189.

[101] UN Human Rights Office of the High Commissioner, *Guiding Principles on Business and Human Rights: Implementing the United Nations "Protect, Respect and Remedy" Framework* (2011), www.ohchr.org/sites/default/files/Documents/Publications/GuidingPrinciplesBusinessHR_EN.pdf.

governments.[102] Additionally, the ISO 26000 Guidance on Social Responsibility provides that an organisation should recognise its social responsibility within its sphere of influence and have the ability to affect the decisions or activities of other parties with whom it has political, contractual, economic or other relationships.[103] Literature on corporate governance outlines the number of approaches and strategies that companies are implementing, both goal-based and rule-based, while corporate governance has also spurred a whole new dimension of Environmental and Social Governance (ESG) investing, often interchangeable with or similar to 'sustainable' investing that places 'ethical business practices' as a top priority over other good governance categories such as 'strong management'.[104]

Despite the proliferation of sustainable supply chain initiatives, ESG investing, and soft law instruments for best business practice, the problem of effectiveness still remains. A lack of effectiveness hampers accountability and has resulted in growing greenwashing allegations against companies with seemingly good intentions. 'Greenwashing' refers to a company strategy of not 'walking the talk' – ie where a company's communicated practices are seemingly green and responsible, whilst their actual practices are irresponsible in respect of the environment.[105] Pizzetti et al note that most greenwashing takes place in the supply chain and is 'vicarious', meaning that a company's suppliers misbehave in way that is inconsistent to the company's communicated green strategies.[106] There is one, largely neglected, tool that can combat such issues of implementation and the negative implications associated with greenwashing: *contracts*.

Sustainable supply chains are already starting to shift attention to contractual clauses embodying binding green supplier commitments, integrated codes of conduct, and increased enforcement remedies.[107] An alternative theory is needed to recognise the limitations of public law-makers and to supersede the legitimacy debates of corporate authority by focusing on gaps and problems surrounding the implementation and enforcement of standards – whether these be imposed by regulators or privately adopted. Contract governance can arguably go further than theories of corporate governance and private authority in respect of environmental problem-solving.[108] This is because corporate governance and private

[102] OECD, OECD Guidelines for Multinational Enterprises on Responsible Business Conduct (2023), doi.org/10.1787/81f92357-en.

[103] ISO (the International Organization for Standardization) is a worldwide federation of national standards bodies (ISO member bodies) offering guidance instead of requirements, iso26000.info.

[104] John Hill, *Environmental, Social, and Governance (ESG) Investing* (Academic Press, 2020) 1.

[105] Kent Walker and Fang Wan, 'The harm of symbolic actions and green-washing: Corporate actions and communications on environmental performance and their financial implications' (2012) 109 *Journal of Business Ethics* 227.

[106] Marta Pizzetti, Lucia Gatti and Peter Seele, 'Firms Talk, Suppliers Walk: Analyzing the Locus of Greenwashing in the Blame Game and Introducing "Vicarious Greenwashing"' (2021) 170 *Journal of Business Ethics* 21.

[107] Kateřina Peterková Mitkidis, 'Sustainability Clauses in International Supply Chain Contracts: Regulation, Enforceability and Effects of Ethical Requirements' (2014) 1 *Nordic Journal of Commercial Law* 3.

[108] Albeit contract governance has not yet been applied as such and is generally discussed in an economic and antitrust context.

authority do not delve deeply enough into questions of market transactions and contracts.[109] The next section looks at why contracts have been left out of the governance discussion for so long when today's contracts are essentially what 'links entrepreneurial innovations to the efforts and finance necessary to transform ideas into value'.[110] At present, the seemingly fixed doctrines of contract law are creating a friction with the implementation of energy efficiency and innovation. This is particularly true of maritime law which is 'often wedded to the past, often the distant past, refusing to move with the times'.[111]

B. Why has Contract Law been Largely Left Out of the Regulatory Response to Climate Change?

Contract law may seem like a suitable target for re-regulation and state intervention because it is a powerful legal institution that can accommodate government interference (eg as seen with consumer rights) within the enforcement of private agreements.[112] Yet despite the early cognisance of the role of contract-governed financial instruments and transactions in the 'pre-crisis speed-up of securitization markets', laissez-faire contract law has remained very resilient to any attempt at embedding it a wider socio-political context.[113] Formalist opinions of contract law recognise that contract law and its doctrines comprise of default rules regarding formation, remedies and interpretation; yet the default rules should meet a strict test of 'the minimum decencies … which the court will insist upon as essential to [or] inherent in a bargain of that type'.[114] As a result, default rules should be clear, simple and kept to a minimum, thus preserving the freedom of contract.[115] Maritime contracts, like most international commercial transactions, are predominantly governed by an English common law system. English law remains inherently formalistic, more so than in other Western jurisdictions, meaning that it is not susceptible to considerations of moral imperatives nor socio-political policy, but by established doctrines centred on an objective theory of contract law.[116]

[109] Peer Zumbansen, 'Law, Economics, and More: The Genius of Contract Governance: Comment on T. Kameda, K. Inukai, T. Wisdom, and W. Toyokawa, "The Concept of Herd Behavior: Its Psychological and Neural Underpinnings"' in Grundmann et al (n 79) 85.

[110] Ronald Gilson, Charles Sabel, Robert Scott, 'Contract, Uncertainty, and Innovation' in Grundmann et al (n 79) 155.

[111] Martin Davies, 'When Was the Last Time You Were Restrained by a Prince? Conservatism and the Development of Maritime Law' in P Mukherjee P et al (eds), *Maritime Law in Motion. WMU Studies in Maritime Affairs*, vol 8 (Springer, 2020) 153, 171.

[112] James 'Jay' Varellas, 'Contract law, securitization and the pre-crisis transformation of banking' (2016) in Bertram Lomfeld, Alessandro Somma and Peer Zumbansen (eds), *Reshaping Markets: Economic Governance, the Global Financial Crisis and Liberal Utopia* (Cambridge University Press, 2016) 45–59.

[113] ibid 130–31.

[114] Morgan (n 82) 114, quoting K Llewellyn, *Book review* (1938–39) 52 *Harvard Law Review* 701, 703.

[115] ibid 166.

[116] PS Atiyah, 'Form and substance in contract law' in *Essays on Contract* (Oxford University Press, 1988).

This stands in stark contrast to post-colonial democracies where the private law is not isolated from constitutional influence and the horizontal application of rights between private actors. The arguments put forward for contract law maintaining an isolated neutrality from public law, social-justice, or sustainability agendas are that:

(1) The courts should not be involved in economic micro-regulation as not even trained economists cannot 'derive determinate recommendations from neoclassical economic analysis of law'.[117]
(2) Judges would be overwhelmed by conflicting socio-economic data and making decisions of policy in the private law would result in political decision-making.[118]
(3) Imposing cooperative norms such as good faith and trust are counterproductive and have the opposite effect.[119]
(4) Parties will always act in their own self-interests.[120]

The problem with this formalistic minimalist approach is that it assumes that the common law remains the general regulator of agreements.[121] Indeed, a reversion to this very classical-style model can be attributed to the decreasing role of the judiciary in the creation of contract law rules.[122] Mitchell argues that this has had the unfortunate result of a stagnation in the common law and an isolation of many modern contracting relationships from legal scrutiny.[123] The reality of modern-day contracts is that innovative forms and clauses emerge in the markets to implement the contemporary objectives of private actors, yet the common law is playing catch-up and is failing to adopt judicial frameworks for such contractual innovation.[124]

There is also the practical aspect of researching bilateral documents that are protected by non-disclosure provisions.[125] Contractual developments are difficult to register whilst public bodies may only have access to the standard forms and template clauses that companies make available on a generic basis. Indeed, this book draws from template clauses provided by drafting associations in finance and shipping, as well as voluntary initiatives, without knowing the extent to which these clauses are being used in day-to-day commercial dealings. This sort of empirical study would be difficult to conduct due to the nature of professional privilege,

[117] Morgan (n 82) 121; Hugh Collins, *Regulating Contracts* (Oxford University Press, 1999) 85 (this 'goes beyond the expertise of ordinary courts'); M Pargendler, 'The Role of the State in Contract Law: The Common-Civil Law Divide' (2018) 43 *Yale Journal of International Law* 143 (NYU Law and Economics Research Paper No 17-01).
[118] Maimon Schwarzschild, 'Keeping it private' (2006) 25 *University of Queensland Law Journal* 215.
[119] Morgan (n 82) 125–37.
[120] See *Gold Group Properties Ltd v BDW Trading Ltd* [2010] EWHC 1632 (TCC).
[121] Mitchell (n 83).
[122] ibid 3.
[123] ibid.
[124] Gilson, Sabel and Scott (n 110) 158.
[125] Peterková Mitkidis (n 80) 68.

yet there is evidence to support that the insertion of sustainability clauses in commercial contracts has become a widespread practice.[126] 'Sustainability provisions' refer to a broad range of clauses that implement minimum social and/or environmental standards, and are generally incorporated as express provisions, by way of reference to policy documents, codes of conduct, or separate agreements.[127] Various economic sectors are providing template provisions on the responsibility of environmental compliance and energy-efficiency standards between contracting parties, yet these clauses remain relatively weak in comparison to core commitments under the agreement.

Studies on sustainability provisions in contracts highlight that contract law is largely inept at enforcing the vagueness, aspirational value and normative basis that characterises these sorts of commitments.[128] Yet the fact that contract law does not generally support a specific type of clause does not necessarily infer that contract law needs to be developed, parties are still free to expressly include what they like.[129] It is also arguable that if contracting parties need to pursue sustainability ends, then contract law offers suitable enforcement mechanisms. However, this book seeks to elucidate that traditional contractual architecture and common law default rules do not always adequately implement party intentions in the decarbonisation and energy-efficiency context. English contract law struggles with environmental or sustainability provisions because it was designed to pursue an entirely different set of priorities. Contract law grapples with defining and implementing cooperative norms, data-sharing obligations, anticipating contractual breach (where the occurrence of the breach could result in detrimental impacts for the environment), third-party rights for classes of persons impacted by climate change, and the remoteness of damages when dealing with reputational harms and negative climate externalities.

Climate change is a problem that inherently impacts on third parties, yet third parties are unable to evaluate the impact of commercial relationships on their interests. Arguments could be made that the law of torts is the better equipped private law sister that should protect third parties to whom the contracting parties have no relationship with. Hence, the wave of torts-based class actions that have characterised environmental litigation in the United States and are forming the basis for transnational climate litigation.[130] In the context of sustainable contracting,

[126] V Ulfbeck, O Hansen and A Andhov, 'Contractual enforcement of CSR clauses and the protection of weak parties in the chain' in V Ulfbeck, A Andhov and K Mitkidis, *Law and Responsible Supply Chain Management* (Routledge, 2019) 46–52.

[127] Pia Rebelo, 'Sustainable Supply Chain Finance: The Incorporation of Green Principles into SCF Agreements (2020) 26 *International Trade Law and Regulation* 260; Byron Keating et al, 'In pursuit of a sustainable supply chain: insights from Westpac Banking Corporation' (2008) 13 *Supply Chain Management* 182.

[128] Vibe Ulfbeck and Ole Hansen, 'Sustainability clauses in an unsustainable contract law? (2022) 6 *CEPRI Studies on Private Governance.*

[129] ibid 3.

[130] Kim Bouwer, 'Substantial Justice?: Transnational Torts as Climate Litigation' (2021) 15 *Carbon & Climate Law Review* 188.

the notion of third-party benefits arising from a contractual relationship requires some departure from the doctrine of privity of contract. Determining whether or not third parties fall within one of the exceptions to the doctrine is not a straightforward matter. The complexity in English law arises as a result of the co-existence of both the remaining common law rules and the introduction of the Contracts (Rights of Third Parties) Act 1999. The 1999 Act uses intention as the basis for creating third-party rights and creates only two circumstances where such a right is created, allowing the third party to sue on the contract: 1) where 'the contract expressly provides that [the third party] may', which can refer to both a positive obligation (eg payment) or reliance on an exclusion or limitation clause;[131] and 2) if 'the term purports to confer a benefit on him'.[132] This is subject to the qualification that on a proper construction of the contract, it must appear that the parties intended the term to be enforceable by the third party.[133] If it does not appear so, then subsection 1(b) does not apply. Purporting to 'to confer a benefit' on a third party requires that the purpose of the parties' bargain must have been to benefit the third party and it is not good enough that it be an incidental benefit (ie a third party is benefited if the contract is performed).[134] The proper construction of the contract depends, once again, on intention, yet the courts have interpreted subsection 1(b) as affording a strong presumption in favour of enforcing third-party rights.[135] Despite the strong presumption in favour of third-party rights, to extend the presumption to the environment or communities impacted by climate change is a tenuous and untested line of argument. Furthermore, the Law Commission has made it quite clear that the application of subsection 1(b) does not allow 'cutting across the chain of sub-contracts', which would apply to supply chains and transport networks.[136] Another limitation which the 1999 Act places on third parties is found in subsection 1(3), which provides that the 'third party must be expressly identified in the contract by name, as a member of a class or as answering a particular description but need not be in existence when the contract is entered into'.[137]

[131] s 1(1)(a). This provision also works both ways, in the same way a third-party right can be expressly included, it can be expressly excluded – provided that s 3 of the Unfair Contract Terms Act 1977 (UCTA) is considered. See s 1(6), which negates the need for overly complex drafting to allow a third party to rely on an exclusion clause, as illustrated by *New Zealand Shipping Co Ltd v AM Satterthwaite & Co Ltd (The Eurymedon)* [1975] AC 154.

[132] s 1(1)(b).

[133] s 1(2).

[134] *Dolphin Maritime & Aviation Services Ltd v Sveriges Angfartygs Assurans Forening* [2009] EWHC 716 (Comm), [2009] 2 Lloyd's Rep 123.

[135] The Law Commission, *Privity Of Contract: Contracts For The Benefit Of Third Parties Item 1 of the Sixth Programme of Law Reform* (LAW COM No 242 July 1996) at 80 (7.17); *Nisshin Shipping Co Ltd v Cleaves & Co Ltd* [2003] EWHC 2602 (Comm), [2004] 1 Lloyd's Rep 38; *Prudential Assurance Co Ltd v Ayres* [2007] EWHC 775 (Ch), [2007] 3 All ER 946.

[136] The Law Commission (n 135) 7.18 (iii).

[137] *Avraamides and another v Colwill and another* [2006] EWCA Civ 1533.

Yet, torts is not without its own hurdles when construing environmentalism and climate harms into a duty of care. As Kysar (2012) writes:

> At each stage of the traditional tort analysis – duty, breach, causation, and harm – the climate change plaintiff finds herself bumping up against doctrines that are premised on a classical liberal world view in which threats such as global climate change simply do not register.[138]

Despite the constraints of the elements of tortious liability, attribution science is overcoming issues of causation,[139] and litigants are strongly advancing arguments for a duty of care to be imposed on big carbon emitters for their greenhouse gas contributions.

Landmark cases have succeeded in making rights-based arguments for private climate litigation, such as *Milieudefensie v Royal Dutch Shell plc*.[140] In this torts action, Milieudefensie argued that RDS has an obligation as per the unwritten standard of care under the Dutch Civil Code,[141] to assist efforts to prevent climate change through its corporate policy which applies across its Shell group.[142] The unwritten standard of care is to be interpreted by the *Kelderluik* criteria[143] for risk assessment, as well as human rights. Milieudefensie particularly highlighted the right to life and the right to respect for private and family life, as well as soft law instruments such as the UN Guiding Principles on Business and Human Rights, the UN Global Compact and the OECD Guidelines for Multinational Enterprises.[144] The Milieudefensie case also highlighted the relationship between the success of public law litigation aimed at governments, in particular the case of *Urgenda Foundation v The Netherlands*,[145] and the growing success of private avenues of climate liability. Kim Bouwer writes that there is no 'holy grail' torts case that marks a turning point in torts-based transnational climate litigation;[146] yet enthusiasm in the area of torts climate action is not waning.[147]

[138] Douglas Kysar, 'What Climate Change Can Do About Tort Law' (2012) 42 *Environmental Law Reporter* 10739, 27.

[139] *Luciano Lliuya v RWE AG, Appeal against the Judgment of the District Court of Essen*, Az 2 O 285/15, of 15 December 2016 (2/23/2017) 27.

[140] *Milieudefensie et al v Royal Dutch Shell plc*, ECLI:NL:RBDHA:2021:5339, Hague District Court, Judgment of 26 May 2021.

[141] Book 6, s 162 Dutch Civil Code.

[142] *Milieudefensie et al v Royal Dutch Shell plc* (n 140) [3.2].

[143] Supreme Court, 5 November 1965, ECLI:NL:HR:1965:AB7079 (*Kelderluik*). 'The Dutch Supreme Court has held variations on the Kelderluik judgment to be applicable to a wide variety of risk situations, such as workplace accidents, toxic torts in the workplace, product liability and governmental liability'; see Ivo Giesen, Elbert de Jong and Marlou Overheul, 'How Dutch Law responds to Risks' in Matthew Dyson (ed), *Regulating Risks through Private Law* (Intersentia, 2018) ch 7, 165.

[144] *Milieudefensie et al v Royal Dutch Shell plc* (n 140) [3.2].

[145] *Urgenda Foundation v The Netherlands* [2015] HAZA C/09/00456689 [4.43]; *The State of the Netherlands v Urgenda Foundation*, The Hague Court of Appeal (9 October 2018), case 200.178.245/01 (English translation).

[146] Kim Bouwer, 'Lessons from a Distorted Metaphor: The Holy Grail of Climate Litigation' (2020) 9 *Transnational Environmental Law* 347, 352–56.

[147] Bouwer (n 146).

In addition to the success of these landmark cases, the case of *Begum v Maran (UK) Ltd* could potentially advance the duty of care argument to overcome the issues surrounding privity of contract.[148] Although not a climate nor environmental case per se, this Supreme Court ruling does look down the contractual chain to evaluate whom owes the duty of care. The main issue in this judgment is whether the defendant owed the deceased a duty of care, despite not being a party to an ultimate sale agreement that sold the vessel to unreputable shipbreaking yard where the plaintiff's husband tragically died due to hazardous working conditions. The claimant put forth two arguments (routes) for establishing a duty of care owed to her late husband who was killed in a shipbreaking accident. The first route was based on the vessel being a 'dangerous product' and therefore the principles of *Donoghue v Stevenson* apply.[149] However, the Court was in agreement with the opinion that the danger arose from the demolition process rather than the vessel itself.[150] Nevertheless, the Court could not find such a line of argument to be 'so fanciful' as to strike it out and the question should proceed to trial.[151]

The second, and most plausible route for establishing a duty of care (in the Court's opinion), is that the owner/agent is liable on the basis that it is liable for the actions of third parties such as the shipyard and its management, on the basis that it created the source of danger; therefore falling within the exception of the rule that the law does not impose liability on a person for harm caused to another due the interventions of a third party.[152] This second route was considered arguable and 'not fanciful' and 'may properly be described as an unusual extension of an existing category of cases where a duty has been found, but it would not be an entirely new basis of tortious liability'.[153]

Whilst the matter remains unsettled, the consideration of a torts duty of care will also raise questions of whether freedom of contract carries a responsibility to ensure that vessels will not be sold on to buyers and subsequent buyers who are highly likely to violate international and national laws, causing personal injury and damage to the natural environment. Torts developments cannot therefore be seen in isolation of contract law discussions in the sustainability and human rights context. The *Begum* case raises the question of 'value chain' negligence cases which is, at its core, a network of contracts endeavour. Developments in climate change litigation will no doubt require contractual solutions to not only protect private companies from associated risks, but to also converge risk management with the public law sustainable development agenda. It is therefore long overdue that contract law be examined as a site of climate action solutions as well as other agendas within the sustainable development triage of interests.

[148] *Begum v Maran (UK) Ltd* [2021] EWCA Civ 326.
[149] [38]–[50].
[150] [43].
[151] [50].
[152] [51]; this rule was established in *Smith v Littlewoods Organisation Ltd* [1987] AC 241, 270.
[153] [65].

C. Key Aspects of Contract Governance

'Governance' refers to the 'institutional matrix within which transactions are negotiated and executed'.[154] Therefore, contract governance contemplates a wide range of rule and decision-makers, and the 'interplay between external and internal impacts on decision-making in institutions (state or corporation) and the analysis of 'weak spots' within a scheme of collaboration'.[155] Contract governance incorporates some key considerations and objectives: 1) modernising contract law studies to achieve an integrated view of regulation and private law in market transactions; 2) regulation is not viewed as limiting freedom of contract but as a way of restoring and contributing to party autonomy, therefore viewing regulation and private law as furthering a common goal; 3) steps to close the gaps between regulation and private law remedies are already underway; 4) contracts are not viewed as bilateral instruments, but as a tripartite process between the legislature and contracting parties.[156] Where contract governance exceeds other theories, is that it comprises both traditional and progressive assertions that contracts *govern*, and that we are also concerned with the *governance* of contracts.[157] The author of this book cannot articulate contract governance more eloquently than Zumbansen:

> Contract governance cannot be reduced to a theory of social norms independent from the theory of society, in which it is embedded. This theory, however, is not fully accessible for the law itself, as it has its own – legal – 'rhymes and reasons'. But the differentiation of the legal system occurs as the law 'reacts to the world' over time. In doing so, it receives impulses from economics, politics, and religion and these perturb, impregnate, and challenge the law and its toolkit. This is where we are.[158]

Contract governance necessarily incorporates theories of 'corporate governance' and 'private authority', which have for a long time recognised reflexive governance mechanisms, including 'regulated self-regulation' and ways of connecting the corporate world and state-centric world.[159] In the absence of an international authority which can prescribe and enforce laws which apply to all private actors, multinational enterprises could capitalise on regulatory gaps, externalise costs and employ low standards. Private and corporate governance have therefore proposed new approaches to collective action problems surrounding environmentalism which transverse various scales of regulation.[160] A private governance model identifies the pressures which influence company behaviour *other than*

[154] Oliver E Williamson, 'Transaction-Cost Economics: The Governance of Contractual Relations' (1979) 22 *Journal of Law and Economics* 233, 239.

[155] Grundmann et al (n 79) 5.

[156] ibid.

[157] Zumbansen (n 109) 81.

[158] ibid.

[159] Martin Herberg, 'Private authority, global governance, and the law' in Gerd Winter (Ed.), *Multilevel Governance of Global Environmental Change: Perspectives from Science, Sociology and the Law* (Cambridge University Press 2006) 149–178.

[160] Michael P Vandenbergh, 'Private Environmental Governance' (2013) 99 Cornell L Rev 129.

state regulation.[161] This model also identifies why private forms of governance are more flexible, easier to implement, and less costly to individual interests.[162] Political concerns and issues of state-sovereignty are also less relevant to private relationships, which are premised on freedom of contract, and thus pose less of a barrier to private regulation.

Yet, corporate governance and private authority theories do not delve deeply enough into questions of market transactions and contracts.[163] As such, a broader theoretical framework is needed to frame legal research in contract law where the objectives of the study extend beyond the accepted intrinsic norm of sheer market efficacy. Legal research is predominantly doctrinal and it has therefore been suggested that a narrower normative legal framework is seemingly more appropriate than a general theoretical framework.[164] Westerman (2011) goes further to argue that this distinction is superfluous because the legal system is used as the implicit theoretical framework and doctrinal legal research is inherently normative, using principles of the legal system as standards.[165] On the other hand, Vranken (2011) strongly disagrees with Westerman's idea of the legal system as a theoretical framework and places the system as the subject of a range of theoretical and normative perspectives.[166] This book supports Vranken's view and therefore views contract law as requiring a theoretical approach which can incorporate a number of normative values to obtain a desired outcome. Contract law needs to be adequately structured and modernised to adopt the contextual enquiries that characterise contract governance. As such, contract governance addresses the following broad 'problems', which require multidisciplinary enquiries from not just law and economics, but the full spectrum of social sciences.[167]

(1) Contract and third parties: the problem that legal frameworks and the drafting of contracts have varying impacts on third parties and third parties exert influence on contracts.
(2) Contracts and networks: the problem that contracts form one component of a larger network of relationships – both as individual and interdependent contracts.
(3) Contract and organisation: the problem that contracts have more than an individual exchange function, but also an organisational one in that they constitute the basis of long-term collaboration.

Contract governance is also hugely concerned with combatting 'herd behaviour' – 'when a group of people behave in the same way without being aware of it' and

[161] Michael P Vandenbergh, 'Private Environmental Governance' (n 160).
[162] Michael P Vandenbergh (n 160).
[163] Zumbansen (n 109) 85.
[164] Mark Van Hoecke debates the nature of legal discipline and its methods in *Methodologies of legal research: Which kind of method for what kind of discipline?* (Hart, 2011).
[165] Pauline Westerman, 'Open or autonomous? The debate on legal methodology as a reflection of the debate on law' (2011) in Van Hoecke (n 164) 87–110.
[166] Jan BM Vranken, 'Methodology of legal doctrinal research: A comment on Westerman' in Van Hoecke (n 164) 111–21.
[167] Grundmann et al (n 79) 6–7.

therefore without being critical of it and capable of independent and rational action.[168] International shipping is arguably not immune to herd behaviour as the whole system is entrenched in oil dependency which went unchallenged for many years. Rhetoric of shipping being sustainable compared to other modes of transport and the perceptions of green technology as risky and unsafe, although once rooted in fact, are now commonly accepted as the prevailing rebuttal to calls for innovation. Herd behaviour ultimately contributed to the mass retirements of fleets, their scrapping, and orders for newbuilds resulting in the hazardous recycling practices along developing nation shorelines.[169] However, the concept of herding has not yet received attention from a legal perspective. Legally, it is hard to define and it is largely irrelevant to lawyers and legal scholars until such time that it negatively impacts on others with a tangible causal link.[170] Micklitz writes that an analysis of herd behaviour leads to a number of preliminary conclusions including, inter alia:[171]

- The public/private law divide serves no purpose as contract governance must include all relevant actors, private parties and regulatory/supervisory authorities.[172]
- Supervisory authorities have broader functions than enforcement and compliance, but must monitor the markets including contract making – this means considering the interests of all actors: the financial service provider, private parties and the consumers.[173]
- Cooperation in the spirit of trust and confidence between actors is key.[174]
- The actions of private parties reach beyond the interests of the firm, therefore collective action is needed.

Micklitz proposes that combatting herd behaviour with a contract governance approach recognises the need for: 1) incentives for cooperation; 2) responsible lending and responsible investment; 3) ranking and labelling of risky financial instruments; 4) access to, and disclosure of, information versus advice; 5) contract and corporate governance; and 6) communication (advertising and sales promotion).[175] The overall vision propounded by contract governance is that

[168] Herd behaviour was indeed the cause of the 2008 financial crisis as identified by Bruno S Frey and Reto Cueni, 'Moral Hazard and Herd Behaviour in the Financial Crisis' in Grundmann et al (n 79) 87.

[169] NC Papapostolou, PK Pouliasis and I Kyriakou, 'Herd behavior in the drybulk market: An empirical analysis of the decision to invest in new and retire existing fleet capacity' (2017) 104 *Transportation Research Part E: Logistics and Transportation Review* 36.

[170] Hans-W Micklitz, 'Herd Behaviour and Third Party Impact as a Legal Concept: On Tulips, Pyramid Games, and Asset-backed Securities' in Grundmann et al (n 79) 113.

[171] Micklitz (n 170) 137.

[172] See also Fabrizio Cafaggi and Horatia Muir-Watt, *Making European Private Law, Governance Design* (Edward Elgar Publishing Ltd, 2008).

[173] Micklitz in Grundman et al (n 79) 137.

[174] Micklitz (n 170).

[175] Micklitz (n 170).

when regulators draft the rules, they consider both public supervision and private contracting, bearing in mind 'a realistic vision of the behaviour and the decision-making process of the actors in mind'.[176]

A contract governance approach to environmental management of shipping therefore recognises the pressures on private behaviour *in addition* to state regulation. By placing all emphasis on the IMO and state administrations to bring about protection of the marine environment from vessels, one ignores other critical transboundary forms of governance. Despite the proliferation of private governance attempts in the sector, the IMO and its signatory states are still viewed as the relevant actors for solving environmental challenges and a set of top-down laws are viewed as the necessary action. This outlook fails to recognise that environmental preferences and collective climate objectives can be expressed through a number of private transactions, such as lending, investing, purchasing, supply-chain contracts and major shipping contracts (ie charter parties). Standard-setting already occurs within these negotiated arrangements between private stakeholders and not only for the purpose of achieving compliance with the prevailing public law regime. Enforcement can occur through many private means, such as internal inspections, corporate shaming, non-renewal or termination of agreements, and preferential purchases. Disputes are increasingly resolved through private arbitration without recourse to state courts. All these private activities within the sector generate a type of environmental behaviour which is not determined by a public body.

III. The Importance of Green Contractual Norms

In order for a collective action target to be met, the environmental norms legitimised by international instruments need to more pervasively permeate the private law whilst contract law should also be recognised as an inherent site of norm creation.[177] Utilitarian private law theorists have thus far suggested that the private law creates incentives, not norms.[178] Yet private law institutions are inherently normative, as they use the language of obligations and prescribe how private actors *should* act in relation to each other.[179] Perhaps contract law has been largely excluded from meaningful discussions on normativity as the main legal subjects of contract law are considered to be companies who are supposedly only motivated by economic incentives.[180] This accords with the formalist perspectives discussed in section II.B

[176] ibid 138.

[177] Generally, collective action problems embodying either a social dilemma or tragedy of the commons require cooperative norms; see Jonathan Crowe and Lucy Agnew, 'Legal Obligation and Social Norms' (2020) 41 *Adelaide Law Review* 217, 229.

[178] Stephen A Smith, 'The Normativity of Private Law' (2011) 31 *Oxford Journal of Legal Studies* 215, 215.

[179] ibid 225.

[180] ibid.

above; ie that contract law should not concern itself with norms, as this would require judges to engage with socio-economic policy and moralistic reasoning.[181] It also accords with the preference shown towards market based incentives in meeting decarbonisation targets. Yet economic theories are beginning to recognise that in managing environmental risk, it is not exclusively market incentives that impact on company behaviour, but also external social norms.[182] There is extensive literature on legal norms as a 'type' of social norm,[183] but this section seeks only to assert that maritime law already enjoys a number of environmental legal norms as legitimised by IMO instruments.[184] For the purposes of this discussion, the main question is how these public law green norms can influence maritime contracts, as well as how the contract law infrastructure that governs shipping can simultaneously serve to implement and enforce new social norms (ie from non-legal to legal).

This is an important question as normative approaches have historically been helpful where formal and rigid laws cannot always address the changing legal needs of a commercial environment in flux.[185] In economics and marketing science, it is also recognised that cooperative norms are needed to enhance performance in times of transactional uncertainty.[186] In uncertain times with new emerging risks, performance deteriorates when contracts are not supported by norms while, on the other hand, cooperative norms become unnecessary in times of stability.[187] Relational contract theorists, although often dismissed by formalists and contractual minimalists, have increasingly proposed the idea of improving contractual arrangements for not only the contracting parties but also other stakeholders.[188] The prevalence of relational and 'pro-social' contracting ideas has increased following the power imbalances highlighted by the COVID-19 pandemic in supply chains.[189] Theses pro-social contracting ideas recognise that contracts have the capacity to enshrine values and have expressive powers.[190] Similar to the idea of cooperative norms in economic literature, relational contracting for pro-social values recognises contracts need to operationalise a shared-responsibility model between parties to achieve the social performance of the contract.[191]

[181] Braucher (n 81) 697, 701, 702.

[182] Botao Qin and Jason F Shogren, 'Social norms, regulation, and environmental risk' (2015) 129 *Economic Letters* 22, 22.

[183] H Peyton Young, 'The Evolution of Social Norms' (2015) 7 *Annual Review of Economics* 359, 373.

[184] Michael Tsimplis, 'Environmental norms in maritime contracts' in *Environmental Norms in Maritime Law* (Edward Elgar Publishing, 2021) ch 8.

[185] Hanri du Plessis, 'Legal Pluralism, uBuntuand the Use of Open Norms in the South African Common Law of Contract' (2019) 22 *Potchefstroom Electronic Law Journal*: this article provides an account of how ancient Roman lawyers introduced flexible legal procedures and a more normative approach to a changing commercial environment.

[186] Ulf Bernitz, 'Commercial Norms and Soft Law' (2013) 58 *Scandinavian Studies in Law* 29.

[187] ibid.

[188] Sarah Dadush, 'Prosocial Contracts: Making Relational Contracts More Relational' (2022) 85 *Law and contemporary problems* (0023–9186) 153.

[189] ibid 157.

[190] Jonathan C Lipson, 'Promising Justice: Contract (As) Social Responsibility' (2019) *Wisconsin Law Review* 1109, 1151–52.

[191] Dadush (n 188) 156.

This book posits that cooperative norms are needed in the same way to achieve sustainability or net-zero objectives. Shipping actors require shared-responsibility norms for energy efficiency and shipping contracts need to embed models where the costs and benefits of energy efficiency are shared. This is perhaps best illustrated in the shipowner and time charterer relationship, where the problem of 'split incentives' or the 'principal-agent' has been identified as a major obstacle in achieving an energy transition.[192] The characteristics of this problem are discussed more fully in chapter four on charterparties, yet the idea of shared responsibility is relevant to all the contractual relationships between shipping actors that are discussed in this book. Yet shared-responsibility models can only operate where there is cooperation in the spirit of trust and confidence, also acknowledging that the actions of private parties reach beyond the interests of the firm – a key observation of contract governance theory.[193] A premise of this book is that contracting for net-zero should be supported by norms which can be developed in a number of ways. In maritime contracts, norms predominantly emerge from:[194]

(a) International instruments, binding rules, and legislation governing contract law
(b) Illegality of Contract
(c) The 'Law of Standard Agreements'

i. Binding Rules

In the climate change context, there is a marked absence of binding rules and international instruments which impose environmental or decarbonisation rules on shipping contracts. Here, the regulation and governance of contracts occurs when binding rules such as the Hague-Visby Rules,[195] the Hamburg Rules,[196] or the Rotterdam Rules[197] are implemented and widely adopted. Although such rules have been adopted for contracts of carriage covered by a bill of lading or equivalent document of title, English common law still remains the governing regime for maritime contracts generally speaking.[198]

[192] Seyed Vahid Vakili et al, 'A Conceptual Transdisciplinary Framework to Overcome Energy Efficiency Barriers in Ship Operation Cycles to Meet IMO's Initial Green House Gas Strategy Goals: Case Study for an Iranian Shipping Company' (2022) 15 *Energies* 2098.
[193] Micklitz (n 170) 137.
[194] Tsimplis (n 184).
[195] A final amendment was made in 1979 by the Protocol Amending the International Convention for the Unification of Certain Rules of Law Relating to Bills of Lading (adopted 21 December 1979; in force 14 February 1984). Many countries did not adopt the Hague–Visby Rules and stayed with the 1924 Hague Rules; whilst some countries which chose to upgrade to the Hague-Visby Rules subsequently failed to adopt the 1979 protocol.
[196] The UN Convention on the Carriage of Goods by Sea (adopted 31 March 1978, in force 1 November 1992) A/CONF.89/13.
[197] UNCITRAL Convention on Contracts for the International Carriage of Goods Wholly or Partly by Sea (New York, 2008).
[198] The Rules applicable to charterparty agreements and the prevalence of environmental norms therein, are discussed in ch 4.

Under English common law, parties are given a high degree of autonomy, and that autonomy is only restricted or regulated where there are strong public policy reasons to do so. The Sale of Goods Act 1979 and the Consumer Rights Act 2015 are key examples where the interests of the buyer have been afforded protection in contracts for the sale of goods, as well as services where the latter is concerned. There are thus only two ways to develop norms using binding contract law rules: 1) parliamentary intervention; or 2) via the doctrine of precedent (ie judge-made law). At present, parliamentary intervention only exists in some limited capacity with regards to public procurement contracts, while no case law to date accepts sustainability or its pillar of environmentalism as an underpinning contractual norm.

At certain junctures, this book explores arguments for the implication of green terms or the construction of terms to include green objectives, yet there is no English law precedent as of yet to support these arguments. A 'greening' of the common law is probably an unlikely possibility at present,[199] yet it is argued that such normativity becomes a closer reality. Indeed, such arguments are more likely to succeed in post-colonial constitutions embedding environmental rights capable of horizontal application.[200] The EU has also introduced ecological concerns into the legitimate consumer expectations standard under EU sales law[201] and therefore introduces the idea of ecological sustainability in the criterion of reasonableness, 'which is applied at the stage of interpretation of every act undertaken by a private law subject'.[202] There are thus incremental steps occurring in the Global North, while the Global South presents untapped potential for the alignment of the private law with climate change targets.

ii. Illegality of Contract

Shipping contracts are subject to the ordinary requirement of contract law that obligations cannot be enforceable if they contravene public laws and standards.[203] There are a number of conventions that impose standards on private shipping actors and these instruments are inherently normative. Specifically, MARPOL recognises a principle of prevention yet this falls short of the precautionary principle of international environmental law as harmful substances are only controlled where 'liable to' create damage or harm to humans and the marine environment.[204]

[199] David Gibbs-Kneller, 'Corporate Strategy on Climate Risk in the Courtroom: Not Worth Powder in Shot' (2023) 25 *Sage Journals* 326.

[200] Pia Rebelo and Xavier Rebelo, 'Rights-Based Climate Change Litigation Against Private Actors' in Kim Bouwer et al (eds), *Climate Litigation and Justice in Africa* (Bristol University Press, 2024) 187–219.

[201] Directive (EU) 2019/771 of the European Parliament and of the Council of 20 May 2019 on certain aspects concerning contracts for the sale of goods, amending Regulation (EU) 2017/2394 and Directive 2009/22/EC, and repealing Directive 1999/44/EC.

[202] Katarzyna Południak-Gierz, 'Eco-Reasonableness. Possibilities of Incorporating Green Principles Into General Private Law Clauses' in M Andenas and M Heidemann (eds), *Quo vadis Commercial Contract?* (LCF Studies in Commercial and Financial Law, vol 1, Springer, 2023) 107–27.

[203] *Holman v Johnson* (1775) 1 Cowp 341.

[204] Art 2(2) MARPOL.

As Tsimplis notes, this reflects the outcome of such events happening, not being entirely guarded against.[205] MARPOL does reflect a norm of cooperation and implementation, yet this applies only to states and their jurisdiction to investigate contraventions of MARPOL.[206] Furthermore, MARPOL does not embody principles of sustainable development, which are understandably beyond its original scope which dealt almost exclusively with oil pollution. However, the IMO has committed itself to sustainable development and the realisation of the Sustainable Development Goals (SDGs) in its contemporary work.[207] The CII standard is supposed to reflect the IMO's 2023 GHG Strategy and its objectives, and perhaps proffers the best prospect for a normative commitment between actors to improve energy efficiency over time.

Up until the adoption of the CII standard, contractual compliance clauses implementing environmental standards have not been a lucrative site for norm creation and have not had the cumulative effect of establishing normative guidance for contractual performance.[208] Environmental compliance is ordinarily dealt with through the use of boilerplate clauses as recommended by shipping associations such as BIMCO and INTERTANKO. Instead of creating cooperative norms, environmental compliance is usually handled in such a way that the responsibility of compliance unequally burdens one party who bears the risks and costs.

Chapter four of this book presents an analysis of how very recently published clauses on GHG emissions such as BIMCO's EEXI Clause[209] as well as its ETS Clause[210] for time charters, appear to fit squarely within the traditional boundaries of duties that polarise and juxtapose party interests. Much like BIMCO's previous compliance clauses for sulphur emission standards,[211] these clauses are not intended to provide normative foundations for the interpretation of other duties and isolate environmental factors to the confines of lesser warranty provisions, ie those not generally serious enough in nature to afford termination rights upon breach. However, BIMCO's CII Operations for Time Charters Clause illustrates a marked and progressive difference in the way that parties deal with net-zero targets.[212] This clause will be discussed in greater detail in chapter four.

iii. *The 'Law of Standard Agreements'*

Much of the contractual governance of international commerce takes place through standard form agreements. Standard form agreements are, 'generally speaking, the

[205] Tsimplis (n 184).

[206] Article 6 MARPOL.

[207] It did so in its Strategic Plans since 2016; see Strategic Plan for the Organization (2016–2021), Assembly Resolution A.1097(29) 1 December 2015.

[208] Pia Rebelo, 'BIMCO's Carbon Intensity Indicator Clause (CII) for time charters: towards a new era of climate drafting' (2022) 28 *Journal of International Maritime Law* 240.

[209] BIMCO, EEXI Transition Clause for Time Charter Parties (2021).

[210] BIMCO, Emission Trading Scheme Allowances Clause For Time Charter Parties (2022).

[211] BIMCO, 2020 Marine Fuel Sulphur Content Clause for Time Charter Parties (2020).

[212] Pia Rebelo, 'BIMCO's Carbon Intensity Indicator Clause (CII) for time charters: towards a new era of climate drafting' (2022) 28 *Journal of International Maritime Law* 240.

most important instrument nowadays for norm creation in business',[213] particularly in an international sector where standard forms comprise sources of transnational private law.[214] Maritime law is no exception, and the prevalence of standardised forms has created a series of customs and implied duties in relation to contractual performance. This is particularly true with charterparty forms which enjoy a circular relationship with common law duties. Many of the common law duties placed on private parties under voyage and time charters have arisen from customary trade practices embodied in standardised documents, whilst standard forms inevitably include recognisable common law obligations that would be implied where not express.

Despite the changing landscape of global commerce, the shipping sector remains notoriously conservative in adopting new forms or accepting amendments to existing recognisable agreements.[215] There is also a small pool of charterparty standard forms to choose from, with the classic and most prevalent time charterparty form existing in three iterations: NYPE46, NYPE93 and NYPE2015. Despite having more suitable revised iterations of the NYPE form, the NYPE46 remains the most widespread.[216]

However, environmental norms have emerged from other maritime relationships characterised by standard forms, such as the RECYCLECON and salvage removal forms. The RECYCLECON contract provides a standardised document for the sale of vessels for recycling a vessel in 'a safe and environmentally sound manner consistent with the international and national law and relevant guidelines'.[217] This contract thus covers vessels sold for recycling *only*; it does not cover previous trading arrangements prior to the vessel being recycled.[218] This contract can bind private actors to the Hong Kong Convention for The Safe and Environmentally Sound Recycling of Ships (HK Convention)[219] as Clause 17 requires that the buyer 'undertake and warrant that the Vessel will be recycled at a Ship Recycling Facility in accordance with the Ship Recycling Facility Plan and the Ship Recycling Plan'. As such, the norms of the HK Convention are imposed on actors as a way to guide contractual performance for an environmental benefit. In standard forms for salvage, contractors 'shall use their best endeavours to prevent or minimise damage to the environment',[220] as well as adhere to duties

[213] Bernitz (n 186) 40.
[214] Joanne Braithwaite, 'Standard Form Contracts as Transnational Law: Evidence from the Derivatives Markets Standard Form Contracts as Transnational Law' (2012) 75 *Modern Law Review* 0026–7961, 779.
[215] Paul Todd, 'NYPE 2015: Wholesale Reform or an Invitation to Cherry-Pick?' (2016) *Lloyd's Maritime & Commercial Law Quarterly* 306.
[216] ibid.
[217] BIMCO, RECYCLECON (2012), *Preamble.*
[218] c' 17.
[219] Hong Kong International Convention for The Safe And Environmentally Sound Recycling Of Ships, 2009 SR/CONF/45 (HK Convention).
[220] Lloyd's Standard Form Of Salvage Agreement 2020, cl B.

from the 1989 Salvage Convention.[221] Although the Salvage Convention permits contractual variation or exclusion of its provisions, environmental obligations cannot be excluded.[222]

Standard forms have the capacity to include sustainability or decarbonisation norms which could be inferred from the totality of the environmental commitments expressed in such forms, and heightened by reference to international standards, soft law and voluntarily adopted commitments to decarbonisation targets. The contractual techniques available to do so are discussed in specific transactional contexts in each upcoming chapter of this book. However, the standard form agreements in current use are likely to only achieve this if substantively modified by parties.

IV. Concluding Remarks

This book employs a contract governance approach to facilitating and achieving GHG reductions in the shipping sector through targeted contractual mechanisms. This calls for a *re-evaluation* of private agreements to *implement*, *enforce* and *achieve* a higher level of shared commitment to transition the sector from fossil fuel propulsion to renewable and environmentally sustainable sources of energy.

Although 'green' shipping can comprise a myriad of activities with environmental sustainability benefits, the scope of the book is confined primarily to net-zero objectives aimed at tackling climate change. Contractual agreements can *incentivise* better practices through providing commercial certainty on how the responsibility for enhanced energy efficiency is to be shared amongst parties, whilst simultaneously providing an interpretive framework for the manner in which all obligations and sub-contracted obligations are carried out. Contractual arrangements can also provide *new ways of self-regulation* in addressing the gaps in compliance and enforcement created by the public law regime.

As recognised by contract governance theories, the term 'contract' is defined not only in a legal sense of comprising of its constituent elements under English law, but it is recognised as a tool upon which the effects of governance are contingent.[223] Contracts embody exchange relationships which operate within a social framework of norms and ideals.[224] A fundamental assertion of this book is that contracts can either promote the achievement of such ideals or maintain the status quo.

[221] 1989 International Convention on Salvage (adopted 28 April 1989) 1953 UNTS 193.

[222] Art 6(3).

[223] Thomas G Noordewier, George John and John R Nevin, 'Performance Outcomes of Purchasing Arrangements in Industrial Buyer-Vendor Relationships' (1990) 54 *Journal of Marketing* 80.

[224] Russell Hardin, 'The New Social Contract: An Inquiry into Modern Contractual Relations, Ian R. Macneil' (1982) 93 *Ethics* 168.

2

Green Finance for Shipping

Energy transitions and the achievement of climate objectives require huge capital investments from both the public and private sector.[1] This reality has catalysed a diverse range of financial products, policy responses and regulatory interventions.[2] However, these responses are still very much in their infancy and teething problems have emerged in the form of new legal risks stemming from the notion of financial 'green washing' – ie where the sustainability performance of a financial product misleads investors and stakeholders.[3] Similar to ordinary greenwashing, where a company's communicated practices are seemingly green whilst their actual practices are unsustainable,[4] 'financial greenwashing' refers to misleading information suggesting that a bank's portfolio is climate-aligned or environmentally sustainable. As such, a number of regulatory and voluntary frameworks have emerged to deal with the lack of consistency and clarity on what constitutes 'green', 'sustainable', 'climate-aligned', or conversely, 'brown' or 'unsustainable'. Despite these significant developments, research and guidance on the contractual implementation of green finance has been largely ignored or deliberately avoided.[5] Even in the context of regulatory frameworks, the most notable example of which is the EU Taxonomy Regulation,[6] there is a reluctance on the part of state administrations to interfere with the private law. Cherednychenko notes that:

> While a flawed contractual design of financial products and a failure of contract law to ensure their economic and social utility were at the root of the global financial crisis, the EU policy discourse has traditionally focused on economic activities (for example

[1] UNFCCC, 'Summary of Global Climate Action at COP 28' (2023), unfccc.int/sites/default/files/resource/Summary_GCA_COP28.pdf.

[2] G20 Green Finance Study Group, G20 Green Finance Synthesis Report (5 September 2016) 10.

[3] European Banking Authority, EBA Progress Report on Greenwashing Monitoring and Supervision (31 May 2023) EBA/REP/2023/16.

[4] Kent Walker and Fang Wan, 'The harm of symbolic actions and green-washing: Corporate actions and communications on environmental performance and their financial implications' (2012) 109 *Journal of Business Ethics* 227.

[5] Federica Agostini, 'From "Green Bond Principles" to "Green Bond Clauses": Mitigating Greenwashing Through Contract Law' in Mads Andenas and Maren Heidemann (eds), *Quo vadis Commercial Contract? Reflections on Sustainability, Ethics and Technology in the Emerging Lawand Practice of Global Commerce* (Springer Nature Switzerland AG, 2023) 151.

[6] Proposal for a Regulation of the European Parliament and of the Council on the establishment of a framework to facilitate sustainable investment COM/2018/353 final; The Taxonomy Regulation came into force on 12 July 2020.

financial services) rather than the legal mechanisms used to carry out such activities (for example contracts) and enforcement avenues available to private parties.[7]

Similarly, developments in the green bond market have focused on what makes a bond 'green' without addressing how green bond clauses have adjusted to regulatory frameworks and their effectiveness in safeguarding the 'greenness' of funds and securities.[8] This chapter focuses on this particular gap in legal research and views contract law as a quasi-regulatory tool for the implementation of green standards in ship financing. In keeping with a contract governance theory, private actors must translate a set of converged climate objectives into their day-to-day transactions to carry out the objectives of the green finance framework in question, whilst also minimising greenwashing risks and protecting commercial interests.

Furthermore, the impacts of green finance frameworks reach further than simply controlling lender–borrower relationships. The loan agreement is the first contract in a chain of contracts that determines the shipowner's commercial decisions. To avoid 'vicarious' greenwashing in this chain of contracts, comparable to what is prevalent in supply chain greenwashing,[9] the loan agreement will need a set of contractual prescriptions that impacts the shipowners' subsequent transactions with third parties – ie with shipyards, charterers, fuel suppliers, freight forwarders, recycling yards, etc. The loan agreement may even directly impact on contractual arrangements between third parties exclusively (ie where the shipowner is not a party to the contract), such as between charterer and bunker supplier. Contract governance theory literature has recognised, specifically in the context of product safety standards, that 'effective implementation would require a network structure rather than a sequence of bilateral contracts'.[10] The same applies to the implementation of green or sustainability standards that are equally dependent on compliance by multiple interdependent actors and must increasingly focus on control points along the chain.[11] Bilateral contracts cannot govern high degrees of interdependence which need to be governed in a cooperative setting.[12] As such, green finance frameworks can provide the basis for a series of cooperative norms across networks along sustainability or green objectives. Indeed, cooperative norms are expressly incorporated into climate clauses and can assist

[7] Olha O Cherednychenko, 'EU Financial Regulation, Contract Law and Sustainable Consumer Finance' (2019) University of Groningen Faculty of Law Research Paper Series No. 4/2020.

[8] Agostini (n 5) 152.

[9] Meaning that a company's suppliers misbehave in way that is inconsistent to the company's communicated green strategies. See Marta Pizzetti, Lucia Gatti and Peter Seele, 'Firms Talk, Suppliers Walk: Analyzing the Locus of Greenwashing in the Blame Game and Introducing 'Vicarious Greenwashing'' (2021) 170 *Journal of Business Ethics* 21.

[10] Fabrizio Cafaggi and Paola Iamiceli, 'Private Regulation and Industrial Organization: Contractual Governance and the Network Approach' in Stefan Grundmann, Florian Möslein and Karl Riesenhuber (eds), *Contract Governance: Dimensions in Law and Interdisciplinary Research* (Oxford University Press, 2015) 353.

[11] ibid 345.

[12] Gunther Teubner, 'Coincidentia Oppositorum: Hybrid Networks Beyond Contract and Organisation' in Marc Amstutz and Gunther Teubner (eds), *Networks. Legal Issues of Multilateral Cooperation* (Hart Publishing, 2009).

with the effective implementation of green finance frameworks within contractual networks. The purpose of this chapter is to conceive the transaction between lender and borrower for the obtainment of green finance as the first arrangement in a network of contracts that will realise the decarbonisation of shipping.

This chapter first sets out the green finance landscape for shipping (section I). It outlines the purpose of green finance frameworks as key risk-management tools and tracks the recent progress that has been made to provide shipping with a set of 'green' definitions and scope for eligible activities. Emphasis must also be placed on emerging risks that stem from green finance, namely greenwashing in the financial markets. This also emphasises that new risks involve a network approach to contracts as litigants are seeking to follow the money trail and pierce the 'contractual veil' in environmental and climate-related disputes.[13] Second, the chapter provides an overview of regulatory (section II) and private voluntary green finance frameworks (section III) that have included shipping. Third, it analyses the contractual mechanisms available for the implementation of green finance frameworks. As debt-financing remains dominant in ship finance, the loan agreement will be evaluated for its effectiveness in implementing green finance frameworks and for 'weak spots' where enforcement measures require development. Contracts must seek ways to effectively implement green finance frameworks between parties to maximise their normative value in achieving shared climate goals and to provide for effective risk management. This is a largely technical enquiry based within the common law principles of English law as the prevailing legal system of the international maritime sector; as the majority of shipping loan agreements are governed by English law principles.[14] Although there is a lack of standardised green clauses specifically for ship finance, voluntary initiatives are starting to provide template clauses and contractual guidance.

I. The Green Finance Landscape and Shipping

Green finance is endorsed by the UN as 'all the initiatives taken by private and public agents (e.g. businesses, banks, governments, international organizations, etc.) in developing, promoting, implementing and supporting projects with sustainable impacts through financial instruments'.[15] The United Nations Global Compact also recognises financial intermediation by banks as critical in creating a link between global capital and private financial solutions for the realisation of the SDGs.[16] From a regulator's perspective, green finance is concerned with

[13] See for example, *Begum v Maran (UK) Ltd* [2021] 3 WLUK 162.

[14] Lucy French, 'Introduction' in Stephenson Harwood (ed), *Shipping Finance*, 3rd edn (Euromoney, 2006).

[15] ITC, 'What is Green Finance?', www.intracen.org/What-is-green-finance.

[16] UN Global Compact, *Scaling SDG Finance for the Sustainable Development Goals: Foreign Direct Investment, financial intermediation and public–private partnerships* (Report, 2019) 23, www.unglobalcompact.org/library/5721.

de-risking energy transitions by mobilising the necessary capital for low-carbon or zero-carbon technologies and guiding industry actors on technology selection. Many theoretical frameworks exist to categorise the barriers to energy transitions, yet most recognise that the problem of climate change requires a radical transformation of modern industrial socio-technological regimes.[17] These transformative transitions are generally hindered by: 1) uncertainty regarding regulatory change and technical capacity; 2) disagreements about optimal solutions, costs and benefits; and 3) the distribution of power between state and non-state actors.[18] Green finance poses solutions to all three of these barriers by directing actors towards a verified set of activities that investment should be channelled towards, thereby providing capital for pre-selected methods and technology for optimal energy performance.[19] As such, regulators and policy-makers have done much work to establish frameworks embodying such criteria to avoid a taxonomy diversification and to unify the inconsistencies that have emerged from piece-meal ESG and CSR initiatives on a private governance level.

From a banking perspective, green finance is largely concerned with risk. Private financial institutions have for a long time acknowledged the concept of 'environmental risk'. Environmental risks generally have three aspects: credit risk, lender liability and reputational risk.[20] Credit risk is influenced by the growing body of restrictive environmental regulations imposed on borrowing companies which weakens their position to repay loans, whilst security offered in the form on real property[21] can mean impaired value of collateral and saleability if non-compliance occurs.[22] Lender liability is directly linked to the bank's own governing environmental legislation which can result in costly rehabilitation, clean-ups and damages caused by the bank's borrowing companies. Reputation risk refers to the public's perception of the bank, as well as by its key stakeholders who significantly contribute to the long-term viability of the institution.[23] Banks with shipping portfolios need to prepare for these risks, and green finance frameworks are a good way of managing regulatory risks imposed by tightening environmental standards as well as the demand-side risks of consumer preferences for green supply chains.[24]

[17] Jonathan Köhler et al, 'An agenda for sustainability transitions research: State of the art and future directions' (2019) 31 *Environmental Innovation and Societal Transitions* 1.

[18] Frank W Geels et al, 'The Socio-Technical Dynamics of Low-Carbon Transitions' (2017) 1 *Joule* 463.

[19] Pia Rebelo, 'Legal Tools for Overcoming Perceived Risks' in Green Shipping in Regulation of Risk (Brill | Nijhoff, 2022).

[20] Yinshuo Xu et al, 'The Impacts of Environmental Risks on Bank Loan Covenants and the Cost of Bank Loans: an Australian Case Study and the Implications for China' in *Proceedings of the 2018 International Conference on E-Business and Applications* (ICEBA, 2018).

[21] For example, contaminated land in respect of terrestrial activities or a vessel which can only use HFOs.

[22] Phil Case, *Environmental risk management and corporate lending: a global perspective* (Woodhead Publishing Limited, 1999).

[23] Katherine Taken Smith, Murphy Smith and Kun Wang, 'Does brand management of corporate reputation translate into higher market value?' (2010) 18 *Journal of Strategic Marketing* 201.

[24] Share Action, 'Changing Course: Bank Financing of the Shipping Industry' (*Investor Briefing*, May 2019).

Ships built with short-term investor perspectives typically underperform and have a much higher risk of depreciating and becoming illiquid.[25] This consequently poses a risk of ships becoming stranded assets – a phenomenon which usually occurs during times of an oversupply market whereby ships lose 'economic value well ahead of … anticipated useful life'.[26] In fact, the high exposure that banks face in respect of their shipping portfolios has often led to opinions that 'shipping and banking don't mix' and that capital sources such as sovereign wealth funds, financial conglomerates, and pension funds are better suited to handle the risks and cyclicity of the industry.[27] The financial volatility of shipping is exacerbated by the greater climate risks that banks are facing which comprise both the physical risk of climate-related disasters and transition risks to low-carbon or zero-carbon economies.[28] Although this chapter is not concerned with a full exposition of the types of climate risks that banks are exposed to, it is worth noting that climate activism is creatively engaging new legal avenues for holding corporations accountable for both direct and indirect contributions to climate change. Inroads have already been made in the areas of torts liability,[29] company law,[30] advertising and competition law[31] and financial sector greenwashing claims. Germany has already seen a financial product advertised by Commerz Real Fund Management Sàrl subjected to greenwashing claims.[32] In this particular case, investors were able to make use of the Fund's website to calculate their personal CO_2 footprint and then offset that figure with a calculable investment. The Regional Court found this to be misleading and in violation of § 5(1) of the Act against Unfair Competition.

To deal with greenwashing complaints, a number of market regulators are taking action accordingly. The US Securities and Exchange Commission has set up a Climate and ESG Task Force, whilst the UK's Financial Conduct Authority is

[25] UMAS, *Navigating Decarbonisation: An approach to evaluate shipping's risks and opportunities associated with climate change mitigation policy* (2017), rmi.org/wp-content/uploads/2017/03/Shipping_Navigating_Decarbonization_Report_2017.pdf.

[26] Generation Foundation, *Stranded Carbon Assets: Why and How Carbon Risks Should Be Incorporated in Investment Analysis* (2013), www.genfound.org/media/1374/pdf-generation-foundation-stranded-carbon-assets-v1.pdf.

[27] Zam Kahn, 'It's time we faced the fact that banks and shipping don't mix' (*TradeWinds*, 20 September 2019), www.tradewindsnews.com/opinion/it-s-time-we-faced-the-fact-that-banks-and-shipping-don-t-mix/2-1-670495.

[28] TCDF, *Final Report on the Recommendations of the Task Force on Climate-related Financial Disclosures* (15 June 2017), www.fsb-tcfd.org/wp-content/uploads/2017/06/FINAL-2017-TCFD-Report-11052018.pdf.

[29] *Milieudefensie et al v Royal Dutch Shell plc*, Hague District Court, Judgment of 26 May 2021 (ECLI:NL:RBDHA:2021:5339); *Luciano Lliuya v RWE AG* Case No. 2 O 285/15 Essen Regional Court (15 December 2016); and possibly *Begum v Maran* (UK) Ltd [2021] 3 WLUK 162.

[30] *Australasian Centre for Corporate Responsibility v Commonwealth Bank of Australia* [2016] FCAFC 80; *Minister of Water Affairs and Forestry v Stilfontein Gold Mining Company* (2006) 5 SA 333 (W).

[31] See *FossielVrij NL v KLM*, whereby KLM airline has been sued for falsely advertising to consumers that they can fly sustainably under its 'Fly Responsibly' campaign, available at climatecasechart.com/non-us-case/fossielvrij-nl-v-klm; also see Climate Case chart for more examples: climatecasechart.com/non-us-case-category/misleading-advertising.

[32] *Verbraucherzentrale Baden-Württemberg eV v Commerz Real Fund Management Sàrl* Regional Court Stuttgart, judgment of 10 January 2022, docket no 36 O 92/21 KfH.

working to build trust in ESG-labelled instruments.[33] The UK's Financial Services and Market Act 2000 makes provision for compensation for losses suffered as a result of misleading and inaccurate ESG claims and disclosures made in published information and corporate governance documents or statements.[34] The European Securities and Markets Authority has stated in its Roadmap for Sustainable Finance (2022–2024) that it will tackle greenwashing and promote transparency.[35]

Although these risks might be complex considerations for banks to manage and overcome, they also present real opportunities to adapt and offer increasingly competitive products. Banks can improve credit quality and loan portfolio resilience by effectively identifying climate-related risks. Through promoting energy-efficiency in lending practices, banks can enhance the quality of collateral thus raising recovery rates in the event of default. This is because the energy efficiency of a ship influences its asset value in the second-hand market in a number of ways: 1) by restoring profit margins, where fossil energy prices are expected to increase; 2) by increasing competitiveness because charterers and end users are conscious of damaging environmental practices; and 3) the environmental profile of an asset may translate into how the vessel is used, eg energy-efficient vessels may have less idle time between contracts.[36] In the same way, retrofits can also improve the quality of assets to assist ship portfolios in minimising risk. This should be accompanied by standardised reporting amongst banks so as to not affect competition by certain banks offering 'relaxed' reporting measures. Green finance frameworks can assist banks in creating taxonomy aligned financial products for shipowners.

Whilst other economic sectors have benefited from a wide range of banking and finance initiatives for the funding of industrial projects,[37] shipping has only enjoyed inclusion in green finance initiatives recently. To incentivise shipping companies to order energy efficient newbuilds, purchase green second-hand vessel, or to upgrade existing technology within their fleets, green finance must be readily available that allows for preferential access to funds for these green actions. This process is practically facilitated through commercial contracts which have been characterised by the standard forms governing product offerings and loan disbursements. Whilst bank debt-financing prevails as the traditional method of ship finance, green finance frameworks are relevant to a number of contractual arrangements prevalent in the diversification of ship finance such as the capital markets, leasing and mezzanine financing.[38]

[33] FCA, Sustainability Disclosure Requirements (SDR) and investment labels (CP22/20), www.fca.org.uk/publication/consultation/cp22-20.pdf.

[34] ss 90 and 90A.

[35] European Securities and Markets Authority, 'Sustainable Finance Roadmap 2022–2024' 8, www.esma.europa.eu/sites/default/files/library/esma30-379-1051_sustainable_finance_roadmap.pdf.

[36] Roar Adland, Pierre Cariou and François-Charles Wolff, 'Does energy efficiency affect ship values in the second-hand market?' (2018) ffhalshs-01706627f, halshs.archives-ouvertes.fr/halshs-01706627/document.

[37] An early example is the Equator Principles: equator-principles.com.

[38] Fotis Giannakoulis, 'Overview of ship finance' in Manolis Kavussanos and ID Visvikis, *The International Handbook of Shipping Finance* (Palgrave Macmillan, 2016) 71–94.

II. Regional Frameworks: EIB Green Shipping Programmes, the EU Taxonomy Regulation, UK

The inclusion of shipping in the EU Taxonomy Regulation is an important development for shipowners given the difficulties in accessing finance since the 2008 financial crisis which saw the implementation of the Basel criteria and shipping projects classified as 'riskier' – hence, the withdrawal of certain stakeholders and the reduction of accessible liquidity for shipping actors.[39] Prior to the EU's Action Plan on Disclosed Finance of 2018, shipowners were able to access green finance in a limited way under the European Investment Bank's (EIB) Green Shipping programme. The EIB provides targeted financial products and finances green shipping projects in three ways:

(1) Under its traditional lending programme with large shipping corporates.
(2) The Green Shipping Guarantee Programme (GSG): structured as an EU Connecting Europe Facility (CEF) and the European Fund for Strategic investments (EFSI) debt instrument in cooperation with shipping banks.[40]
(3) The Green Shipping Loan Programme (GSL): structured as programme loan for a series of sub-loans to for ship owners with eligible projects primarily in European shipyards and aligned with the TEN-T policy.[41]

In respect of the GSG, a number of requirements are to be fulfilled by a 'promoter': an acceptable corporate that can demonstrate significant experience and competence for the work proposed; that can demonstrate that EU procurement procedures have been implemented for shipyard selection and all relevant regulatory standards are met; whilst also seeking to enhance environmental and social capability through the adoption of non-regulatory standards applicable to the maritime industry (ie ISO).[42] For the GSL, projects must meet the eligibility criteria in the Bank's Transport Lending Policy which requires satisfactory forecast economic returns and consistency with EU Maritime policy on green, sustainable shipping.[43] Both types of schemes require EIAs for multi-investment projects which are to be determined at the appraisal stage, and both also exist within the EU regulatory and policy framework more generally. Chuah has written quite comprehensively on the difficulties in incorporating these requirements into core contractual undertakings.[44]

[39] Manolis G Kavussanos and Dimitris A Tsouknidis, 'Green Shipping Finance: Existing Initiatives and the Road Ahead' in Byoung-Wook Ko and Dong-Wook Song (eds), *New Maritime Business. WMU Studies in Maritime Affairs* Vol 10 (Springer, 2021).

[40] EIB, Green Shipping Guarantee Programme, www.eib.org/en/projects/all/20150334.

[41] ibid.

[42] EIB GSG, 'Environmental and Social Data Sheet' (11 May 2018), www.eib.org/attachments/registers/67288970.pdf. Recent promoters include: Spliethoff's Bevrachtingskantoor BV (SBK); BAI – Mont St-Michel II Financing for Brittany Ferries Group; Eureka Shipping Holdings.

[43] ibid.

[44] Jason Chuah, 'Legal Aspects of Green Shipping Finance – Insights from the European Investment Bank's Schemes' in P Mukherjee P et al (eds), *Maritime Law in Motion. WMU Studies in Maritime Affairs* Vol 8 (Springer, 2020) 131–52.

Some guidance on contractual implementation is given in the EIB's 2014 contract terms for environmental matters.[45] The environmental undertakings of borrowers by these proforma clauses is one of applicable national and EU law, including principles and standards, national laws and regulations, and applicable international treaties – all 'of which a principal objective is the preservation, protection or improvement of the Environment'.[46] The EIB is also an institution which furthers the objectives of the EU and is constrained by its own legislation which gives it its competence to grant loans.[47] EIB Investments should 'be carried out in the territories of Member States' and 'to the extent that funds are not available from other sources on reasonable terms'.[48] The criterion of 'reasonable terms' is a matter of policy and commercial consideration.[49] This is informed by the EIB Transport Lending Policy 2011, which sets out lending policy and selection criteria.[50] This, in turn, is primarily articulated through the 2011 Transport White Paper, which envisions a maritime 'blue belt' and market access to ports in terms of shipping activities. Shipping is discussed in relation to easing encumbrances on maritime transport within the Union, which does little to classify maritime projects in alignment with EU sustainability objectives. The EIB Transport Lending Policy also outlines a commitment to the Trans-European Transport Network (TEN-T);[51] which is committed to a gradual incorporation of climate change considerations in all its transport and related activities.[52] The TEN-T policy focuses on the development of two main transport pillars: the 'Motorways of the Sea' (MoS), and the European Railway Transport Management System.[53] The primary aim of the MoS

[45] cl 1(a) of 'EIB template contractual clauses on environmental matters' (2014) www.eib.org/attachments/documents/eib_standard_contractual_clauses_on_environmental_information_en.pdf.

[46] cl 1(g).

[47] Art 16 of the Consolidated version of the Treaty on the Functioning of the European Union Protocol (No 5) on The Statute Of The European Investment Bank OJ C 202, 7.6.2016, p. 251–264 (EIB Statute), read in conjunction with Art 309 of the Consolidated versions of the Treaty on European Union and the Treaty on the Functioning of the European Union (TFEU) [2016] OJ C202/1; Art 18(1) also restricts these competencies.

[48] Art 16, EIB Statute. This adds two important requirements, centred on two concepts: 'territories' and 'reasonable terms'.

[49] See Chuah (n 44); and EU Parliament and Council in a Decision No 1080/2011/EU of the European Parliament and of the Council of 25 October 2011 which specifically states the competency of the EU to finance projects outside the Union (in particular Recital 8).

[50] EIB, *EIB Transport Lending Policy* (13 December 2011), www.eib.org/attachments/strategies/transport_lending_policy_en.pdf.

[51] European Commission, *The TEN-T project* (2013), ec.europa.eu/inea/en/ten-t/ten-t-projects; based on Regulation (EU) No 1315/2013 of the European Parliament and of the Council of 11 December 2013 on Union guidelines for the development of the trans-European transport network and repealing Decision No 661/2010/EU Text with EEA relevance. This Regulation is currently being revised to align the TEN-T policy with the European Green Deal and the Sustainable and Smart Mobility Strategy. See Proposal for a Regulation of The European Parliament And of the Council on Union guidelines for the development of the trans-European transport network, amending Regulation (EU) 2021/1153 and Regulation (EU) No 913/2010 and repealing Regulation (EU) 1315/2013, COM/2021/812 final.

[52] EIB (n 50).

[53] European coordinators were appointed to lead the harmonised realisation of these projects, for which work plans were drawn up in 2015. There are currently five workplans, the latest being the Rhine-Alpine TEN-T Core Network Corridor.

it to accomplish a 'European Maritime Transport Space without barriers, connecting Core Network Corridors by integrating maritime links with hinterland',[54] which is fundamentally a strategy aimed at development and infrastructure to facilitate economic growth.

Contractual implementation and the underlying purport of EIB green financing for shipping is therefore difficult to conceive given the matrix of governing EU environmental law, EIB governing law, and EU transport policies. In addition to criticisms that the EIB's green shipping schemes are 'too demanding' on users,[55] available template clauses do not provide interpretative guidance for contractual loan terms whilst regulatory compliance is listed as a check-box activity of all applicable environmental laws. This is not necessarily a bad strategy in terms of protecting against regulatory risk, but is arguably insufficient for the growing body of climate risks emerging from the financial markets. Nevertheless, the administrative complexity of the programmes means that many shipowners are ineligible for EIB support.[56]

Given the growing risks emerging from ESG-labelled instruments, the European Commission delivered its Action Plan on Sustainable Finance in 2018,[57] which develops sustainability criteria under the EU's Framework to Facilitate Sustainable Investment (the 'Taxonomy Regulation') which provides an EU-wide classification system in identifying environmentally sustainable economic activities and providing technical screening criteria.[58] Article 3 of the Taxonomy Regulation provides four overarching criteria for environmentally sustainable economic activities.[59] Determining the degree to which an investment is environmentally sustainable is measured according to whether the economic activity:

(1) contributes to one or more of the environmental objectives set out in Article 9 (in accordance with Articles 10 to 16);[60]
(2) does not significantly harm any of the environmental objectives (set out in Article 9 in accordance with Article 17);

[54] European Commission, *Motorways of the Sea*, ec.europa.eu/transport/themes/infrastructure/motorways-sea_en ('MoS website').

[55] Monitor Deloitte, *EU Shipping Competitiveness Study: International benchmark analysis* (Study commissioned by the European Community Shipowners' Associations (February 2017).

[56] ibid; other criticisms include that the EIB Transport Lending Policy focuses heavily on supporting inland water transport, ports and logistics, whilst only providing funding to vessels flying an EU state flag.

[57] Action Plan: Financing Sustainable Growth COM/2018/097 final (updated 5 August 2020).

[58] Proposal for a Regulation of the European Parliament and of the Council on the establishment of a framework to facilitate sustainable investment COM/2018/353 final; The Taxonomy Regulation came into force on 12 July 2020. The Action Plan also initiated an amendment to the Benchmarks Regulation on law carbon and positive carbon impact benchmarks (Regulation (EU) 2019/2089 of the European Parliament and of the Council of 27 November 2019).

[59] Regulation (EU) 2020/852.

[60] These are: (a) climate change mitigation; (b) climate change adaptation; (c) the sustainable use and protection of water and marine resources; (d) the transition to a circular economy; (e) pollution prevention and control; (f) the protection and restoration of biodiversity and ecosystems.

(3) is carried out in compliance with the minimum safeguards (laid down in Article 18);[61] and

(4) complies with technical screening criteria that have been established by the Commission (in accordance with Article 10(3), 11(3), 12(2), 13(2), 14(2) or 15(2)).

The Taxonomy Regulation is supplemented by delegated acts, informed by the recommendations of the Technical Working Group on Sustainable Finance, containing technical screening criteria for eligible economic activities.[62] The first Delegated Act ('Climate Delegated Act') includes activities that contribute to the first two objectives listed in Article 9 of the Taxonomy Regulation: (a) climate change mitigation; and (b) climate change adaptation.[63] This was amended by Complimentary Climate Delegated Act focusing on specific nuclear and gas energy activities only.[64] The second delegated Act, known as the Environmental Delegated Act, was published in June of 2023 and came into force in January 2024.[65] It focuses on the four remaining non-climate objective under Article 9: (c) the sustainable use and protection of water and marine resources; (d) the transition to a circular economy; (e) pollution prevention and control; (f) the protection and restoration of biodiversity and ecosystems.[66] Furthermore, the Disclosures Delegated Act sets out sets out the details of the Key Performance Indicators (KPIs) to be used by non-financial and financial undertakings when making disclosures under Article 8 of the Taxonomy Regulation.[67]

Under the Climate Delegated Act (for activities contributing to mitigation and adaptation) maritime transport and related infrastructure are included within the technical screening criteria under the following categories:

- inland passenger water transport;
- inland freight water transport;
- retrofitting of inland water passenger and freight transport;
- sea and coastal freight water transport, vessels for port operations and auxiliary activities;
- sea and coastal passenger water transport; and
- retrofitting of sea and coastal freight and passenger water transport.

[61] The minimum ensures alignment with the OECD Guidelines for Multinational Enterprises and the UN Guiding Principles on Business and Human Rights, including the principles and rights set out in the eight fundamental conventions identified in the Declaration of the International Labour Organisation on Fundamental Principles and Rights at Work and the International Bill of Human Rights (Article 18).

[62] The EIB is the first issuer to have aligned its Climate Awareness Bonds and Sustainability Awareness Bonds with the EU Taxonomy in order to extend loan eligibilities in line with adapting legislation.

[63] Commission Delegated Regulation (EU) 2021/2139 of 4 June 2021 ('Climate Delegated Act').

[64] Commission Delegated Regulation (EU) 2022/1214 of 9 March 2022.

[65] C(2023) 3850 final.

[66] Draft available at ec.europa.eu/finance/docs/level-2-measures/taxonomy-regulation-delegated-act-2022-environmental_en.pdf.

[67] Commission Delegated Regulation (EU) 2021/2178 of 6 July 2021.

These activities will make a substantial contribution to climate change mitigation if, inter alia, the vessel has zero direct (tailpipe) CO_2 emissions; or derives at least 25 per cent of its energy from zero direct (tailpipe) CO_2 emission fuels or plug-in power for their normal operation at sea and in ports until 31 December 2025.[68] The inclusion of shipping in the Taxonomy Regulation is helpful for the financing of green vessels, yet concerns about maritime technology's more general access to bank financing should also be balanced. In an Opinion of the European Economic and Social Committee (EESC) on 'An industrial strategy for the maritime technology sector' published in April 2023, the EESC expressed grave concern that the maritime technology sector faces increased difficulties in obtaining bank loans and public financing.[69] The EESC also demanded that funds be collected from infringements of FuelEU Maritime and the revenues from the EU Emission Trading Scheme to help support the sector. In addition, it called for 'EU taxonomy rules that support sustainable investments in the maritime sector, promote its inclusiveness and ensure legal certainty for technological investments'.[70]

The UK has been critical of the EU's approach and seems likely to adopt a more qualitative approach within its forthcoming green finance taxonomy. In November 2020, the UK Government announced that following its departure from the EU, it will implement its own green taxonomy for determining environmentally sustainable activities.[71] The Green Technical Advisory Group (GTAG), comprising of financial and business stakeholders, taxonomy and data experts, academic subject matter experts, NGOs, the Environment Agency, the Committee on Climate Change, and chaired by the Green Finance Institute, has been appointed as the independent expert group to deliver the Green Taxonomy.[72] The minutes of the GTAG's first meeting on 23 June 2021 reflect that a key issue is the 'need for the taxonomy to be applied in a way that is decision-useful and easy to apply for investors as well as real economy actors'.[73] It realises that there may be a divergence from the EU Taxonomy, but this is necessary to address UK-specific needs. Although, this does not say much about the metrics or methods employed to determine eligible projects and little information is available as of yet. This Strategy was informed by the previous Treasury Committee's inquiry into the decarbonisation of the UK economy and green finance in June 2019 wherein it received evidence on its terms of reference, including the potential economic opportunity offered by decarbonisation, the Treasury's strategy in facilitating clean growth and its response to the

[68] See Technical Screening Criteria 6.7– 6.12 respectively under the Climate Delegated Act (n 63).

[69] Opinion of the European Economic and Social Committee on 'An industrial strategy for the maritime technology sector' (Own-initiative opinion) (2023/C 100/05).

[70] ibid 1.9.

[71] HM Treasury, 'Chancellor sets out ambition for future of UK financial services' (9 November 2020), www.gov.uk/government/news/chancellor-sets-out-ambition-for-future-of-uk-financial-services.

[72] HM Treasury, 'New independent group to help tackle "greenwashing"' (9 June 2021), www.gov.uk/government/news/new-independent-group-to-help-tackle-greenwashing.

[73] Green Technical Advisory Group (GTAG) Meeting Notes, Meeting 1: 23 June 2021, www.greenfinanceinstitute.co.uk/wp-content/uploads/2021/08/GTAG-Meeting-1_Public-minutes_23rd-June-2021.pdf.

Climate Change Committee's net-zero recommendation, and green finance.[74] However, the latest 2023 update has not provided anything tangible on the progress of the Taxonomy, other than to say that the government will work with its Green Technical Advisory Group to develop the taxonomy.[75]

III. Private Frameworks and Initiatives

To fill some of the gaps created by taxonomy diversification or the underdevelopment thereof, private banking initiatives have emerged to largely assess green activities from an environmental risk assessment perspective. Private banking initiatives have been emerging for sustainable finance as early as the Equator Principles, which initiated a framework for determining, assessing and managing environmental and social risk in projects and have established minimum standards for due diligence and monitoring to support sustainable risk decision-making.[76] With increasing pressure on the shipping sector to align itself more closely with climate ambitions, maritime transport is being increasingly included in existing frameworks yet shipping-specific initiatives have also emerged. The following subsections provide a brief overview of the green finance landscape for shipping in respect of available private and voluntary frameworks.

A. Common Principles for Climate Change Adaptation Finance Tracking

In 2015, the Common Principles for Climate Change Adaptation Finance Tracking were developed by a group of Multilateral Development Banks (MDBs)[77] and the International Finance Development Finance Club (IDFC), to work towards an improved and harmonised set of working definitions, understandings, and principles for climate change adaptation finance tracking.[78] The Common Principles guidelines provide lists of activities and details on quality control procedures which are to be prioritised by each institution, without covering aspects of

[74] Treasury Select Committee, 'Decarbonisation of the UK economy and Green Finance terms of reference', old.parliament.uk/business/committees/committees-a-z/commons-select/treasury-committee/inquiries1/parliament-2017/decarbonisation-of-uk-economy-and-green-finance-17-19.

[75] HM Treasury, 'Mobilising green investment: 2023 green finance strategy' (Policy, updated 11 April 2023), www.gov.uk/government/publications/green-finance-strategy/mobilising-green-investment-2023-green-finance-strategy-annexes.

[76] Equator Principles, equator-principles.com.

[77] Consisting of the African Development Bank (AfDB); the Asian Development Bank (ADB), the European Bank for Reconstruction and Development (EBRD); the European Investment Bank (EIB); the Inter-American Development Bank (IDB); and the International Finance Corporation (IFC) and World Bank (IDA/IBRD) from the World Bank Group (WBG).

[78] Mainstreaming Climate Action within Financial Institutions Emerging Practices, www.mainstreamingclimate.org/wp-content/uploads/2017/03/fi_mainstreaming_epp_en-1.pdf.

implementation.[79] The guidelines provide a list of activities eligible for classification as 'climate mitigation finance' – these are broadly defined as those activities which promote 'efforts to reduce or limit GHG emissions or enhance GHG sequestration'.[80] Transport features on this list of eligible activities, yet it seems that urban transport modal change, transport oriented urban development, and inter-urban transport are the only further sub-categories. Shipping may be placed within those activities categorised as 'energy-efficiency', in particular under the subcategory of 'vehicle energy efficiency fleet retrofit' which refers to 'Existing vehicles, rail or boat fleet retrofit or replacement (including the use of lower-carbon fuels, electric or hydrogen technologies, etc.)'.[81] This is not particularly helpful in addressing the broad range of environmental impacts from shipping in addition to the emission of greenhouse gases. In any event, ocean-going vessels do not seem to be targeted as a form of transport.

B. Green Bond Principles

Green bonds are important instruments for raising the necessary capital for energy transitions. In 2016, green bonds were defined as:[82]

> [D]ebt instruments used to finance green projects that deliver environmental benefits. A green bond is differentiated from a regular bond by its commitment to use the funds raised to finance or refinance 'green' projects, assets or business activities. Green bonds can be issued by either public or private actors up front to raise capital for projects or for refinancing purposes, freeing up capital and leading to increased lending.

Before then, not one definition had prevailed but rather benchmark indices and exchange listings emerged with the growth of green investment.[83] A lack of a common framework prompted the International Capital Market Association (ICMA) to first publish its Green Bond Principles in 2014. It has since updated its criteria to further support issuers in financing 'environmentally sound and sustainable projects that foster a net-zero emissions economy and protect the environment'.[84] The ICMA has also provided guidance for other sustainability development themes such as the Social Bond Principles (SBP), the Sustainability Bond Guidelines (SBG) and the Sustainability-Linked Bond Principles (SLBP). What makes Green Bonds unique is that proceeds will be exclusively applied to

[79] Common Principles for Climate Mitigation Finance Tracking (Version 3–18 October 2021), www.eib.org/attachments/documents/mdb_idfc_mitigation_common_principles_en.pdf.
[80] ibid.
[81] ibid.
[82] OECD et al, Green Bonds: Country Experiences, Barriers And Options (In support of the G20 Green Finance Study Group, 2016), unepinquiry.org/wp-content/uploads/2016/09/6_Green_Bonds_Country_Experiences_Barriers_and_Options.pdf.
[83] OECD, *Green Bonds: Mobilising the debt capital markets for a low-carbon transition* (Bloomberg Philanthropies, 2015).
[84] ICMA, *Green Bond Principles: Voluntary Process Guidelines for Issuing Green Bonds* (June 2021), www.icmagroup.org/assets/documents/Sustainable-finance/2022-updates/Green-Bond-Principles-June-2022-060623.pdf.

finance or re-finance projects with clear environmental benefits.[85] All types of bond issuers can issue a Green, Social, Sustainability or Sustainability-Linked Bond subject to prevailing law. The Handbook on a Harmonised Framework ('Handbook') for Impact Reporting purports to harmonise the MDBs – IDFC Common Principles (above) and successive frameworks for Green Bonds, with the objective of enhancing the usability of the initial documents and to avoid repetitions.[86]

Clean Transportation activities are directed by an 'Avoid-Shift-Improve' (ASI) method that envisions avoiding the need to travel or reducing the length of travel, moving people or freight to a more sustainable and less polluting means of transportation, and reducing the emissions (both GHG and local pollutants) of vehicles or the transport system, respectively. The Handbook goes further than the MDBs – IDFC Common Principles in recognising that an indicator of clean transportation can also be a 'reduction of air pollutants: particulate matter, sulphur oxides, nitrogen oxides, carbon monoxide (CO), and non-methane volatile organic compounds (NMVOCs)'.[87] It also recognises benchmark standards for Clean Transport, including MARPOL by way of example as well as the EURO VI Standard and World Health Organization (WHO) guidelines for particulate matter concentration.

To assure investors that the capital raised by issuing green bonds is actually directed towards green activities, green bonds requirements must necessarily inform how the use of proceeds is controlled under loan agreements. As such, Green Loan Principles have also been developed by the Loan Market Association.

C. Loan Market Association's Green Loan Principles and Sustainability-Linked Loan Principles

The Loan Market Association (LMA) launched the Green Loan Principles (GLP) to provide a framework for market standards and guidelines for green bonds whilst also maintaining flexibility in loan products.[88] To provide market consistency, the LMA has modelled its initiatives on the ICMA's various bond principles by providing corresponding guidance for lenders who make use of the capital raised by green bonds, although this does not need to be the case. Accordingly, the LMA has published the Social Loan Principles,[89] and the Sustainability-Linked Loan Principles. The Sustainability-Linked Loans are different to Green Loans as they are not aimed at channelling loan proceeds towards certain categories of projects.

[85] ICMA, Guidance Handbook (January 2022), www.icmagroup.org/assets/GreenSocialSustainabilityDb/The-GBP-Guidance-Handbook-January-2022.pdf.

[86] ICMA, Handbook Harmonised Framework for Impact Reporting (June 2022), www.icmagroup.org/assets/documents/Sustainable-finance/2022-updates/Harmonised-Framework-for-Impact-Reporting-Green-Bonds_June-2022-280622.pdf.

[87] ibid 23.

[88] Loan Market Association, 'Green Loan Principles' (February 2023), www.lma.eu.com/application/files/8916/9755/2443/Green_Loan_Principles_23_February_2023.pdf.

[89] Loan Market Association, 'Social Loan Principles' (February 2023), www.lma.eu.com/application/files/3716/7715/0338/Social_Loan_Principles_23_February_2023.pdf.

Rather, the LMA Sustainability Linked Loans aim to support a borrower's efforts in improving its sustainability profile over the term of the loan.[90] The borrower should select relevant and measurable key performance indicators (KPIs) which can be benchmarked, in order to illustrate this improvement.

The Green Loan Principles are voluntary recommended guidelines to be applied by market participants on a 'deal-by-deal basis'.[91] The GLP provides uses with non-exhaustive categories of Green Projects that contribute to climate change mitigation and adaptation, natural resource conservation, biodiversity conservation, and pollution prevention and control. There are four core components to the GLP:

(1) Use of Proceeds
(2) Process for Project Evaluation and Selection
(3) Management of Proceeds
(4) Reporting

These directly correspond to the core components of the ICMA's Green Bond Principles, except that the Green Bond Principles do not include a Process for Project Evaluation and Selection. The use of proceeds must be for one of the broad non-exhaustive categories that are also aligned with the ICMA's categories for green activities under the Green Bond Principles. Green shipping could easily fit within the category of Clean Transportation (such as electric, hybrid, public, rail, non-motorised, multi-modal transportation, infrastructure for clean energy vehicles and reduction of harmful emissions) or Green Technologies (such as carbon extraction technologies and energy storage systems).[92] Borrowers are then recommended to make certain information available to lenders in respect of the sustainability of the Green Project and the methods used to determine this. Borrowers should also have a dedicated account to which the green loan proceeds are credited to and should keep strict records on the use of such proceeds which should be reported on an annual basis. Transparency is key to the GLP and achieved impacts should also be included in the borrower's reports.

In 2021, Hapag-Lloyd relied on the LMA's Green Loan Principles for acquiring a USD 417 million syndicated green loan with a 12-year maturity, to finance three of six 23,500 TEU containerships, with the remaining three vessels financed by a lease financing agreement.[93] Both of these debt transactions fulfil the Green Loan Principles of the LMA, illustrating that voluntary green frameworks are already being used by shipping actors to access capital.[94]

[90] Loan Market Association, 'Sustainability-Linked Loan Principles' (February 2023), www.lma.eu.com/application/files/9216/9755/2878/Sustainability_Linked_Loan_Principles_23_February_2023_v.2.pdf.

[91] ibid 2.

[92] ibid 3.

[93] Marc Allen, 'DNV supports Hapag-Lloyd's milestone green financing' (Maritime Direct, 4 March 2021), maritime.direct/en/2021/03/04/dnv-supports-hapag-lloyds-milestone-green-financing/?utm_source=rss&utm_medium=rss&utm_campaign=dnv-supports-hapag-lloyds-milestone-green-financing.

[94] DNV GL acted as the independent expert in order to provide second-party opinion for verification under the terms of the green financing. According to Hapag, the new vessels ordered in December 2020 are extremely fuel-efficient, containing high-pressure dual-fuel engines that can provide a 15–25% reduction in CO_2 emissions.

Unlike Sustainability-Linked-Loans, the LMA has not yet provided model additional clauses for green loans. This is probably because Sustainability-Linked Loans are now arguably one of the most popular sustainable loan products in the market as they incorporate greater flexibility in comparison to use of proceeds products (such as green loans). However, it does state that the use of proceeds component of the green loan should be clearly identifiable in the finance documents for Revolving Credit Facilities.[95] Despite the lack of contractual guidance, it is evident that the loan should include details of the four components of the GLP. Although not officially provided by the LMA itself, the Chancery Lane Project (TCLP) has provided a Green Loan 'Starter Pack' which provides practitioners with suggested clauses for the LMA's GLP.[96] Harrison's clause is structured around the four components in alignment with LMA documents. It provides comprehensive definitions, representations, warranties, undertakings, events of defaults which extend to the scope of the green project, account management and reporting requirements. Both of the LMA's model clauses for Sustainability-Linked-Loans and TCLP's Green Loan Starter Pack are frequently referred to in section II of this chapter. Although the focus of this book is on green shipping and therefore green loans seem more relevant, it is also entirely possible that shipping actors may make use of more flexible products like sustainability-linked loans. The LMA Sustainability-Linked-Loan provisions are therefore helpful in analysing contractual tools for the implementation of external frameworks with sustainable objectives that can be inclusive or adapted to green-specific objectives.

D. Climate Bonds Initiative

The Climate Bonds Initiative (CBI) certification standard provides standards and guidance to its programme members as well as banks, non-governmental organisations, other stakeholders and government bodies.[97] In addition to working on market intelligence and the dissemination of information and data, its core work is focused on developing a trusted standard and providing policy models and advice. Its trusted standard has been the development of a Climate Bonds Taxonomy which clearly defines what projects are climate aligned and will drive a low carbon economy. The CBI uses a traffic light system for projects included in its taxonomy; namely 'green light' (meaning automatically compatible), 'orange light' (meaning compatible if compliant with a screening indicator), or 'red light' (not compatible).

Due to the 2020 sulphur cap and IMO targets for carbon reduction, the CBI announced early in 2019 that its Shipping Technical Working Group (TWG) and Industry Working Group (IWG) would develop a framework criterion for shipping

[95] LMA (n 88).
[96] The Chancery Lane Project, Green Loan 'Starter Pack' (19 October 2022), chancerylaneproject.org/climate-clauses/green-loan-starter-pack.
[97] See CBI Climate Bonds Taxonomy (October 2021), www.climatebonds.net.

investments. The Shipping Criteria form part of the Climate Bonds Standard and provide concise decision rules for determining the compatibility of shipping projects and assets with a low-carbon, climate resilient economy, and are therefore eligible for certification under the Climate Bonds Standard. The TWG and IWG received input from a number of representatives from 'academia, civil society, ship owners, operators, investors and international policy bodies from around the world'.[98] The CBI Shipping Criteria can also be used to certify related infrastructure that is dedicated to recharging and refuelling zero emissions (eg charging stations and fuel bunkering for eligible fuels). The CBI includes the following table of activities in its Shipping Criteria Document while a separate table includes a list of projects that are specifically excluded from the criteria.

Table 2.1 Assets and projects included in the CBI Shipping Criteria (source: climatebonds.net)[99]

Assets	**Example Use of Proceeds**	**Mit.**	**Adapt.**
Ships above 5,000 GT for which data is collected under the EU MRV[100] and/or IMO DCS data collection regimes.[101]	Ships classified as Bulk Carriers, Chemical Tankers, Containers, General Cargo, Ferry-pax only, Cruise, Ferry-RoPax, Refrigerated Bulk, Ro-Ro and Vehicle, and are not in the list of excluded assets.	□	○
Ships below 5,000 GT **<u>if zero emissions.</u>**	Zero emissions ships which are propelled and powered by batteries, or zero-emissions fuels and are not in the list of excluded assets.[102]	○	○
Infrastructure that is dedicated to refuelling or recharging zero emissions ships	Charging stations and refuelling assets that are dedicated for storing and delivering chemical or electric energy to power and propel ships, consistent with the definition of zero-emissions fuels.	○	○

□ = Automatically fulfil requirements for Certification.
○ = Must meet CBI Shipping Criteria for Certification.

E. Poseidon Principles

The Poseidon Principles (PP) comprises a group of banks led by Citi, Société Générale and Danske Bank that have noted the pivotal enabling role that financing

[98] CBI, *Shipping* (2020), www.climatebonds.net/standard/shipping.
[99] Shipping Criteria Document, www.climatebonds.net/standard/shipping.
[100] The EU MRV data regime is available for voyages that include ports within EU Member States.
[101] The IMO DCS data regime for ships performing international voyages.
[102] These fuels are listed in 'Managed Reduction Plan' guidance on p 9 of the Shipping Criteria Document.

plays for the shipping sector and the need for a framework that integrates climate considerations into lending decisions with the objective of achieving decarbonisation in the industry.[103]

The PP are aimed at aligning the shipping industry with the IMO 2050 Strategy through requiring signatories to assess the sustainability of vessels within their shipping portfolios using an annual efficiency ratio of grams of CO_2 per ton-mile. Signatories will commit to disclosure requirements on whether their shipping portfolios are aligned with the PP, meaning that 'bank liquidity will be prioritised for those clients supporting IMO target levels'.[104] Compliance with the PP is to be incorporated into contractual agreements between signatories, clients and partners, through a standardised covenant clause (SCC) which will be continuously updated in the annual review process.[105] This SCC makes direct reference to Annex VI of MARPOL and mandates compliance with Regulation 22A for collection and reporting of ship fuel oil consumption data for a ship's SEEMP.

Technical guidance is provided for PP signatories on accountability and enforceability.[106] This guidance offers specific accountability requirements for each 'information data flow step' to ensure accurate calculation of climate alignment and compliance with IMO standards. These flow steps are as follows:

- Step 1: Sourcing vessel IMO DCS data
- Step 2: Calculating vessel carbon intensity and climate alignment
- Step 3: Calculating climate alignment of portfolio
- Step 4: Disclosure

At each step there are 'preferred' pathways for obtaining information and 'allowed pathways' that are also acceptable to the PP framework. For Step 1 and Step 2, it is preferable that this data is sourced from an IMO recognised organisation. Other allowed sources could be the shipowner itself for Step 1, and Step 2 could be carried out by a third party or done internally by the signatory. Under Step 3, climate alignment should be calculated using climate alignment data from step 2 and the signatories' loan book data. The signatory can perform this calculation itself or outsource it to a third party. Finally, disclosure serves as a quality control mechanism and provides its climate alignment score along with other data to the Secretariat of the PP.

[103] Poseidon Principles, www.poseidonprinciples.org.

[104] Paul Taylor, Global Head of Shipping & Offshore, Société Générale CIB was quoted as making this statement at the launch of the Poseidon Principles in New York, June 2019, as reported by Barry Parker, 'The Poseidon Principles and a green transformation" of shipping' (*Seatrade Maritime Review*, 20 June 2019), www.seatrade-maritime.com/americas/poseidon-principles-and-green-transformation-shipping.

[105] Poseidon Principles, *Technical Guidance* (Version 4.2, April 2023), www.poseidonprinciples.org/finance/wp-content/uploads/2019/07/Poseidon_Principles.pdf.

[106] ibid 24.

In order to obtain the necessary information at Step 1, signatories can use the SCC in relevant vessel financing documents with shipowners.[107] The SCC requires the Shipowner to

> upon the request of [any Lender] and at the cost of the [Owner], on or before [31st July] in each calendar year, supply or procure the supply to [the Facility Agent] [such Lender] of all information necessary in order for [any Lender] to comply with its obligations under the Poseidon Principles in respect of the preceding year.

The owner also acknowledges that any such information will form part of the Lender's published information informing portfolio climate alignment as required by the PP. Definitions are also provided for clarity, whilst the guiding comment states that the SCC is not intended to impose more onerous reporting requirements than other obligations for periodic reporting to Lenders and should benefit from grace periods.

Although the Poseidon Principles does not specifically define a set of 'green shipping activities', it uses a carbon-efficiency metric which measures 'Climate alignment', being the 'degree to which a vessel, product, or portfolio's carbon intensity is in line with a decarbonisation trajectory that meets the IMO ambition of reducing total annual GHG emissions by at least 50% by 2050 based on 2008 levels'.[108] This tool could perhaps advance a comparability system which is more effective than merely listing certain activities, although detailed technical guidance on each activity could achieve the same level of comparability. However, as it stands, the PP do not require holistic contractual integration into financing agreements between signatories and borrowers. The SCC is not an onerous reporting requirement and if shipowners are supposed to assist signatories in improving upon climate alignment scores over time, then there should be contractual requirements for such. At present, the contractual obligation requires nothing more than mere regulatory compliance with the IMO EEXI and CII measures.

F. Getting to Zero Coalition

The Global Maritime Forum is presently managing a business coalition of over 200 organisations that are involved in maritime, energy, infrastructure and finance.[109] By 2030, the coalition aims to have zero-emission vessels (ZEVs) operating on key trade corridors with plans to expand production of ZEVs and develop new

[107] Poseidon Principles, Standard Covenant Clause (January 2020), www.poseidonprinciples.org/finance/wp-content/uploads/2020/01/PP-Standard-Covenant-Clause.17.1.20.pdf.

[108] ibid.

[109] Global Maritime Forum, Getting to Zero Coalition, www.globalmaritimeforum.org/getting-to-zero-coalition.

corridors.[110] The coalition has also called for governments in its 2021 'Call to Action for Shipping Decarbonisation' to:

(1) 'Commit to decarbonizing international shipping by 2050
(2) Support industrial scale zero emission shipping projects through national action
(3) Deliver policy measures that will make zero emission shipping the default choice by 2030'.[111]

Signatory companies are given some limited guidance on their role in getting to zero. Financial institutions are guided to integrate climate considerations in lending and investment decisions, to provide finance for ZEVs and de-risk investments for such.[112] As the coalition involves a wide range of sectoral actors, no contractual guidance is given on how to integrate the coalition's ambitions into transactional arrangements. Some competition law guidance is given on how to avoid breaching competition and antitrust laws,[113] yet little is said about how to integrate net-zero ambitions into day-to-day business transactions.

IV. Contractual Implementation of Green Finance Frameworks

The Green Finance for shipping landscape illustrates that although huge strides have been made to tackle the de-risking of the green transition through the development of frameworks and product offerings, scant attention has been given to the contractual implementation of these initiatives. This gap in attention is not unique to maritime contractual frameworks. As the Paris Agreement does not establish an international climate tribunal nor any enforcement mechanisms under international law, climate finance or green finance needs to seek out its own systems of enforcement. In most countries, financial obligations have come to rely on a 'naming and shaming' system for private entities known as, 'the threat or use of public opprobrium to affect reputation'.[114] Contract law can therefore provide a quasi-regulatory method for solving disagreements relating to reputational damage and the 'greenness' of finance. Given that green finance must be mobilised

[110] Getting to Zero Coalition, 'Industry Roadmap' (2019), www.globalmaritimeforum.org/content/2019/09/Getting-to-Zero-Coalition_Industry-Roadmap.pdf.

[111] 'Call to Action for Shipping Decarbonisation' (2021), www.globalmaritimeforum.org/content/2021/09/Call-to-Action-for-Shipping-Decarbonization.pdf.

[112] 'Role of Companies in Getting to Zero Coalition' (2022), www.globalmaritimeforum.org/content/2022/08/Getting-to-Zero-Coalition-role-of-companies-July-2022.pdf.

[113] 'Appendix 1: Guidelines on Competition Law' (2022), www.globalmaritimeforum.org/content/2022/08/Guidelines-on-Competition-Law.pdf.

[114] Samantha Daisy, 'Choosing Words Wisely: Climate Agreements Viewed Through a Legal Contractual Framework' (2022) 48 *Columbia Journal of Environmental Law* 41, 151; Jennifer Jacquet and Dale Jamieson, 'Soft but Significant Power in the Paris Agreement' (2016) 6 *Nature Climate Change* 643, 645.

from investors, generally through green bond issuance, the indenture agreement (ie bond documentation) is an initial site of regulation which manifests in a principal–agent relationship: the agent must maximise the principal's interest in a way that adheres to a set of green principles.[115] The principal's interests do not only include financial return but other desired performance such as carbon reduction. As such, it becomes particularly important to adopt a relational contract approach that allows an impact investor to personally identify when desired performance is achieved.[116] Within this bond documentation contractual clauses must necessarily secure this outcome for the principal, which is dependent on the performance and monitoring of subsequent contractual sites in the contractual network.

Greenwashing can already occur within this relationship if bond issuers do not tightly control the use of proceeds for green investments. To achieve such control, there would be merit in implementing an overarching 'green' element in loan documentation that reflects investor priorities[117] – these are manifest in the green finance framework that sets out what these priorities are. The focus of this section is therefore on the contractual framework employed for integrating green finance standards into the ship loan agreement between lender and borrower. The capital deployed in this relationship may or may not have been mobilised through the use of green bonds, but if the bank communicates the product as green in adherence with either a regulatory or private framework, the same risks apply. This section is concerned with bank debt-financing as the prevailing practice for ship finance; this is traditionally described, in simplistic terms, as the advancement of a large sum of money to one or more owning companies with a mortgage on the ship as security.[118] Loan agreements govern the basis upon which finance is advanced from the bank to the shipowner, usually with an undertaking to register a first priority mortgage over the vessel in favour of the lender/bank.[119]

Whilst green finance frameworks are concerned with *governing* contracts (both in respect of defining project eligibility and providing a normative direction), this section is concerned with how contracts can *govern* a set of behaviours that are aligned with the overarching financial framework.[120] Banks are not new to the integration of CSR policies into financial instruments; this can take place in many ways, including sustainability clauses, codes of conduct, or environmental and social covenants.[121] Many types of contracts and standardised forms

[115] Agostini (n 5) 161.

[116] Madeleine Evans, 'Meeting the challenge of impact investing: how can contracting practices secure social impact without sacrificing performance?' (2013) 3 *Journal of Sustainable Finance & Investment* 138, 148.

[117] Agostini (n 5) 161.

[118] *Citibank NA v Hobbs, Savill & Co (The Panglobal Friendship)* [1978] 1 Lloyd's Rep. 368, 371; other forms of financing consist of the capital markets for equity, bond finance, and mezzanine financing.

[119] *The Panglobal Friendship* (n 118).

[120] This forms the basis of a contract governance approach to contract theory (ch 1).

[121] Katerina Peterkova Mitkidis, 'Sustainability Clauses in International Supply Chain Contracts: Regulation, Enforceability and Effects of Ethical Requirements' (2014) 1 *Nordic Journal of Commercial Law*.

govern various financial product offerings, whilst it is also important to note that other forms of financing are also available to shipowners, such as the capital markets and mezzanine financing. This section will focus on debt-financing which uses traditional ship loan forms to govern the relationship between bank and shipowner.

Traditional loan forms for shipping have managed to deal with specific project-related risks and systematic industry risks.[122] These risks are often holistically considered and assessed to manage risk by way of inclusion in the company's general lending policies or specifically in loan agreement clauses.[123] Green finance frameworks present additional compliance and financial greenwashing risks for banks, yet equally provide directional guidance for managing such risk through the provision of definitions and criteria for the use of proceeds. The green framework criteria must necessarily provide a foundational basis for all of the loan terms whilst also requiring banks to adopt a more relational contract approach with lenders in that: there is an underlying mutual goal centred on decarbonisation or environmental sustainability, a high level of communication is required to report on emissions and satisfy investors of green performance, and a commitment to collaboration with substantial financial commitments.[124] At the same time, relational contracts run the risk of being too 'fluffy' without formal elements and enforcements that establish a shared trust between parties.[125]

Traditional loan forms already comprise of such formal elements that are initially summed up in a 'term sheet' and are later formalised into the binding Loan Facility Agreement which has typical inclusions such as 'Events of Default and Acceleration' clauses.[126] These clauses are informed by the principles of English contract law whereby terms of a contract can be classified as either conditions, warranties or intermediate/innominate terms.[127] These distinctions and their consequential remedies play a role in determining the importance given to environmental provisions in loan agreements. It follows logically that the stronger the obligation, the stronger the remedy. How environmental standards are included in loan forms is set out below by looking at the various components of the loan agreement, bearing in mind that although each bank has its own contractual forms, most will try to adhere to the LMA standard as the documentary praxis in shipping

[122] Orestis Schinas and Sebastian Kewitsch, 'Loans and Risk Management Considerations' in Orestis Schinas et al, *HSBA Handbook on Ship Finance* (Springer, 2014) ch 2.

[123] ibid 54.

[124] For relational contracts, see *Yam Seng Ptd Ltd v International Trade Corporation Limited* [2013] EWHC 111 (QB) [725].

[125] David Frydlinger et al, 'Welcome to the Contracting Paradox' in *Contracting in the New Economy* (Palgrave Macmillan, 2021).

[126] Sarah Paterson and Rafal Zakrzewski (eds), *McKnight, Paterson and Zakrzewski on The Law of International Finance*, 2nd edn (Oxford University Press, 2017) 1.1. Preliminary Points.

[127] For more on contractual terms, see Paul S Davies, *JC Smith's The Law of Contract* (Oxford University Press, 2016); see also LexisNexis® Practical Guidance, 'Contract interpretation – conditions, warranties and intermediate terms', *Practice Note: Commercial, Dispute Resolution* (LexisNexis, 2020).

finance.[128] This section will analyse the formal components of loan documentation for ship finance with a view to making such forms 'fit for a green purpose'. This comprises both traditional shipping finance loan clauses and new green or sustainable loan clauses that are becoming common practice in their respective lending markets. It is posited that green finance frameworks require holistic and comprehensive implementation in loan documentation, with most clauses being informed by a green normative element.

i. Interpretation and Definitions

Most loan agreements start with a series of definitions, and this terminology is clearly understood in a commercial context. However, if the loan agreement is in accordance with a green finance framework, then the terminology of the framework needs to be repeated in the Definitions section, or reference should be made to a document containing a taxonomy or glossary of terms. For example, the Equator Principles provides a Glossary of Terms for Equator Principles Financial Institutions (EPFIs) for incorporation into loan documentation, although it does not specify whether the entire glossary should be included in the definition section or incorporated by way of reference.[129]

Similarly, the Loan Market Association provides a Sustainable Lending Glossary to assist with developing a common language surrounding green or sustainable lending.[130] However, the LMA's glossary was not created for contractual interpretation, but is rather aimed at providing explanations for users on scientific and economic language, UN agencies, relevant government policies, and its own green loan principles. Nevertheless, the LMA provides other drafting guidance to users for sustainable finance. TCLP has gone one step further than the LMA, to provide free-template green loan clauses that are aligned with LMA's green loan principles with reference to the LMA style drafting.[131] As expected, the definitions provided by the TCLP Green Loan Starter Pack for drafting green loans matches the glossary explanations provided by the LMA and the language used in its Green Loan Principles. However, the TCLP's definitions are specifically intended for contractual incorporation and have been adapted accordingly.

[128] Stefan Otto and Thilo Scholl, 'Legal Treatment of Ship Finance Loans: Analysis of the Ship Loan Contract' in Orestis Schinas, Carsten Grau and Max Johns (eds), *HSBA Handbook on Ship Finance* (Springer, 2015) 59.

[129] Equator Principles, Guidance For EPFIs On Incorporating Environmental And Social Considerations Into Loan Documentation (December 2020), equator-principles.com/app/uploads/Loan_documentation_EP_Dec2020.pdf.

[130] LMA, Sustainable Lending Glossary (August 2021), www.lsta.org/content/sustainable-lending-glossary-of-terms.

[131] TCLP, *Harrison's Clause* in 'Green Loan Starter Pack' (1 July 2020, updated 19 October 2022), chancerylaneproject.org/climate-clauses/green-loan-starter-pack.

ii. Purpose of the Loan

This clause generally outlines the bank's commitment to make the loan on its standard terms.[132] This clause also includes that the loan is to be used to finance the purchase price of the vessel (or part thereof) or for refinancing. Generally, the bank includes a proviso that it is not obligated to ensure that the loan is used for this purpose, which puts the bank in a vulnerable position if repayment is compromised.[133] The position is different under German law, where the bank has to monitor that the contractual obligations are being fulfilled and that the borrower is using the loan for its intended purpose, especially where the loan is a special-purpose loan (which would generally be the case for ship finance).[134] Clause 3 in both the LMA investment grade facility agreement and the LMA leveraged facility agreement provides a purpose for the loan which can be tailored to reflect the unique circumstances of the relevant transaction.[135] If the borrower does not use the loan for its intended purpose, this should be included under 'Events of Default'.[136] However, as discussed in section vi below on Events of Default, this is not usually the case for environmental provisions. Nonetheless, the 'greenness' of the loan is of paramount importance where the loan adheres to a green finance framework. Here, the purpose of the loan is not simply to advance finance to assist the shipowner in acquiring a newbuild, a second-hand vessel, or retrofitting an existing fleet; the purpose is also one of net-zero emissions or attaining a level of energy-efficiency. Unsurprisingly, TCLP makes reference to a Green Loan framework (which could directly refer to the Green Loan Principles) in its Purpose section as set out below:[137]

> 3.1 The Borrower shall apply all amounts borrowed by it under the Green Facility towards:
>
> a) The financing of the Eligible Green Project in accordance with the Green Loan Framework; and
>
> b) Payment of the Green Project Costs (other than periodic fees) [as described in the Funds Flow Statement].

Although the objectives of the green finance framework are not an exclusive purpose of the loan, it should be unequivocal that proceeds are not to be used for projects outside of the scope of the applicable framework. Lenders may also want to consider if they intend to include an additional 'Background' or 'Preamble/Recital' clause, more commonly used in shipbuilding agreements. Preambles and recitals offer powerful interpretive guidance for the construction

[132] Harwoo (n 14) 23.

[133] ibid 23.

[134] Translation of Circular 34/2002 (BA) to all credit institutions in the Federal Republic of Germany.

[135] Slaughter & May, *The ACT Borrower's Guide to the LMA Facilities Agreement for Leveraged Transactions* (The Association of Corporate Treasurers, October 2008).

[136] In the case of very specific purposes or exclusive purpose clauses, a Quistclose trust could naturally arise. See *Quistclose Investments v Rolls Razor* [1970] AC 567.

[137] TCLP (n 131).

of other contractual terms. These are discussed more extensively in chapter four pertaining to charterparty agreements, yet it is worth stating here that recitals provide evidence of the relevant 'factual matrix' at the date of execution – an established factor in the construction of terms.[138] As such, including reference to the green finance framework and its objectives in the loan's purposive provisions, a preamble, or recital, could assist with the interpretation of other duties to align contractual performance with attaining emission reduction targets.

Expressly referring to a green finance framework may also assist with the implication of terms if the loan agreement is silent. A practical example of where one might expect that a duty is implied into a loan agreement is where a green product offering prescribes to a principled taxonomy that sets specific technical criteria for eligible projects. Although the loan may reiterate these technical criteria for the purpose of proceeds or as a condition of vessel design or operational performance, it may not necessarily set out that the activity may not contravene other environmental objectives of the taxonomy. For example, projects financed under the EU Taxonomy Regulation require that Article 9 environmental objectives are not harmed, yet this may not be evident if the loan agreement simply refers to the financing of a newbuild vessel with zero direct (tailpipe) CO_2 emissions. Is it implied that the vessel's construction did not contravene an environmental objective, eg construction at a unsustainable shipyard? Thus far, there is no precedent for implication *by law* of green obligations in loan documentation, where the term is considered necessary to a particular and definable type of contractual relationship.[139] This may change if green loans form the subject of increasing dispute and are subjected to arguments on the implications of terms. Yet, for now it is only worth considering whether implication *by fact* is plausible. Although the courts are hesitant to imply terms into agreements, it is possible to do so as a matter *of fact* if it is evident where the 'intention of the parties (objectively ascertained) is sought',[140] and 'collected from the words of the agreement and the surrounding circumstances'.[141]

Lord Simon in *BP Refinery (Westernport) Pty Ltd v Hastings Shire Council* explained that the following conditions must be satisfied to imply a term as matter of fact into contract:[142] (1) it must be reasonable and equitable; (2) it must be necessary to give business efficacy to the contract, so that no term will be implied if the contract is effective without it; (3) it must be so obvious that 'it goes without saying'; (4) it must be capable of clear expression; and (5) it must not contradict any express term of the contract. Despite the courts subsequently pursuing alternative approaches,[143] Lord Simon's test was confirmed as the correct test by

[138] *Blackpool FC (Properties) Ltd. v JSC Baltic International Bank* [2018] EWCA Civ 732.
[139] *Bank of Nova Scotia v Hellenic Mutual War Risk Association (Bermuda) Ltd* [1989] 3 All ER 628 at 665.
[140] *Liverpool City Council v Irwin* [1977] AC 239, Lord Edmund-Davies at 266.
[141] *Ali v Christian Salvesen Food Services Ltd* [1997] 1 All ER 721, Waite LJ at 726.
[142] (1977) 52 ALJR 20.
[143] *Attorney-General of Belize v Belize Telecom Limited* [2009] UKPC 10, [2009] 2 All ER (Comm) 1.

Lord Neuberger in *Marks and Spencer plc v BNP Paribas Securities Services Trust Company (Jersey) Ltd.*[144] As such, the Supreme Court effectively reaffirmed the traditional officious bystander and business efficacy tests.

In applying these tests to the implication of green terms, the requirement of 'business efficacy' may pose a significant hurdle. As contract law does not recognise an environmental sustainability agenda, it is hard to conceive how sustainable contractual performance enhances business efficacy. However, the express commitment to a green finance framework in a recital or purpose clause can assist in making this point trite. Loan disbursements are entirely dependent on achieving the purpose of the green finance instrument, therefore business efficacy is conflated with a set of environmental sustainability principles. The two cannot be artificially separated as the framework itself is a risk management tool which has already contextualised the climate agenda as a business endeavour for long-term economic sustainability. This argument is aligned with Lord Neuberger's sentiments that necessity for business efficacy involves a value judgment. The test is not one of 'absolute necessity' – 'a more helpful way of putting Lord Simon's second requirement is … that a term can only be implied if, without the term, the contract would lack commercial or practical coherence'.[145]

iii. Conditions Precedent

Condition Precedents (or Conditions of Utilisation in LMA language) are a set of requirements that must be satisfied as a conditionality upon which the loan is contingent.[146] These include a large amount of documentation which must be presented to the Lender's lawyers, including, inter alia: the company's constitutional documents, certificates of good standing for borrower and guarantor, company searches, valid permits, certificates or government-requested documents, legal opinions, or other information relating to the parties' security.[147] Within an English law context, these stipulations arguably go to the root of the contract as non-compliance with these terms (ie failure to provide documentation or providing inadequate documents), will enable the lender to withhold funds until the conditions are satisfied.[148] As lenders have the option to withhold funds, breaches of these provisions do not usually trigger an Event of Default.

[144] *Marks and Spencer* [2015] UKSC 72.

[145] ibid [21].

[146] *Wickman Machine Tool Sales Ltd v L Schuler AG* [1974] AC 235, 235, 250H; *Total Gas Marketing Limited v. ARCO British Limited and Others* [1998] UKHL 22, [1998] CLC 1275 at 1281–82; Otto and Scholl (n 128).

[147] Harwood (n 14) 24–25; Dora Mace-Kokota and Danaë Hosek-Ugolini, 'The Financing of Second-Hand Vessels' in Stephenson Harwood, *Shipping Finance: A Practical Handbook* (Globe and Law Business, 2018).

[148] Kyriakos Spoullos, 'Key Clauses of a Shipping Loan Agreement' in Manolis G Kavussanos, and Ilias D Visvikis (eds), *The International Handbook of Shipping Finance: Theory and Practice* (Palgrave Macmillan UK, 2016) 217.

In an environmental context, these requirements are extended to corrective action plans and mitigation measures. For example, the Equator Principles in its guidance to EPFIs, provides that as a condition precedent to all disbursements, the borrower has to furnish the lender with a certificate certifying that the project is operational and complies with all environmental requirements, as well as a completeness status for the actions referenced in the Principles Action Plan.[149] In TCLP's Green Loan starter pack, 'Principle Two: Project Evaluation and Selection' entails documentary requirements as conditions precedent, also termed as 'conditions of utilisation'.[150] These include, a 'copy of the Borrower's and/or the Group's environmental sustainability strategy materials (to the extent not already included in the Green Loan Framework'. It is important to note that the Green Loan Starter Pack is neither sector nor transaction specific, therefore additional shipping-specific information would have to inserted for ship finance documents. It is likely that this will include IMO-mandated surveys and certificates, CII ratings, and additional information required by the green finance framework. For newbuilds, evidence of the vessels' energy efficiency design is likely necessary in addition to proof of the shipping company's sustainability plans.

It is also important to note that for newbuilds, financing the vessel has traditionally taken place in one of two ways: the buyer/shipowner obtains debt-finance to buy the vessel in full on delivery (or to finance its pre-delivery instalments); or the seller/builder provides 'yard credit' in that the buyer and seller negotiate a payment schedule, generally on the yard's payment terms.[151] The latter method of finance has recently been revived in the UK with the launch of the Department of Business and Trade's Shipbuilding Credit Guarantee Scheme by UK Export Finance, which enables the shipyard to receive payment as though there is a cash contract in place, while the buyer is able to access extended repayment terms.[152] Lenders are protected against non-payment of the instalments of the principal amount and interest by the guaranteed loan. UK Export Finance will also consider a number of factors in considering an application including Environmental, Social and Human Rights risk management that identifies risk and requires due diligence to be carried out.[153] This process is supported by legal documents such as the OECD Recommendation of the Council on Common Approaches for Officially Supported Export Credits and Environmental and Social Due Diligence (The 'Common Approaches'),[154] the OECD Recommendation of the Council on

[149] Equator Principles, 'Guidance for EPFIs on Incorporating Environmental and Social considerations into Loan Documentation' (December 2020).

[150] TCLP (n 131).

[151] Harwood (n 14) 46.

[152] UK Government, 'Shipbuilding Credit Guarantee Scheme', www.gov.uk/guidance/shipbuilding-credit-guarantee-scheme#eligibility-criteria.

[153] UK Export Finance, 'Guidance: What UKEF considers in your application form' (updated 26 November 2021), www.gov.uk/government/publications/processes-and-factors-in-uk-export-finance-consideration-of-applicants/what-ukef-considers-in-your-application-form.

[154] OECD, Recommendation of the Council on Common Approaches for Officially Supported Export Credits and Environmental and Social Due Diligence (The 'Common Approaches'), OECD/LEGAL/0393.

Sustainable Lending Practices and Officially Supported Export Credits,[155] and the OECD Recommendation of the Council on Bribery and Officially Supported Export Credits.[156]

If shipyard finance is acquired under this guarantee scheme, then the financing bank may request documentation as a condition precedent in relation to the borrower's compliance with the scheme's requirements to protect itself in the event of non-payment. Shipbuilding agreements implementing such lending provisions are discussed further in chapter three.

iv. Representation and Warranties

Representations and warranties comprise a series of statements of fact on the basis of which the parties enter into the agreement. Loan agreements will often contain a warranty that the financier has been furnished with a full set of complete and accurate documents pertaining to the purchase of the specified property and that relevant environmental laws have been complied with. However, in the context of ship loan agreements, representations and warranties specifically relating to the vessel may also be included in the in the mortgage, or in the mortgage only.[157]

Under LMA loan documentation, representations cover a number of legal and factual issues with the result that if any representations are 'untrue or misleading in any material aspect on the date which it was expressed to be given', then the misrepresentation will be an Event of Default.[158] It is also a condition precedent to any utilisation that the repeating representations are true in all material aspects. For Sustainability-Linked Loans, an additional representation should be made to the borrower that all sustainability information is true and not misleading at the date it was provided.[159] This representation will likely be repeated annually as a Sustainability Compliance Certificate, Sustainability Report and Verification Report will need to be submitted containing representations laid out in the contents of the certificate, such as and external review of KPI performance.

v. Covenants/Undertakings

The main function of a covenant is to ensure that the borrower's financial condition, assets, security over assets, and business operations remain within the ambit

[155] OECD, Recommendation of the Council on Sustainable Lending Practices and Officially Supported Export Credits, OECD/LEGAL/0442.

[156] OECD Recommendation of the Council on Bribery and Officially Supported Export Credits, OECD/LEGAL/0447.

[157] Julie Clegg, 'The Ship Mortgage – Introduction' in Stephenson Harwood, *Shipping Finance: A Practical Handbook* (Globe and Law Business, 2018).

[158] Slaughter and May, *The ACT Borrower's Guide to LMA Loan Documentation for Investment Grade Borrowers* (The Association of Corporate Treasurers, April 2013).

[159] Slaughter and May, *A Borrower's Guide To Sustainability-Linked Loan Terms* (The Association of Corporate Treasurers, August 2023).

of the bank's initial credit approval of the loan.[160] Positive covenants in shipping loan agreements have traditionally included the responsibilities of the borrower to, inter alia, comply with the terms and conditions of their financial obligations, to register the ship in a ship register acceptable to the lender and to provide any information in the event of default.[161] Negative covenants are also considered a form of undertaking, these require the borrower to refrain from taking certain actions. In shipping loans, these generally include obligations not to encumber any assets with a liens, transfer or dispose of the vessel, or enter into any further agreements relating to the operation or chartering of a vessel.[162]

Specific environmental covenants, which now form a common part of industry practice, are ordinarily aimed at environmental risk exposure with a consistent view that the environmental covenant comprises a promise by the borrower to undertake or avoid certain environmental-related activities.[163] These covenants typically involve legal compliance with applicable legislation, regulations or standards,[164] and periodic reporting requirements pertaining to the borrower's environmental performance.[165] Covenants are distinct from conditions and warranties and could be classed as an innominate term. It is unusual to find the term 'covenant' in English contract law literature, whereas in American literature it is more clearly defined. This is because a covenant is essentially an express undertaking for future action or inaction and does not really permit its own species of term under English law. It seems similar to a warranty in that it is a promise of a future condition; however, if the covenant is material enough it could afford more than compensatory damages and may give rise to a right of termination. Generally, the loan agreement itself will determine whether a breach of covenant results in an event of default. It is also common practice to attach a grace period to a breach of covenant allowing the borrower to remedy the default.

For LMA Sustainability Linked loans, there are certain undertakings that the borrower must undertake to ensure the sustainability classification of the loan. Draft clause 26.13 pertains to sustainability information whereby the borrower undertakes to supply additional information reasonably requested by the lender to confirm Sustainability Performance Targets or compliance with other sustainability provisions, to promptly notify the lender of sustainability breaches, and to notify the lender of changes to the appointment of an external reviewer.[166]

The Poseidon Principles also provide a standard covenant clause (SCC) to contractually enforce signatory commitments, as described above in section III.E.

[160] Spoullos (n 148) 218.

[161] Otto and Scholl (n 128) 64.

[162] ibid.

[163] Mohammed A Bekhechi, 'Some observations regarding environmental covenants and conditionalities in World Bank lending activities' in Armin von Bogdandy and Rüdiger Wolfrum (eds), *Max Planck yearbook of United Nations law* (Kluwer Law International Ltd, 1991) 287–314.

[164] ibid 301.

[165] Xu et al (n 20).

[166] LMA, Model Provisions for Sustainability-Linked Loans (May 2023); Slaughter and May (n 159).

Currently, no guidance is given as to what remedies should be available in the event of a breach of this covenant whilst it remains ambiguous as to how serious such a breach would be in determining whether the lender has termination rights.[167] Thus the question remains whether mere non-compliance with the requisite periodic reporting would deprive the lender 'substantially of the whole benefit' of the contract either.[168] A borrower could argue that failure to comply with the standard covenant clause has not prejudiced the lender in any way, caused any tangible damage or adversely affected its ability to repay the loan. Nevertheless, most breaches of covenants will trigger an event of default as is the case with LMA documentation that provides that any breach of an obligation (in addition to non-payment or financial covenants) will amount to an event of default. However, the LMAs Sustainability Linked loans reflect the practice of carving out sustainability-related aspects of the loan agreement from the Events of Default provisions.[169] The justifications for this are set out in the next section, but the LMA approach seems to support the proposition that the Poseidon Principles SCC will not trigger an event of default if breached. This makes the Poseidon Principles SCC and LMA sustainability provisions less onerous than ordinary covenants.

The perception that the sustainable lending market is 'relatively benign to borrowers' is problematic from a greenwashing perspective,[170] yet understandable in encouraging borrowers to undertake such onerous sustainability reporting requirements within the early establishment of the green lending market. It is also important to note that the LMA Sustainability Linked Loans are aimed at improving the borrower's sustainability over the duration of the loan period, as opposed to loans under the Green Loan Principles, which direct funds to certain types of eligible projects. Perhaps the LMA will adopt a stricter approach to green covenants if it is to draft model provisions for green loans. Until such time, the TCLP clause for Green Loans remains the most useful set of draft provisions for green loans.

The TCLP Green Loan Starter Pack clause (ie Harrison's Clause) provides a number of undertakings for borrowers, including the borrower's compliance with the provisions of the Green Loan Framework in all material respects, not amending the framework in a way that undermines the Paris Agreement, maintaining policies and procedures to track the allocation of funds towards the eligible project and evaluate it on an ongoing basis in accordance with the Green Loan Framework.[171] It gives lenders an option to include these obligations, along with

[167] *Poussard v Spiers and Pond* (1876) 1 QBD 410.

[168] *Hong Kong Fir Shipping Co. Ltd. v Kawasaki Kisen Kaisha Ltd* [1961] 2 Lloyd's Rep 478 (CA).

[169] cls 29.3 and 29.4 (Events of Default) of LMA, Model Provisions for Sustainability-Linked Loans (May 2023).

[170] Norton Rose Fulbright, 'What do you need to know about the new LMA drafting for sustainability-linked loans?' (May 2023), www.nortonrosefulbright.com/en/knowledge/publications/15ccc56b/what-do-you-need-to-know-about-the-new-lma-drafting-for-sustainability-linked-loans.

[171] 28.42 Green Loan Undertakings of Harrison's Clause.

other covenants, in the list of events of default if breached. This is similar in the approach to the LMA Sustainability Linked Loan and the main reason for doing so is that there are also 'Declassification' and pricing remedies available to lenders. These are discussed below.

vi. Events of Default

Like 'covenant', the term 'default' is not a clearly defined legal term in English law yet is commonly understood in commercial practice to refer to express 'events of default' in a loan agreement,[172] or any failure to abide by the contract on the part of the shipowner in a mortgage agreement.[173] Defaults occur when the mortgagor or borrower breaches one of the undertakings specified in the relevant agreement, after which a default will occur if the shipowner has not remedied the default within a stipulated grace period.[174] Most loan agreements contain a comprehensive list of events that, upon occurrence, would entitle the lender/bank to cancel the transaction and declare the outstanding balance of the loan as well as accrued interest repayable (known as acceleration). It is important that these clauses make clear that it is not the event itself that accelerates the loan, but the financial institution's declaration or notice – this is to avoid the borrower pleading limitation as a defence in future litigation whereby the financier claims the outstanding amounts.[175] In shipping loans, the most common events of default include if the vessel is sold or encumbered, registration of the ship or the mortgage is challenged, or the vessel becomes a loss and the loan is not repaid within the agreed period.[176]

A primary benefit of listing certain breaches as being events of default is that it becomes unnecessary to determine whether a clause is material or repudiatory in order for the non-breaching party to be afforded adequate remedy. There is thus more certainty when it comes to the lender's enforcement rights as classifying the term breached as either a condition, innominate term, or warranty becomes irrelevant.[177] The lender can therefore accelerate payment and enforce remedies, including taking possession of the ship if it is mortgaged and selling it to enforce the mortgage.[178] However, the Privy Council did retain its discretion to assess the seriousness of an event of default in the case of *Cukurova Finance Ltd v Alfa Telecom Ltd*.[179] In this case the court considered whether the lender did

[172] David Osborne, Graeme Bowtle and Charles Buss, *The Law of Ship Mortgages* (Informa law from Routledge, 2017) 221.

[173] *Doe ex dem Gertrude Baroness Dacre v Mary Jane Roper Dowager Lady Dacre* 126 ER 887 (CCP), (1798) 1 Bos & P 250, 258.

[174] ibid 223.

[175] Mace-Kokota and Hosek-Ugolini (n 147) 98.

[176] Mace-Kokota and Hosek-Ugolini (n 147).

[177] *Ashmore v Corporation of Llyod's (No 2)* [1992] 2 Lloyds Rep 620, 226: where the same argument is applied to a mortgagee's enforcement rights in the event of default.

[178] ibid 217, 226.

[179] *Cukurova Finance International Ltd & Anor v Alfa Telecom Turkey Ltd (British Virgin Islands)* [2013] UKPC 2 (30 January 2013).

have forfeiture rights in respect of events of default as set out by the loan facility agreement. Here the event of default was triggered by the borrower's (Cukurova Finance Ltd) involvement in arbitration proceedings which resulted in an award being made against it and which the lender (Alfa Telecom) believed would have a 'material adverse effect on the financial condition, assets or business' of Cukurova and therefore amounted to an event of default under the loan agreement.[180]

Alfa Telecom argued that a number of events of default in the loan agreement had been triggered and they were therefore entitled to appropriate the loan security. On the particular facts of the case, the Privy Council found that 'the Award, giving rise to an event of default relating to "material adverse effect", involved a decision on a strongly contested issue', and the lender was kept fully aware of this claim.[181] Furthermore, the other events of default relied on by the lender, 'even if they had all been established, demonstrate no bad faith' on the part of the borrower and 'caused no significant damage' to the lender.[182] Although the facts of this case were complicated, the Privy Council essentially considered issues of 'serious damage' and 'good faith' in determining that the mere occurrence of an event of default will not necessarily result in the range of remedies afforded by the loan agreement, namely the enforcement of a mortgage and the appropriation of security. The Privy Council therefore sought some sort of prejudice to the lender in order to allow forfeiture. For environmental provisions, this sort of prejudice to lenders or 'serious' or 'significant' damage may be hard to determine or quantify in a financial sense. The damage may be purely reputational or simply exposes the lender to the risk of greenwashing without immediate damage. Nevertheless, the inclusion of green provisions in events of default would expand the lender's remedy and its control over the use of proceeds.

It has already been suggested that impact investors protect their interests by conceptualising 'greenness' as an event of default in indenture documentation.[183] If breaches of green provisions are elevated to this status in indenture documentation, then the bank could arguably default on its obligations to investors if similar enforcement mechanisms do not exert control over borrowers. Terminating a loan, accelerating payment, and forfeiture of secured assets are likely to have the strongest deterring effect on borrowers – all of which can only follow a lender issuing a notice of default. In *Lombard North Central Plc v European Skyjets Ltd*,[184] the court set out some key guidance on terminating and accelerating a loan by notice following an event of default:

(1) Lenders can waive their right to declare an event of default through positive action such as communicating to the borrower that it is permitted additional time to clear the payment arrears and accepting the late payments

[180] ibid 22.
[181] ibid 125.
[182] ibid.
[183] Agostini 171.
[184] *Lombard North Central Plc v European Skyjets Ltd* [2022] EWHC 728 (QB).

accompanied with charging late payment fees.[185] Furthermore, a 'no waiver' clause will not prevent such communication having this effect as the positive acts are inconsistent with a lender that is reserving its rights.[186]

(2) There is no requirement that a lender's Notice refer to a valid event of default and such Notice can remain effective if other events of default have occurred following an invalid one (e.g. where the lender has waived its right).[187] The only conditions necessary for the to be effective are: (1) that the Notice be sent after the occurrence of an event of default; and (2) that the Notice cancel the Facility and require the Borrower to immediately repay the loan together with accrued interest.[188]

(3) A contractual right to terminate is an absolute right of the lender to 'exercise for its own purposes, as it sees fit'.[189] This right is not subjected to so called 'Braganza duties',[190] being an implied duty to act in good faith for a proper purpose. In exercising the lender's termination right, there is no duty of good faith.

Lombard North Central Plc v European Skyjets Ltd therefore illustrates the extensive power of events of default, provided that the lender does not act in such a way that waives its rights to termination. However, as noted in the previous section, the LMA's Sustainability-Linked Loan model draft provisions and TCLP's Green Loan Starter Pack generally carve out sustainability or green provisions from events of default. TCLP gives lenders a choice of wording as to whether the following terms will trigger an event of default if breached:

(i) Clause 3.1 (Purpose)
(ii) Clause 25.34 (Green Loan Representations)
(iii) Clause 26.8 (Green Loan Reporting)
(iv) Clause 28.34 (Group Bank Accounts)
(v) Clause 28.42 (Green Loan Undertakings)
(vi) Clause 29.22 (Green Loan Audits)

If the lender elects to exclude the above from events of default, 'the Borrower shall not bear any liability to the Finance Parties as a result of the occurrence of any of the foregoing'.[191] This would remove the possibility of the lender being able to enforce ordinary rights resulting from an event of default such as acceleration and forfeiture. This begs the question of how the lender seeks to adequately enforce green framework principles or criteria if green provisions are not deemed serious enough to justify an event of default. If a single environmental covenant, such

[185] ibid [85].
[186] ibid [89]–[90].
[187] ibid [107].
[188] ibid [104].
[189] ibid [152].
[190] *Braganza v BP Shipping Limited* [2015] UKSC 17, [2015] 1 WLR 1661; considered in *TAQA Bratani Limited v Rockrose UKCS8 LLC* [2020] EWHC 58 (Comm) [44]–[53] where it was rejected that rights of termination were to be analysed as contractual discretions.
[191] cl 29.25 [No] Event of Default of *Harrison's Clause* (n 131).

as the Poseidon Principle's SCC, were the only contractual enforcement mechanism included in a loan agreement, there would be even less available remedy as it becomes doubtful whether the SCC is serious enough to result in repudiatory breach and resultant termination rights. It would be unlikely, as the Poseidon Principles SCC alone is merely a reporting undertaking. Alternative remedies for enforcing covenants are orders of specific performance to order the borrow to adhere to green requirements, or injunctions to prevent proceeds being used for non-green activities (ie for breach of a negative covenant).[192] However, orders for specific performance and injunctions are equitable remedies granted at the discretion of the court.[193] They are therefore not guaranteed remedies for managing the risks of non-compliance and breach.

The fact that sustainability and green provisions are commonly excluded from events of default seems to water down the purpose of green finance frameworks and may see the bank exposing itself to risk. Given mounting greenwashing scrutiny, it may be prudent for banks to include green provisions under events of default. However, loan documentation in the sustainable or green loan market appears to run on the underlying objective of incentivisation over rigid punitive measures. This is aligned with the core principle of green finance to not only mobilise funds necessary for green transitions, but to incentivise actors to adopt green technology and lower their emissions. As such, other clauses are employed to control the sustainability or green purpose of the loan. The main remedy under LMA documentation appears to be 'Declassification' of the loan, or altering the loan price based on sustainability performance, or through specific mechanisms such as an interest ratchet mechanism. Neither declassification provisions nor pricing provisions are common in traditional ship debt-financing documentation. These two types of clauses are set out briefly below as modern additions to ship finance as the sector is increasingly included in green finance frameworks.

vii. Product Pricing: Margin Adjustment or Interest Ratchet Clauses

A key feature of the LMA Sustainability-Linked Loan is that a borrower is rewarded for improved sustainability performance. This is the economic consequence of either underperforming in meeting Sustainability Performance Targets (SPTs), meeting them, or exceeding them. To improve upon this incentive, lenders should consider more than mere *de minimis* savings on interest rates. Both the 'Borrower's Guide to Sustainability-Linked Loans' by Slaughter and May (2023)[194] and the UK Financial Conduct Authority have highlighted that *de minimis* savings on margins are disproportionately outweighed by the administrative reporting burdens of

[192] *Priyanka Shipping Limited v Glory Bulk Carriers PTE Limited* [2019] EWHC 2804 (Comm) where an injunction and damages were claimed in respect of breach of an undertaking.
[193] *Beswick v Beswick* [1968] AC 58; *Araci v Fallon* [2011] EWCA Civ 668.
[194] Slaughter and May (n 159).

sustainability-linked loans as well as meeting SPTs.[195] Nevertheless, margin adjustments should work as follows under LMA Sustainability-Linked Loan forms to deliver adequate incentives to borrowers. Under Clause 15.3 of the LMA SLL draft provisions, parties agree to a margin grid whereby the margin increases, decreases or remains the same depending on how many SPTs are met in the reference period as provided in the most recent Sustainability Compliance Certificate.

Margin adjustments take place on an agreed Margin Adjustment Date, which parties can define as either the start date of the next interest period or a stipulated number of business days following the lender's receipt of the Sustainability Compliance Certificate. If the Sustainability Compliance Certificate contains inaccurate information and a higher margin should have been applied to the reference period, the borrower must back-pay to put the lenders in the same position they would have been had the margin been calculated with accurate information. If sustainability breaches are identified and for so long as it is continuing, the Sustainability Margin Adjustment will default to its highest level. Slaughter and May identify that it would be unfair to borrowers for the highest margin level to be applied to the entire loan reference period and that borrowers should negotiate that it only applies to the next interest period for outstanding loans or subsequent loans in the loan reference period.[196]

This is not dissimilar to how the TCLP Laith & Irsa's Clause on 'Interest Ratchet Clause for Carbon Saving' operates.[197] However, the clause is not specific to Green Loans, but loan facilities more generally. It also aims at lowering the cost of capital for companies who lower or limit their carbon emissions. This clause also operates to reduce the interest rate applicable to a loan for the interest period by applying a 'Rate Reduction corresponding to that Carbon Savings Target'.[198] The borrower shall deliver to the lender a Carbon Savings certificate which sets out the carbon savings for the relevant period ending on a 'Carbon Savings Calculation Date'.[199] If the lender, acting reasonably, does not approve the Carbon Savings Compliance Certificate, then the clause makes provision for the negotiation in good faith between parties to agree to a Revised Carbon Savings Compliance Certificate. If the parties do not reach such an agreement for a Revised Carbon Savings Compliance, they shall together appoint an independent expert.[200]

A key purpose of Margin Adjustment or Interest Ratchet Clauses is incentivisation. As such, failing to evidence carbon savings via a compliance certificate does not amount to an event of default or a declassification event. The 'penalty' or disincentive derives from paying a higher interest rate, although parties may

[195] Financial Conduct Authority, 'Review of the Sustainability-Linked Loans (SLL) Market' (29 June 2023), www.fca.org.uk/publication/correspondence/sll-letter-june-2023.pdf.

[196] Slaughter and May (n 159) 46.

[197] TCLP, Laith & Irsa's Clause – Interest Ratchet Clause for Carbon Saving (14 October 2022), chancerylaneproject.org/climate-clauses/interest-ratchet-clause-for-carbon-saving.

[198] cl 1.1.2 of Laith & Irsa's Clause.

[199] cl 2 of Laith & Irsa's Clause.

[200] cl 2.5 of Laith & Irsa's Clause.

wish to include other stipulations to raise their climate ambitions. For example, the TCLP Laith & Irsa's Clause can be used in conjunction with Nozomi's Clause, which makes receiving finance conditional, as a qualifying criteria, on setting net zero targets.[201] This includes providing the lender with both a 'Net Zero Date' and a 'Net Zero Plan'.[202] A default interest rate applies until such time that environmental targets are achieved, and thereafter a discount is applied. Such discounts could be applied in conjunction with a Margin Adjustment, yet Nozomi's Clause is not designed specifically for this purpose and is more suited to convertible loan note instruments. It would therefore require some adaptation to embed an additional discount incentive to interest rate calculations for achieving specific targets, alongside evidencing ongoing carbon-saving where an interest ratchet clause is already included.

viii. Declassification Events

The main way of mitigating greenwashing risks is through declassification clauses. These allow the lender to declassify the loan as either sustainability-linked or green, and parties are prevented from advertising it as such. Declassification works like a default provision in that it can be triggered by a declassification event. In LMA Sustainability-Linked Loan documentation, a declassification event is narrowly defined as a failure by the parties to agree on sustainability amendments within a specified period of time following a 'Sustainability Amendment Event'. A sustainability amendment clause operates as a *rendez-vous* clause which allows the parties to discuss in good faith changes affecting the borrower's business.[203] The sustainability amendment provisions in loan agreements therefore encourage negotiation on amendments to the loan agreement as required to accommodate new circumstances. These may include a lack of data and inability to report on a specific KPI, changes to the borrower's business such as the acquisition of new business that is not yet low-carbon, or where the KPIs become irrelevant.[204] This process is triggered by a Sustainability Amendment Event, which includes changes in the composition of the group's business (acquisitions, disposals, mergers, etc) which are reasonably expected to impact KPIs or SPTs, the delivery of information impacting KPIs or SPTs, and additional triggers that may be inserted by the parties.[205]

[201] TCLP, 'Laith & Irsa's Clause – Essential notes and guidance' (2022), chancerylaneproject.org/climate-clauses/interest-ratchet-clause-for-carbon-saving.

[202] TCLP, Nozomi's Clause – Net Zero Convertible Loan Note (updated 1 November 2021), chancerylaneproject.org/climate-clauses/net-zero-convertible-loan-note.

[203] Greg Brown, 'Sustainability-linked loans: how 'greenwashing' risk is mitigated in documentation' (Allen & Overy LLP Publications, 2023), www.allenovery.com/en-gb/global/news-and-insights/publications/sustainability-linked-loans-how-greenwashing-risk-is-mitigated-in-documentation.

[204] Slaughter and May (n 159) 65.

[205] cl 42.6 (Sustainability amendments) of LMA Sustainability Linked Loan Model Provisions.

If no agreement within a specified time is reached, an agent of the lender may by notice declassify the facility as 'sustainability linked'.[206] Following the Declassification Date, the consequences are as follows:

(1) The margin adjustment mechanism and sustainability provisions cease to apply;
(2) No future publicity of the facility as sustainability-linked is permitted.

Under the LMA draft provisions, this is an irreversible event as nothing in the LMA documentation permits reclassification of the product as sustainability linked. This is important for risk mitigation as it would be misleading to label something as sustainable when it did not meet sustainability criteria at any given time.

With respect to use of proceeds products such as green loans, declassification is more straightforward as it is not contingent on a sustainability amendment event. This is for the obvious reason that the loan is not targeted at improving the sustainability performance of the borrower, but at using the loan proceeds for a very specific purpose. Under the TCLP Green Loan Starter Pack (Clause 29.23 of Harrison's Clause), declassification events are triggered where:

(a) any representation, warranty or statement made or given or deemed to be made or given by the Borrower relating to a Green Loan is or proves to have been incorrect or misleading in any material respect when made or deemed to be made;
(b) the Borrower fails to comply with any of the provisions referred to in:
 (i) Clause 3.1 (Purpose);
 (ii) Clause 25.34 (Green Loan Representations);
 (iii) Clause 26.8 (Green Loan Reporting);
 (iv) Clause 28.34 (Group Bank Accounts);
 (v) Clause 28.42 (Green Loan Undertakings); or
 (vi) Clause 29.22 (Green Loan Audits).

If a failure to comply with the above provisions is not remedied within a stipulated period of time following notice of the breach or the borrower becoming aware that Certification of the Eligible Green Project is revoked or has not been renewed by the external reviewer, the borrower must cease all communications and publications that the loan is a Green Loan and amend all of its marketing materials accordingly. A declassification event can also trigger an event of default if the lender elects to insert it as such in the loan agreement. Harrison's clause gives parties the option of choosing language to reflect their agreed position. The Guiding Notes accompanying Harrison's clause state that declassification events, 'should not serve to end an otherwise commercially viable project and accordingly other remedies, short of a declared default, may be appropriate'.[207] Although this seems logical from a commercial viability perspective, it fails to protect the lender's key objectives and purpose of the loan, particularly if the lender has advertised

[206] cl 28.41 (Declassification Event) of LMA Sustainability Linked Loan Model Provisions.
[207] TCLP, Guiding Notes on Harrison's Clause in Green Loan 'Starter Pack' (updated 2022).

itself as no longer investing in non-green or brown activities. For example, some lenders may extensively advertise their commitment to not investing in fossil fuel enterprises. As such, the lender may opt to include declassification as an event of default or to omit declassification procedures all together and only have listed events of default following non-compliance with green provisions. If the consequence is merely to stop the borrower from advertising the loan product or eligible project as green, the lender may also want to consider product pricing or interest rate adjustments. However having a pricing adjustment should arguably operate within certain margins of greenness, not to completely change the intended purpose of the use of proceeds.

ix. Reputational Harm

Following a declassification event or the triggering of an event of default, the common law categories of contractual damages available to an innocent party can present problems where significant harm is caused to a lender's reputational interests. In order for the lender to claim damages for the breach of a loan covenant, the lender would need to either claim damages in the conventional way, showing that it has lost profit or incurred additional expenses,[208] or illustrate that negotiating damages can be awarded where, 'the loss suffered by the claimant is appropriately measured by reference to the economic value of the right which has been breached or considered an asset' and 'the breach of the contract results in the loss of a valuable asset created or protected by the right which was infringed'.[209] Where a bank's reputation has been impugned by a non-compliant shipowner, but no economic loss is proven, it could be difficult to extend the term 'valuable asset' to reputational rights. The 'valuable assets' referred to by negotiating damages are ordinarily proprietary rights or rights such as intellectual property rights and rights of confidence.[210] A lender/bank would have a difficult time trying to argue that its green image is tantamount to a right which is lost through the breach of the contract.

One way of addressing the problem of reputational harm could be to include a liquidated damages clause. However, the LMA SLL does not make provision for liquidated damages, as the loan architecture is built around incentivisation rather than punitive measures. Use of proceeds loans, like the LMA Green Loan, also focus on declassification events as opposed to more severe consequences that may terminate or hinder an otherwise commercially viable arrangement. Mounting greenwashing risks and increased regulation may see lenders seeking out additional remedies beyond mere interest rate adjustments and declassification. Parties may which to consider alternative mechanisms to protect interests such as 'ESG controversies'. These refer to events that are generally serious in nature, like an oil

[208] *Morris-Garner and another v One Step (Support) Ltd* [2018] UKSC 20, 95(1)–(9).
[209] ibid 95(10).
[210] *Priyanka Shipping Limited v Glory Bulk Carriers Pte Limited* (n 192) 193.

spill or an explosion, which can attract immense reputational harm even where other climate risks may be indemnified against. The LMA SLL draft provisions note that they do not include sustainability margin adjustment for 'ESG controversies' nor do they have other clauses dealing with such. A liquidated damages clause can therefore seek to provide remedy where reputational harm might have implications that are initially too remote to justify an ordinary claim in damages following breach.

The English courts have retained their jurisdiction to oversee such clauses due to the controversy surrounding the distinction between liquidated damages clauses and penalty clauses (the latter being those with an underlying intention to punish).[211] This distinction has traditionally been an important one, as penalty clauses are not accepted in English law and would not be enforced by the court beyond the actual loss of the party seeking to rely on the clause.[212] The distinction would rest on the intention of the parties and is a question of substance not form – punitive damages being a sum of money which exceeds a genuine pre-estimation of loss – with the courts setting out a number of rules to determine the nature of the clause.[213] However, these rules were criticised by Lord Neuberger and Lord Sumption for being a 'quasi-statutory code' in *Cavendish Square Holding BV v Talal El Makdessi and ParkingEye Ltd v Beavis*.[214] The majority of the Supreme Court found that the 'real question' to be asked in the future is whether the agreed damages clause 'is penal, not whether it is a pre-estimate of loss'.[215]

The outcome of *ParkingEye v Beavis* has essentially given contracting parties a greater level of freedom in setting a damages amount to be payable upon breach of a contract without considerable scope for judicial intervention.[216] It has also been submitted that the Supreme Court requires a very high degree of disproportion whilst a 'legitimate' interest does not need to be financial.[217] There are also clever ways to avoid the penalty rule, such as acceleration of a present debt,[218] stipulating a sum payable on an event that is *not* a breach,[219] or avoiding specifying a sum but instead providing that breach of a clause will violate the essence of

[211] There is no equivalent broad ban on penalty clauses in the civil law tradition; in fact, penalty clauses are explicitly recognised and regulated in some civil codes. Some even go so far as to say that a penalty sum may be collected in addition to ordinary damages; see Solène Rowan, *Remedies For Breach Of Contract: A Comparative Analysis Of The Protection Of Performance* (Oxford University Press, 2012), which makes a comparison between English and French law. See also Mariana Pargendler, 'The Role of the State in Contract Law: The Common-Civil Law Divide' (2018) 43 *Yale Journal of International Law* 143, 2018, NYU Law and Economics Research Paper No 17-01.

[212] *Jobson v Johnson* [1989] 1 All ER 621.

[213] *Jobson v Johnson* (n 212).

[214] [2015] UKSC 67, [2016] AC 1172 (two cases were heard as part of the same appeal).

[215] *Cavendish and ParkingEye* (n 214) 31.

[216] Ewan McKendrick, *Contract Law*, 13th edn (Macmillan Law Masters, 2019) 412.

[217] ibid.

[218] *The Angelic Star* [1988] 1 Lloyd's Rep 122; *O'Dea v Allstates Leasing System (WA) Pty Ltd* (1983) 57 ALJR 172, 174; *Edgeworth Capital (Luxembourg) Sarl v Ramblas Investments BV* [2015] EWHC 150 (Comm).

[219] *Alder v Moore* [1961] 2 QB 57.

the contract thus allowing for termination rights and the calculation of a loss of bargain. However, the final option does not afford the convenience of liquidated damages nor does labelling a term a condition necessarily make it one.[220]

V. Conclusions

This chapter has sought to evaluate how a contract governance approach to green finance comprises both an external regulatory or quasi-regulatory tool like a taxonomy framework, coupled with meaningful internal contractual integration of the standards and targets therein. Loan agreements provide a key site for collaboration in respect of risk management and climate governance strategies, yet are only starting to gain attention from drafting associations in relation to developing new mechanisms and remedies. While traditional loan agreements would include environmental standards within existing constituent parts of the ship loan (ie covenants and undertakings), these clauses are largely insufficient for holistically implementing broader sustainability and green agendas. Additional mechanisms enabled by freedom of contract are being increasingly adopted by banks to ensure the accountability of green investments and to protect the bank from climate-related financial risks. Although the primary goal in doing so is risk management, there is an underlying premise that all shipping actors are working towards the realisation of a decarbonisation goal to align the sector with the Paris Agreement. There is a non-financial impetus, although not mutually exclusive from the costs and risk element, that must be taken for granted in this evaluation.

[220] *Lombard North Central Plc v Butterworth* (n 184); *Financings Ltd v Baldock* [1963] 2 QB 104.

3

Green Shipbuilding and Securing Green Fuel

Although the focus of regulatory efforts has been on a ship's operational lifespan, it is important to recognise that a lifecycle approach to decarbonising shipping also embodies shipbuilding, repairs and dismantling. There are few academic studies focusing on decarbonising and limiting the environmental impacts of shipbuilding yards as they are largely seen as small contributors of a ship's overall lifespan emissions, while also playing a key role in domestic markets for driving economic growth.[1] Furthermore, the shipbuilding sector is not subjected to global governance approaches in climate mitigation as it falls within regional and national domains for law-making. Most international instruments regarding shipbuilding standards are exclusively concerned with vessel design as opposed to setting standards for the construction process, sourcing of sustainable materials, and limiting the environmental outputs of such activities. The International Convention for the Safety of Life at Sea 1974 is predominantly concerned with the safety of life and cargo on merchant ships while MARPOL annexes require, inter alia, that the vessel achieves a certain energy-efficiency, has a ballast water management system, and installs SOx or NOx scrubbers where necessary.[2]

In the context of CO_2 emissions, the EEXI standard will have necessary impacts on a vessel's technical features, such as engine power, fuel consumption and cargo capacity (ch 1 section I.A). However, ship construction as an infrastructural sector has far-reaching effects beyond the design and effectiveness of its final product, as GHG emissions and pollutants from shipyards can effect around 400km of the surrounding area.[3] Furthermore, although shipbuilding is only estimated as accounting for at least two–four per cent of a vessel's overall carbon emissions with

[1] Seyedvahid Vakili et al, 'Energy-related clean and green framework for shipbuilding community towards zero-emissions: A strategic analysis from concept to case study' (2022) 46 *International Journal of Energy Research* 20624.

[2] Although some authors disagree that scrubbers have any net benefit for the environment whatsoever; see Ida-Maja Hassellöv et al, 'Effects of seawater scrubbing on a microplanktonic community during a summer-bloom in the Baltic Sea' (2021) 291 *Environmental Pollution* 118251.

[3] Seyedvahid Vakili et al, 'The road to zero emission shipbuilding Industry: A systematic and transdisciplinary approach to modern multi-energy shipyards' (2023) X *Energy Conversion and Management* 100365, 3.

a further one per cent from repairs, this shipbuilding and retrofitting sector is set to grow with increasing demands for cleaner and more energy-efficient vessels.[4] Such growth is also supported by targeted government efforts such at the UK's funding competition for clean maritime and smart shipping projects.[5]

This demand is a very immediate corollary of green finance frameworks which, as discussed in chapter two, aim to channel funds to two key green shipping activities: 1) energy efficient vessels; and 2) alternative fuels. In decarbonising shipbuilding, a lifecycle perspective is instrumental to consider the cumulative emissions of production activities which include scope 2 (indirect) and scope 3 emissions (from the value chain).[6] The same applies to sourcing alternative fuels which have wider impacts than their combustion properties, but must also consider extraction and transportation thereof.[7] Voluntary international standards exist for industrial or economic sectors that require holistic 'cradle to grave' approaches for their products and energy-efficiency management systems. The ISO 14001 and ISO 50001 standards provide useful voluntary environmental management tools and energy management systems respectively.[8] Furthermore, certain countries have adopted circular economy policies and regulations to minimise waste, emissions and reduce material costs.[9] Greener and cleaner fuels will also need to be sourced by shipowners and charterers in a manner that comprehensively evaluates environmental life-cycle impacts and whether such fuels actually do secure meaningful emissions savings overall.[10]

This chapter focuses on two key knock-on effects of green finance frameworks from a contract governance perspective. First, it looks at shipbuilding contracts (section I), which govern a set of prescripts for the design and building phase of a vessel's lifespan. Traditional shipbuilding contracts do not include obligations pertaining to the sourcing of materials and the carbon emissions of the selected yard. However, a green credit facility used to finance a green vessel project could run the risk of exposure to greenwashing if it does not focus on these core aspects of shipbuilding. The second type of agreement that this chapter evaluates is off-take agreements to secure supply of green fuels and increase scalability in availability of these alternative fuels (section IV).

[4] ibid (n 3).

[5] The Clean Maritime Demonstration Competition forms part of the UK's Clean Maritime Plan (2019) by the Department of Transport, apply-for-innovation-funding.service.gov.uk/competition/888/overview?_ga=2.61428395.627485050.1699718893-646967318.1698333333.

[6] Mikhail V Chester and Arpad Horvath, 'Environmental assessment of passenger transportation should include infrastructure and supply chains' (2009) 4 *Environmental Research Letters* 024008.

[7] Paul Gilbert et al, 'Assessment of full life-cycle air emissions of alternative shipping fuels' (2018) 172 *Journal of Cleaner Production* 855.

[8] ISO standards, www.iso.org/standards.html.

[9] Kiara S. Winans et al, 'The history and current applications of the circular economy concept' (2017) 68 *Renewable and Sustainable Energy Reviews* 825.

[10] Gilbert et al (n 7).

I. Green Shipbuilding

Traditionally, legal risks have risen from two types of disputes in shipbuilding: (i) 'party-performance related causes', ie due to defective performance by a buyer or shipbuilder; and (ii) 'extenuating causes', ie events outside of the control of the parties.[11] Party-performance causes often arise from financial difficulties causing payment defaults by buyers, deliberate defaults,[12] insolvency of the shipyard, delays in completion,[13] defects and errors in following design specification,[14] sub-contractor errors,[15] disputes pertaining to novation,[16] or opportunism based on the market that could cause a buyer to want the shipyard to alter the course of construction.[17] Extenuating causes, on the other hand, include *force majeure* events, frustrating events,[18] and market changes which ultimately give rise to financial disputes. The remedies for such disputes stem from the Sale of Goods Act 1979, the common law, law of equity, and the contract itself. In the case of party-performance related defects, a 'prevention principle' applies so that a 'party shall never take advantage of his own wrong'.[19] This principle has developed particularly within a shipbuilding context where late delivery of the vessel has been an issue.[20] Parties are also free to agree to contractual terms that will protect their interests and provide adequate remedy. However, neither of the two types of dispute which these clauses traditionally manage have had to consider the environmental impacts of the shipyard.

This poses immense greenwashing risks where a vessel may be innovatively designed to adhere to green finance project criteria, perhaps even able to achieve net-zero emissions, yet was constructed using energy-intensive practices and unsustainable materials. The same problem has arisen in the context of electric

[11] Amar Vasani, *Shipbuilding disputes: influence of industry norms on law and contracts* (Unpublished Doctoral thesis, City, University of London, 2018) 146.

[12] For example, where a buyer defaults on payment because it no longer requires a tanker. See *Adams Bros v Blythswood Shipbuilding Co (No 2)* (1922) 13 Lloyd's Rep 411.

[13] *Adyard Abu Dhabi v SD Marine Services* [2011] EWHC 848 (Com Ct); *Zhoushan Jinhaiwan Shipyard v Golden Exquisite Inc* [2014] EWHC 4050 (Com Ct).

[14] *Diamante Sociedad de Transportes SA v Todd Oil Burners (The Diamantis Pateras)* (1966) 1 Lloyd's Rep 179 (QB); *Admiralty Commissioners v Cox & King* (1927) 22 Lloyd's Rep 223 (CA).

[15] This can occur when a shipyard does not vet the work of subcontractors who are tasked with portions of a newbuild project, such as installing specific equipment.

[16] *CMA CGM SA v Hyundai Mipo Dockyard* [2009] 1 Lloyd's Rep 213 (Com Ct).

[17] *Northumberland Shipbuilding v Christensen* [1923] 14 Lloyd's Rep 336 (KB) where a shipowner insisted that the shipyard built a different type of vessel instead of the contracted one because ship freight rates had fallen. This was done in the hope of escaping the contract altogether.

[18] *National Carriers v Panalpina (Northern) Ltd* [1981] AC 675 (HL) 854 at 700, Lord Simon defines the doctrine of frustration.

[19] *Rede v Farr* (1817) 6 M & S 121, 105 ER 1188.

[20] *Multiplex v Honeywell* [2007] EWHC 447 (TCC). For a discussion on the development of the prevention principle, see Zoran Tasić, 'The prevention principle and the extension of time clauses in English law shipbuilding contracts' (2020) 59 *Poredbeno Pomorsko Pravo* 121.

road vehicles, whereby electric vehicles based on large batteries require more energy and scarce resources to produce than the potential benefits gained by the operational phase of their lifespan. The extraction and processing of these scarce resources have severe human rights impacts and are a source of conflict and forced displacement in developing nations.[21] What can be learned from electric vehicles is that climate mitigation needs to be seen within its greater context of sustainable development and necessitates *just transitions*. Human rights violations are often at the centre of climate litigation,[22] but shipbuilding contracts have not yet had to comprehensively deal with human rights issues in the context of sustainable development. On the other hand, ship dismantling practices have had greater exposure to such risks. The transactional process for ship recycling usually involves the sale of a vessel to a specialist cash-buyer intermediary for resale to a ship recycling facility. To deal with the prevalent abuse of this process, as seen in *Begum v Maran*,[23] BIMCO introduced the RECYCLECON,[24] which specifies that the vessel is to be sold exclusively for recycling in 'a safe and environmentally sound manner consistent with the international and national law and relevant guidelines', and binds actors to the Hong Kong Convention 2009.[25] In doing so, the standardised documentation considers contractual arrangements that may follow on from the sale agreement and that have significant third-party impacts on workers and coastal communities.

Similar to vessel recycling, shipbuilding contracts are likely going to require a much wider array of sustainability issues than those ordinarily conceived of by existing standardised documentation. 'Ship design' is a concept narrowly captured by shipbuilding contracts, yet green shipbuilding requires a more holistic contract governance approach to 'minimise the offal and harmful emissions during design, manufacturing, service and laying up in order to reduce the pollution to air, water and soil, save resources and improve economic and social benefits'.[26] Given the widening scope of sustainability issues that shipyards are faced with, the distinction between 'clean' and 'green' shipyards becomes useful. The former deals with mitigating all negative environmental outputs excluding air emissions, while the latter deals specifically with energy usage and overall carbon emissions from both production and supporting services.[27] Although the following analysis of shipbuilding contracts focuses on 'green shipbuilding', it is important to note that

[21] Amnesty International and the Initiative for Good Governance and Human Rights, *Powering Change or Business as Usual? Forced evictions at industrial cobalt and copper mines in the Democratic Republic of the Congo* (AFR 62/7009/2023) joint report.

[22] See the landmark case of *Milieudefensie et al v Royal Dutch Shell plc* ECLI:NL:RBDHA:2021:5337.

[23] Such third-party risks were considered in the case in *Begum v Maran (UK) Ltd* [2021] EWCA Civ 326 (discussed in ch 1, section B.ii), although the parties did not make use of RECYCLECON form.

[24] BIMCO, RECYCLECON (2021), www.bimco.org/contracts-and-clauses/bimco-contracts/recyclecon.

[25] Hong Kong International Convention for The Safe And Environmentally Sound Recycling Of Ships, 2009 SR/CONF/45 (HK Convention).

[26] Aevelina Rahman and Mashud Karim, 'Green Shipbuilding and Recycling: Issues and Challenges' (2015) 6 *International Journal of Environmental Science and Development* 838.

[27] Vakili et al (n 1) 20643.

'clean shipbuilding' is equally important as it embodies related sustainability risks for shipyards. Yet these risks are also opportunities for shipyards to be increasingly competitive and attractive to shipowners who are interested in green or clean labelling for their vessels. Shipyards can also align themselves with green finance product offerings to attract eco-conscious shipowners who are subjected to both green loan stipulations and green cargo interests.

II. Negotiating Shipbuilding Contracts

Most shipbuilding projects originate with a buyer's decision to commission a newbuild to either add to or replace vessels within its existing fleet.[28] These decisions need to be aligned with the ship company's overall strategy and its primary objectives, sometimes set out in the company's 'Mission Statement'.[29] The company should also consider its advertised CSR and sustainability agendas, ESG ratings, and both the green prescripts and legislative context of the credit facility used to finance the building of the vessel. According to Deloitte, 63 per cent of shipping companies from a sample of 38 randomly selected, have published at least one ESG report.[30] This number has likely increased since the study was undertaken in 2021, yet at the time, ship companies were showing an average of 'moderate ESG risk' ratings. More recently, Watson Farley and Williams found that 41 per cent of shipowners would forgo a commercial deal for ESG reasons, and 61 per cent of shipowners have formulated due diligence processes to identify ESG risks in suppliers.[31]

From a green finance perspective, the risks for both lenders and borrowers are set out in chapter two. It is worth noting again that simply falling within the technical screening criteria (whether quantitative or qualitative) of a green finance framework does not necessarily mean that all risks have been addressed. Such criteria are to be read in conjunction with enabling legislation so that there is alignment with the overall purpose of the framework's objectives. For example, the EU's Climate Delegated Act (discussed in chapter two) includes activities that contribute to the first two objectives listed in Article 9 of the Taxonomy Regulation: (a) climate change mitigation; and (b) climate change adaptation.[32] Shipping activities under the technical screening criteria that contribute to these objectives

[28] Simon Curtis, Ian Gaunt and William Cecil, *The Law of Shipbuilding Contracts*, 5th edn (Informa Group Ltd, 2020) 8 also noting that newbuildings constructed for the builder's account (ie, without a pre-existing contract of sale) are rare.

[29] George Bruce, 'Shipbuilding Company Strategy' in *Shipbuilding Management*, 1st edn (Springer, 2021) 45.

[30] Deloitte, *ESG in the Shipping sector: The role of ESG in the evaluation of shipping companies* (2021) 14, www2.deloitte.com/content/dam/Deloitte/gr/Documents/consumer-business/gr_esg_in_the_shipping_sector_noexp.pdf.

[31] Watson Farley & Williams, *The Sustainability Imperative – Part 2* (2023) 11, www.wfw.com/reports/the-sustainability-imperative-part-2-report/?intIaContactId=nXBhr5xyjz7BTXN2noycig%3d%3d&intExternalSystemId=1.

[32] Commission Delegated Regulation (EU) 2021/2139 of 4 June 2021 (Climate Delegated Act).

include, inter alia, that the vessel has zero direct (tailpipe) CO_2 emissions; or derives at least 25 per cent of its energy from zero direct (tailpipe) CO_2 emission fuels or plug-in power for their normal operation at sea and in ports until 31 December 2025.[33] However, these activities must be consistent with the 'do no significant harm' principle set out in Article 17 of the Taxonomy Regulation.[34] Article 17 envisions a life-cycle approach to products and services and states that the environmental objective of climate mitigation will be significantly harmed where the activity leads to significant GHG emissions; and that the objective of climate adaptation will be significantly harmed where 'that activity leads to an increased adverse impact of the current climate and the expected future climate, on the activity itself or on people, nature or assets'.[35] It is therefore inconceivable that activities operating within the technical screening criteria should be allowed to indirectly cause harm. These adverse impacts should be considered in ship design, selection of shipyard, and material selection. A zero-emission vessel cannot attain a high degree of 'greenness' if, for example, its metal components are sourced from mines that widely deforest and contaminate natural habitats. The carbon emissions used in its manufacturing may also outweigh its operational benefits to the environment.[36]

On this basis, detailed discussions will then ensue regarding commercial and technical requirements that define the size, type and standard of outfitting of the vessel. Buyers usually seek the assistance of shipbrokers with relevant expertise of the market. Brokers are key actors in this process as they have extensive contacts with shipbuilders and can advise the buyer on the availability of constructions berths, the price of the contract, reasonable delivery times that are suitable to the buyer and the terms likely to be offered by shipbuilders in the market.[37] In accordance with the broker's advice, the buyer will then authorise the broker to approach a shipbuilder that the broker has likely recommended. If the shipbuilder has already developed a standardised design for the vessel that the buyer is seeking, the builder will be in position to immediately furnish the buyer with its specifications, knows as 'Principal Particulars'.[38] It is important that no misrepresentations are made at this stage pertaining to the green attributes of the vessel that the shipbuilder is proposing to build.

Once a buyer has provisionally selected a shipyard, the negotiation phase commences. This stage of pre-contractual exchanges is complex as the shipbuilder must conduct research in respect of the design, performance, and regulatory compliance of the vessel – all within ambit of the buyer's needs. This requires expert consultation,

[33] See Technical Screening Criteria 6.7–6.12 respectively under the Climate Delegated Act.

[34] Regulation (EU) 2020/852.

[35] Art 17(b).

[36] Electric motor cars have been similarly criticised. It has also been shown that although electric cars produce zero-tailpipe emission, they produce the most GHG after taking energy generation, transmission and charging efficiency into accounts, see AE Pg Abas et al, 'Techno-Economic Analysis and Environmental Impact of Electric Vehicle' (2019) 7 IEEE 98565–98578.

[37] Curtis, Gaunt and Cecil (n 28) 8.

[38] The broker may also submit an 'invitation to tender' to a number of shipbuilders recommended by the broker.

running model tests, and consultation with classification societies, legal advisers and regulatory authorities.[39] Although not relevant to the green operation of the vessel once constructed, it should be required of the buyer and financier that the shipyard makes use of green suppliers and ethically sourced materials. This may involve additional research on the part of the builders. Green shipbuilding yards may also want to independently join green labelling and certification schemes, as well as advertising their internal CSR mandates to potential and existing buyers and publishing a list of their approved green suppliers.[40] These development costs are usually borne by the builder on the basis that the buyer will reimburse the costs if the project does proceed. Even if not expressly agreed, the builder may be entitled to restitutionary remedies for its expenses, especially where a benefit has accrued to the buyer for work done by the builder.[41]

In order to protect the interests of each party, it is common to execute a 'letter of intent' setting out mutual understandings.[42] Whether such a letter has contractual effect will be viewed against the 'factual matrix' in which it was prepared and executed.[43] In construing such a document, one should

> look at the document itself, at the surrounding circumstances, and at what happened when [the letter of intent] was brought into existence. The fact that it has the particular label that it has does not brand it at the outset as a contractual document or as a non-contractual document.[44]

Although such a letter does not usually give rise to obligations in contract, they can still constitute misrepresentations in tort or under the Misrepresentation Act 1967. It would be important that the builder accurately describes its ability and capacity to construct a green vessel in accordance with the buyer's requirements. If a builder is unwilling to carry out substantial preliminary work only on the assurance of a letter of intent, it may insist on a bridging contract under which it provides design and technical services in relation to the project for a fee.[45] Such arrangements are ordinarily subsumed by the main shipbuilding contract expressly, and impliedly where no express provision is made.[46] A buyer should ensure that the builder's liability under any design warranties (express or implied) are not discharged by termination of the bridging contract unless stipulated again and re-affirmed in the shipbuilding contract itself.[47]

[39] Curtis, Gaunt and Cecil (n 28) 9.

[40] For example, Green Marine certification requires that participants (including shipowners, shipyards, terminals, and ports) self-evaluate their green performance, the annual self-evaluation report, and submit results to an accredited Green Marine verifier every three years. See Green Marine, Certification Policy: Green Marine Environmental Program (2021), green-marine.org/certification.

[41] Curtis, Gaunt and Cecil (n 28).

[42] ibid.

[43] Lord Wilberforce in *Reardon Smith Line Ltd v Yngvar Hansen Tangen (The 'Diana Prosperity')* [1976] 2 Lloyd's Rep 621 at 625.

[44] *Wilson Smithett & Cape (Sugar) Ltd v Bangladesh Sugar and Food Industries Corporation* (1985) 1 Lloyd's Rep 378 at 379.

[45] Curtis, Gaunt and Cecil (n 28) 13: These arrangements are common in the oil and gas industry where the construction of highly specialised vessels and structures for off-shore use are required.

[46] *British Steel v Cleveland Bridge* [1984] 1 All ER 504.

[47] Curtis, Gaunt and Cecil (n 28) 13.

After such primary work is completed by the builder, final negotiations will commence, usually in the presence of the broker, and specifications will need to be looked over by both parties. Thereafter, the parties usually conclude the main agreement in accordance with the framework of a standard contract form as amended to meet any specific needs. Common standard forms include: Shipbuilders' Association of Japan 1974 (SAJ Form), BIMCO's Standard Newbuilding Contract (NEWBUILDCON), People's Republic China's CMAC Standard Newbuilding Contract (Shanghai Form), the Community of European Shipyards' Association's 'AWES Form' 1999, and the Standard Form Norwegian Shipbuilding Contract 2000.[48] The integration of the same green principles that permeate green finance frameworks as well as the vessel specifications for eligible projects will have to be carried through into these transactions.

III. Structure of Ship Building Contracts and Green Terms

Although the standardised forms may have differences, they are largely similar in structure and stipulated obligations. Such forms usually include:[49]

1. Preamble
2. Allocation of the Design Risk
3. Description and Class of the vessel (design, characteristics, technical specifications)
4. Subcontracting (where the builder requires part of the work to be subcontracted, including direct payments to subcontractors)
5. Performance Guarantees
6. Regulatory Compliance (safety and environmental) and Classification Requirements
7. Quality Assurance
8. Terms of Payment
9. Registration (customary for the buyer to bear all of the costs of registration under the chosen flag)
10. Liquidated Damages provisions[50]

[48] For substantial differences in these forms, see Andrew Tettenborn, 'Contracting by numbers: the different characteristics of the main shipbuilding contracts' in Baris Soyer and Andrew Tettenborn (eds), *Ship Building, Sale and Finance* (Informa Law, 2015) 3.

[49] Curtis, Gaunt and Cecil (n 28) 19.

[50] *Cenargo Ltd v Empresa Nacional Bazan de Construcciones Navales Militares SA* (2002) EWCA Civ 524 confirmed that liquidated damages were applicable in respect of two shipbuilding contracts, however, the general principle espoused by Longmore LJ may present confusion. Nevertheless, liquidated damages pursuant of a legitimate interest are usually enforceable, see *Jobson v Johnson* [1989] 1 All ER 621.

Usually, the buyer acquires financing to make all payments under the agreement on the basis that the contract is paid in full by the time of delivery of the vessel.[51] If the vessel is to be constructed as a 'green' vessel in accordance with a green finance framework, then the buyer needs to ensure that the vessel meets the terms of its loan agreement in respect of performance and targets. This would require that the builder is aware of these terms by way of reference, or that it is given clear specifications on how the vessel is to perform. It is very unlikely that the financier/bank will dictate detailed design specifications. The loan agreement, as seen with the Poseidon Principles SCC, is far more likely to stipulate that the vessel be MARPOL compliant with the necessary software to report and monitor emissions. More stringent frameworks may advance funds on the basis of net carbon emissions or the exclusive use of green supply chains and green construction.

A. Preamble and Green Objectives

Preambles or 'Recitals' for climate drafting are discussed in chapter four (section II.B.i) in relation to charterparties, yet have relevance to both loan documentation and shipbuilding forms. In an environmental context, a preamble or recital referencing a regulatory or voluntary framework and the parties' net-zero commitments would place decarbonisation at the core of the parties' objective intentions. Generally, a preamble serves to identify the 'Buyer' and the 'Builder' and set out the scope of the project, its general terms, and to identify the shipyard where construction is to take place. Although the enforceability of the preamble may not always be straightforward, Curtis et al note that a London arbitration award in 2010 found that the description and identity of the shipyard named in the Preamble was a condition of the contract.[52] It was therefore impermissible for the builders to move construction to another yard.[53] The selection of shipyard is important if the financier requires that the construction take place at a certified or green labelled shipyard. Preambles or recitals can also provide a normative direction for contractual performance as they provide evidence of the relevant 'factual matrix' at the date of execution.[54]

BIMCO already employs a Preamble at the outset of its standardised ship sale form for the recycling of vessels. The RECYCLECON contract provides a standardised document for the sale of vessels for recycling a vessel in 'a safe and environmentally sound manner consistent with the international and national law and relevant guidelines' as per its guiding Preamble.[55] This contract thus

[51] Curtis, Gaunt and Cecil (n 28) 44.

[52] Although the arbitration award remains confidential, Curtis et al briefly set out that the tribunal relied on *Reardon Smith Line Ltd v Yngvar Hansen-Tangen* to establish that the seller's chosen shipyard is a 'substantial ingredient of the "identity" of the thing sold'; see Curtis, Gaunt and Cecil (n 28) 20. (n 43).

[53] Curtis, Gaunt and Cecil (n 28) 21.

[54] *Blackpool FC (Properties) Ltd v JSC Baltic International Bank* [2018] EWCA Civ 732.

[55] ibid, *Preamble*.

covers vessels sold for recycling *only*; it does not cover previous trading arrangements prior to the vessel being recycled.[56] This contract can bind buyers to the HK Convention, as clause 17 requires that the buyer 'undertake and warrant that the Vessel will be recycled at a Ship Recycling Facility in accordance with the Ship Recycling Facility Plan and the Ship Recycling Plan'. The Ship Recycling Plan is defined with reference to the IMO Guidelines for the Development of a Ship Recycling Plan as required by regulation 9 of the Annex to the Hong Kong Convention.[57] Clause 18 of RECYCLECON provides that the buyers, on the seller's request, shall provide a copy of the Ship Recycling Facility Plan (or an attestation that the Facility has such a Plan) and that the buyers should allow the sellers to visit the Facility to verify its compliance.

Although the RECYCLECON cannot provide an all-encompassing solution to overcome the problems associated with harmful cash-buying practices, it does effectively place sustainability at the core of parties' intention – thus unequivocally stating that sustainable recycling goes 'to the root of the contract'.[58] It would be challenging for a buyer to argue that recycling a vessel in an irresponsible manner, not within an agreed and suitable facility, does not amount to repudiatory breach. For the buyer to not recycle the vessel in a *safe and environmentally sound manner* deprives the seller of 'substantially of the whole benefit' which would be obtained under the RECYCLECON.[59] It is clear that by using such a standardised form, the seller intends to sell his vessel to a buyer who can fulfil such obligations, whilst at the same time the contract is priced to enable the buyer to still make a profit. On any interpretation of RECYCLECON's Articles 17 and 18, as supported by the form's Preamble, the undertaking to 'recycle the Vessel in a safe and environmentally sound manner consistent with international and national law and relevant guidelines' is undeniably 'substantial and serious' and a fundamental *condition* of the contract. In such a way, preambles or recitals may assist with the elevation of decarbonisation terms to being fundamental to the intentions of the parties objectively ascertained. Although preambles may not always involve binding terms, they provide a powerful normative effect on the contract as a whole.

In addition to a guiding Preamble, more detailed commitments could be included in a first clause. A prominent 'Clause 1' outlining the green objectives of the buyer would make it explicit that the environmental performance of the vessel or the environmentally sound sourcing of its materials are fundamental obligations. It would also clarify the factual matrix in relation to interpreting and ascertaining the objective intention of the parties in relation to other obligations in the contract.[60] Clause 1(a) of BIMCO's NEWBUILDCON specifically states that, 'the Builder shall design, construct, test and survey, launch, equip, complete, sell

[56] c 17.
[57] Resolution MEPC.196(62) (Aadopted on 15 July 2011).
[58] *Poussard v Spiers and Pond* (1876) 1 QBD 410.
[59] ibid 495.
[60] *Reardon Smith Line Ltd v Yngvar Hansen-Tangen and Sanko SS & Co Ltd* (n 43).

and deliver the Vessel to the Buyer all in accordance with good international shipbuilding and marine engineering practice'.[61] The NEWBUILDCON also provides that the Builder shall:[62]

> Endeavour to take due account of the Vessel's ultimate disposal when designing and constructing the Vessel by:
>
> (i) using materials which can be recycled safely and in an environmentally sound manner; and
>
> (ii) by minimising the use of materials known to be potentially hazardous to health and the environment.'

Such a provision clearly imposes a duty on the builder to warrant that the vessel is designed and constructed in accordance with the contract, taking into account a lifecycle approach to shipbuilding and sustainability. Indeed the exact wording, 'be recycled safely and in an environmentally sound manner' is found in the RECYCLECON thus illustrating BIMCO's cradle to grave approach. A more substantive first clause, or other relevant clause, that sets out the primary purpose of the contract could go further to include the buyer's adherence to a green finance framework, and the parameters of design and construction more generally as 'a green vessel' achieving 'lower' or 'zero emissions'.

B. Design Specification and Compliance

Whilst the Preamble may generally describe the vessel, the 'Description and Class' of the vessel will lay out strict parameters for its design and construction. This description traditionally includes length, breadth and depth, gross tonnage, hold/tank capacity, draught and method of propulsion. However, special requirements for fuel choices, scrubber installations, or battery capacity can all be included. The parties are also free to allocate design risk as they see fit.[63] Problems with design of a newbuild generally emerge much later after the vessel has commenced trading.[64] Express provision should be made for design risk; however, the builder's fundamental commitment to manufacture the vessel will usually entail an obligation to ensure that she meet safety requirements and performance criteria as stipulated under the contract.[65] The builder also guarantees the stipulated

[61] BIMCO, 'NEWBUILDCON' (2007), www.bimco.org/contracts-and-clauses/bimco-contracts/newbuildcon.

[62] cl 4(a).

[63] The SAJ form makes no allocation of design risk, it merely states builder shall 'build, launch, equip and complete' and 'sell and deliver' her to the buyer.

[64] In *The Amoco Cadiz* [1984] 2 Lloyd's Rep 304, an Illinois court found that the shipbuilders were jointly liable with the owners of the tanker for the pollution damage resulting from her stranding.

[65] See *Aktiebolaget Gotaverken v Westminster Corporation of Monrovia and Another* [1971] 2 Lloyd Rep 505. However, where a builder is given a design and instructed merely to build the vessel in accordance with given plans, no warranty can be implied that she must be fit for purpose (*Dixon Kerly Ltd v Robinson* (1965) 2 Lloyd's Rep 404).

performance of the vessel. These guarantees usually relate to standards of performance (speed, deadweight and fuel consumption), a breach of which will usually entitle the buyer to claim liquidated damages or even, where severe, reject delivery of the vessel and rescind the contract.[66]

Regulatory compliance of the vessel with applicable environmental laws is also the responsibility of the builder. Green finance frameworks may require more than mere regulatory requirements, yet bare regulatory compliance is almost invariably the responsibility of the builder. Article 1.2 of the SAJ form requires that on delivery, the vessel shall comply with the 'rules, regulations and requirements of other regulatory bodies as described in the Specifications', which is taken to encompass MARPOL and will implicitly provide for the EEXI and SEEMP where relevant. Clause 3(a) of the NEWBUILDCON similarly requires that the vessel be delivered in compliance with the regulations of the 'Regulatory Authorities'. Other environmental clauses in standardised forms include Protective Coating Clauses and Source of Origin Clauses.[67] If buyers want to impose additional requirements on the builder for outperforming regulatory standards, these would be expressly provided for in the vessel design specifications, whilst performance guarantees may be adjusted accordingly.

C. Climate Clauses for Construction Relevant to Shipbuilding

As they stand, the common forms used for shipbuilding do not go far enough to implement a set of green objectives in design specification and vessel performance. Such forms would need additional terms for alignment with a green finance framework if applicable to the buyer's attainment of finance for payment of the shipbuilding contract. If a vessel is to be categorised as 'green' then a shipbuilder needs to know the performance parameters and consequent design requirements of what constitutes a 'green vessel' in accordance with the framework, as well as knowing what sort of materials and suppliers to procure. Shipbuilding forms can incorporate stronger commitments to climate alignment by introducing additional terms or reworking existing clauses. Shipbuilding contracts can borrow drafting techniques from other construction and infrastructural sectors. Green construction procurement has been recognised as a key way of attaining SDGs, but must be monitored by green logistics services management to have greater effect.[68] Contract governance approaches can ensure that climate mitigation is achieved in sourcing materials and procuring suppliers.

[66] Curtis, Gaunt and Cecil (n 28) 28.

[67] Protective Coating Clauses are found in cl IV(2) Shanghai Form and cl5 NEWBUILDCON. Source of Origin clauses are found in cl IV(3) Shanghai Form and cl 6 of the NEWBUILDCON.

[68] Tsimisaraka Marcelline et al, 'Impact of Green Construction Procurement on Achieving Sustainable Economic Growth Influencing Green Logistic Services Management and Innovation Practices' (2022) 9 *Frontiers in Environmental Sciences* 815928, 12.

In this regard, The Chancery Lane Project (TCLP) has done significant work to introduce a set of climate clauses for the construction sector. The TCLP is a collaborative body of legal practitioners and professionals situated in London which facilitates a number of international events centred on creating climate focused model clauses for commercial contracts.[69] After creative thinking techniques are employed to draft the clauses in question, the clauses are peer-reviewed by sector experts and then published openly and freely on the TCLP website. Each model clause is aimed at a particular climate change issue within a commercial practice area or sector (eg insurance, property, information technology, supply chain, etc) that can be mitigated or adapted through prescribed contractual obligations. Supporting information is also provided, such as separate user manuals and drafting notes. The TCLP has drafted a number of green construction clauses which could be adapted to shipbuilding projects.

For example, its proposed amendments to Joint Contract Tribunal's (JCT) standard Design and Build documents (Mary's Clause) includes in a first clause, a set of environmental objectives and compliance with such objectives.[70] Such a technique is suggested in sections A and B above in relation to shipbuilding. Although, Mary's clause is drafted specifically for JCT design and build agreements in the context of land and building development, there are similarities between vessel construction and other projects. Willow's Clause for 'Construction Materials: Procurement' in the Building and Land sectors also illustrates how a carbon budget can be set for a particular project.[71] A carbon budget is 'the aggregate tons of Greenhouse Gas Emissions permitted for the construction of the Project as set out in the Carbon Budget'.[72] Subclause 1.1. provides that Design-Build team shall provide the owner with a carbon budget which includes details of lower-embodied carbon materials. Optional incentives such as a 'carbon budget bonus' are embedded into the contract should the design-build team meet or achieve better performance than the carbon budget. Optional disincentives include the design team owing the cost of carbon offsets to the owner if the carbon budget is exceeded.

Shipbuilding is also dependent on supply chains for not only materials, but services or specialised equipment. A owner may want to ensure that the shipyard abides by strict criteria or applicable ESG standards for subcontractors and suppliers. Clauses for shipbuilding contracts can be based on sustainable supplier/sub-contractor clauses. The TCLP has drafted a Subcontractor/Supplier Self-Assessment Questionnaire (Robyn's Questionnaire) that obliges subcontractors or suppliers to develop and accelerate climate risk and

[69] The Chancery Lane Project (2022), chancerylaneproject.org/about.

[70] TCLP, *Mary's Clause – JCT Energy Efficiency and Environmental Obligations* (updated 30 November 2022), https://chancerylaneproject.org/clauses/jct-energy-efficiency-and-environmental-obligations/.

[71] TCLP, *Willow's Clause – Construction Materials: Procurement* (updated 20 October 2023), chancerylaneproject.org/climate-clauses/construction-materials-procurement.

[72] Definitions in *Willow's Clause.*

emission reduction strategies.[73] Supplier codes of conduct are not uncommon in procurement and supply chains.[74] The United Nations Global Compact (UNGC) practical guide on supply chain sustainability advises companies to clearly formulate their CSR expectations towards suppliers in a code of conduct and to implement the code through its integration into supplier contracts.[75] Recommendations calling for the use of contractual enforcement mechanisms can also be found in the UN Protect, Respect and Remedy Framework and Guiding Principles,[76] as well as the OECD Guidelines for Multinational Enterprises (2011).[77]

In this regard, international commercial contracts have become a site for transnational forms of private governance. Implementation of sustainability standards is defined by codes of conduct and sustainability principles that are enacted by larger buyers or retailers.[78] Where a chain leader is the drafter of widely incorporated boilerplate clauses, it could be compared to a regulator using a command and control model over passive participants in the chain.[79] Yet the process is not solely dependent on standard-setting, but requires effective monitoring and compliance. Information-sharing makes the process more collaborative and also enables a prospective viewpoint as opposed to a reactive regulatory model which imposes sanctions. Cooperative norms are also embedded in sustainable supply chain clauses. The use of these clauses is also a commitment to improved environmental performance, as evident in Robyn's Questionnaire which places an expectation that 'all members of [the] subcontract/supply chain will be working to improve overall ESG targets during the life cycle of our projects'.

IV. Offtake Agreements for Green Shipping Technology and Fuel

Green shipping will require that bigger shipping companies secure large quantities of alternative fuels and on-shore power. Producers of green fuel and green technologies will, in turn, also require vital enabling cash flow to provide cleaner

[73] TCLP, Robyn's Questionnaire – Subcontractor/ Supplier Self-Assessment Climate Questionnaire (Construction) (published 29 September 2021), chancerylaneproject.org/climate-clauses/subcontractor-supplier-self-assessment-climate-questionnaire-construction.

[74] The equivalent in supply chain finance are 'Know-Your-Client' (KYC) surveys.

[75] UN Global Compact Office and Business for Social Responsibility, *Supply Chain Sustainability: A Practical Guide for Continuous Improvement* (2010) 23.

[76] John Ruggie, 'Protect, Respect & Remedy: A Framework for Business and Human Rights' (2008) 3 *Innovations: Technology, Governance, Globalization* 189.

[77] OECD, *OECD Guidelines for Multinational Enterprises* (OECD Publishing, 2011), Commentary on General Policies, paras 18, 19 and 21.

[78] Fabrizio Cafaggi, 'Regulation through contracts: Supply-chain contracting and sustainability standards' (2016) 12 *European Review of Contract Law* 218, 223.

[79] ibid 223.

fuel solutions for shipping. This can be achieved through the use of offtake agreements which provide a type of project finance that can incentivise a private sponsor to undertake a risky project. Maersk is leading the way in using offtake agreements for transitioning its fleet of vessels. In 2022, it entered into a green fuel agreement with Ørsted to develop the Power-to-X-facility on the US Gulf Coast.[80] In 2023, it also finalised an offtake agreement with a Chinese developer Goldwind for large-scale green methanol supply.[81] The Getting to Zero Coalition and the Energy Transitions Commission has also identified offtake agreements as a key tool for its comprehensive strategy for zero-emission shipping called, 'The Next Wave: Green Corridors'.[82] Offtake agreements are useful in that they make it easier to obtain finance to develop new technologies and green fuels as lenders can see that the producer already has clients and customers lined up before production begins. This section will focus on how these offtake agreements can upscale necessary green infrastructure for shipping by: 1) shipowners and charterers guaranteeing a demand for greener fuels and technologies; and 2) end customers guaranteeing offtake commitments to de-risk ship owners' investments in zero emission-fuelled vessels.

An offtake agreement is a contract under which the 'offtaker' agrees to buy an amount of the product produced by a project.[83] Although this is not a finance agreement per se, project financiers would be interested in the terms of the offtake agreement because the proceeds of sales will ultimately finance the project and repay any lenders. This sort of project finance can counteract the main risks associated with renewable energy or green energy projects, ie a lower rate of return than fossil fuels, and a higher risk of investment in comparison to fossil fuel projects.[84] Key provisions in an offtake agreement include:[85]

(1) Pricing: generally on a take-or-pay basis in accordance with scheduled payments.
(2) The Offtaker's obligations: to take an amount of product at specified times.
(3) Product Specifications: generally related to quality parameters.
(4) Risk allocation: regulatory risk, tax, currency fluctuations.
(5) Credit Support: lenders may require that the offtaker acquires credit from a credit worth entity.

[80] Ørsted, 'Ørsted and Maersk sign landmark green fuels agreement, as Ørsted enters the US Power-to-X market' (22 March 2022), orsted.com/en/media/newsroom/news/2022/03/20220310491311.

[81] Chemical Industry Digest, 'Maersk Signs Landmark Green Methanol Offtake Agreement' (November 2023), www.proquest.com/docview/2894002691?accountid=14510&forcedol=true&pq-origsite=summon&sourcetype=Magazines.

[82] Mission Possible Partnership, *The Next Wave Green Corridors: A special report for the Getting to Zero Coalition*, www.globalmaritimeforum.org/content/2021/11/The-Next-Wave-Green-Corridors.pdf.

[83] LexisPSL 'Offtake contracts – key issues for project finance lenders' (Practice Note, Lexis+ UK, 2023).

[84] Farhad Taghizadeh-Hesary and Naoyuki Yoshino, 'Sustainable Solutions for Green Financing and Investment in Renewable Energy Projects' (2020) 13 *Energies* 788.

[85] LexisPS (n 83).

The quality of the fuel concerned can be dealt with by way of ordinary contractual conditions. Under English law, the sale of fuel is governed by the Sales of Goods Act 1979. Section 14(3) provides that 'there is an implied condition that the goods supplied under the contract are reasonably fit for that purpose'. Ensuring the combustible properties of fuel would be of interest to lenders who have disbursed loan amounts in accordance with a green finance framework. For example, where a shipowner has acquired finance under the EU Taxonomy Regulation, the financing bank may wish to know how the shipowner intends to secure green fuel. Time charters would have the same fuel needs and run the risk of bunker supply shortages through constrained availability. More is said on problems surrounding bunker supply for charterers in chapter four (section II.B.iv) and the shipping sector has prior experience of managing the risks associated with off-spec fuels. However, what is less likely to be managed by an offtake agreement, is the status of a the project as 'net zero' and the extent of scope 1, 2, and 3 emissions throughout the supply chain.

For example, green methanol such as that procured by Maersk in 2023 through its offtake agreement with Goldwind, involves an extensive production process relying on its own sources of energy, storage facilities and transportation of materials and end product. To be truly 'green', it would be assumed that the sources of energy for methanol production are renewable energy sources which are also subjected to the same supply chain concerns regarding scope 2 and 3 emissions. As such, offtake agreements need to manage potential greenwashing risks. As seen in chapter two, a vessel that has obtained green or sustainable finance runs the risk of triggering a declassification event under the loan agreement if the vessel's activities are not green or sustainable. A shipowner or charterer may also be misrepresenting a vessel's overall emissions per-ton mile if it does not take into account the downstream emission of the chosen green fuel. Fortunately, an offtake agreement can benefit from the climate tools already prevalent in supply agreements.

The Chancery Lane Project provides 'The Net Zero Standard for Suppliers' for any supply agreement across all sectors.[86] This clause allows parties to agree to reporting requirement for total carbon emissions, meaning 'the sum of the Supplier's Scope 1, 2 and 3 Emissions, in each case arising out of the performance of its obligations under this agreement during the relevant Reporting Period'.[87] The clause also entails a target that reported emissions should be at least seven per cent lower than those reported in the previous reporting period. To incentivise these types of reporting burdens for the supplier, the clause also embeds a price variation allowing for increases in price where the total emissions are lower than the Target Total Emissions, and for a discounted price where the emissions are higher than the Target Total Emissions.[88] Offtake agreements may need to

[86] TCLP, 'Matilda's Annex – The Net Zero Standard for Suppliers' (10 November 2021), chancerylaneproject.org/climate-clauses/the-net-zero-standard-for-suppliers.

[87] ibid.

[88] A number of options for doing so are provided in the clause.

include such clauses so that it is not only the green fuel's end use emissions that are accounted for. This is particularly relevant for eco-conscious shippers who may start making use of Levi's clause which provides an option to terminate a shipping transport agreement unless the carrier can match or out perform the green credentials of a carrier.

V. Conclusions

This short chapter has dealt with the very immediate key knock-on effects of green finance frameworks from a contract governance perspective. Once a vessel has obtained green or sustainable finance, green shipbuilding and green fuel supply are imminent issues that can present a number of risks for banks and investors. These risks have real effects for borrowers who may trigger declassification events, pay higher interest rates as a result, and may no longer benefit from the reputational advantages of advertising their activities as green. A lender would be very interested in the shipbuilding form to ensure that the vessel does in fact adhere to its energy-efficiency requirements. Offtake agreements are effectively bunker supply arrangements that also involve industrial processes in the same way that shipbuilding is an industry and infrastructural sector. As such, both processes need to be viewed in a much larger supply chain context involving a broader network of contracts. At every contractual phase following the loan disbursement, there is a new site of control for green performance which must be effectively managed through contractual mechanisms. To not include adequate green terms or climate clauses could result in misleading investors on one end, and consumers on the other. Once the vessel is designed in such a way to achieve a desired level of performance with secured fuel sources, a shipowner in the practice of chartering the vessel should then be immediately concerned with the manner in which the charterer operates the vessel. The next chapter looks closely at charterparty agreements as a key area for contract governance approaches. The operational phase of a vessel's lifespan is where a vessel's direct tailpipe emissions stem from and which is the subject of IMO and EU decarbonisation standards.

4

Green Charterparties for Net-Zero

Charterparties are, strictly speaking, contracts of hire and services.[1] The terms of a charterparty, whether time or voyage,[2] need to consider a wide range of matters including duration, rights and obligations in relation to hire and payment thereof, delivery and redelivery of the vessel, and a number of operational matters pertaining to the day-to-day running of the vessel.[3] Generally, these terms are *not* governed by international conventions but by the common law.[4] As such, green matters are not extensively integrated into charterparties, which serve a fundamentally commercial purpose: to govern the charterer's use of the vessel in exchange for payment of hire, and to set out the owner's duties in relation to the vessel's fitness and capacity.[5] Environmental compliance has thus far fitted neatly into a clear demarcation of rights and responsibilities between charterer and owner in relation to bunker selection, agreed routes (eg accounting for ECA's and national environmental laws), the avoidance of delays and performance warranties. There has been no historical need for charterparties to achieve anything more than legality of contract by not contravening applicable environmental standards; nor to consider environmental matters beyond the ways in which they might impact on the traditional categorisation of charterer's and owner's duties: ie those concerned with off-hire or demurrage, seaworthiness, performance, delivery, etc. At present, there are no green commitments beyond mere regulatory compliance that private actors

[1] In *Martrade Shipping & Transport GmbH v United Enterprises Corp (The Wisdom C)* [2014] EWHC 1884 (Comm), [2014] 2 Lloyd's Rep 198, it was observed by Popplewell J that 'the defining characteristic of a time charter is that the vessel is under the directions and orders of the charterer as regards its employment'.

[2] It is also worth noting that a third species of charter party exists called the bareboat charter. In these agreements, the owner delivers the ship and its entire commercial employment and operation to the charterer who will then act as 'quasi-owner' for the agreed period. However, a bareboat charter is essentially a lease agreement as opposed to a contract of carriage. See Anthony Rogers, Jason Chuah and Martin Dockray, *Cases and Materials on the Carriage of Goods by* (Taylor & Francis Group, 2019) 105.

[3] The Hon Mr Justice David Foxton et al, *Scrutton on Charterparties and Bills of Lading*, 24th edn (Sweet & Maxwell, 2021).

[4] See Jason Chuah, 'International Conventions on Carriage of Goods by Sea' in *Law of international trade: cross-border commercial transactions*, 6th edn (Sweet & Maxwell, 2019) 647–48.

[5] This reflects the neoclassical economic underpinnings of contract law which is to 'maximize the wealth of the parties (in a contractual setting) and thereby society as a whole'. See Jonathan Morgan, 'A critique of neoclassical law and economics' in *Contract Law Minimalism: A Formalist Restatement of Commercial Contract Law* (Cambridge University Press, 2013) 43.

in a charterparty need to subscribe to. As far as decarbonisation is concerned, this concept is even newer to the internal milieu of contract law, which has shown extremely limited acceptance of extra-legal norms beyond commercial efficacy.[6]

Unlike the area of green finance, which has seen significant development in catalysing a normative legal framework for financial transactions, chartering has not enjoyed similar developments. Whilst green finance has experienced a proliferation of framework developments and state-led policies for mobilising and directing funds towards green projects and assets (as discussed extensively in chapter two), chartering's only notable progress has been the Sea Cargo Charter and a few niche clauses which are not yet widely used.[7] A major premise of this chapter is that charterparty agreements, being based in English contract law, are lacking in cooperative norms to effectively achieve decarbonisation targets. Indeed, industry commentators and authors have described the contractual regime governing maritime contracts as 'arcane' and a 'Jurassic park where the dinosaurs or classical economics roam free'.[8] Chartering perhaps best illustrates this point as the structural basis for the traditional obligations between owner and charter encourages a system of split incentives and promotes outdated commercial objectives that, in fact, deter environmentally sustainable behaviour. This chapter identifies the existing problems pertaining to how environmental factors are incorporated into charterparties and proposes new ways of implementing green agreements for achieving decarbonisation.

The scope of this chapter is limited to time charters and voyage charters as contracts for the hire of a vessel wherein meaningful negotiation pertaining to green matters including climate considerations *should* take place.[9] Charterparties are contracts that are negotiated in a free market with bargaining power dependent on the prevailing factors influencing supply and demand.[10] Bills of lading, on the other hand, whilst able to be a contract of carriage,[11] generally reflect the terms of an antecedent contract such as a charterparty and are often used in the traditional sense as a receipt for the goods shipped.[12] Furthermore, in liner shipping, the practical realities on the industry place carriers in a dominant position to

[6] Hanoch Dagan, 'The Limited Autonomy of Private Law' (2008) 56 *The American Journal of Comparative Law* 809.

[7] Sea Cargo Charter, www.seacargocharter.org/about. The Sea Cargo Charter is an extension of the Poseidon Principles and provides a global framework for assessing and disclosing the climate alignment of chartering activities.

[8] See Haris Zografakis, 'The third pillar: a contractual architecture for maritime decarbonisation' (Gard Insight, 2021), www.gard.no/web/updates/content/32513672/the-third-pillar-a-contractual-architecture-for-maritime-decarbonisation.

[9] Demise charter parties or bareboat charterparties are excluded from this enquiry as they are not essentially contracts of carriage, but rather lease agreements of the vessel. See Rogers, Chuah and Dockray (n 2) 105.

[10] ibid 13; see also UNCTAD, *Charterparties*, Report from the Secretariat of the UNCTAD (United Nations, 1974).

[11] *Electrosteel Castings v Scan-Trans Shipping & Chartering Sdn Bhd* [2003] 1 Lloyd's Rep 190.

[12] *Rodoconachi v Milburn* (1886) 18 QBD 67, CA.

determine their own obligations and liability through the bill of lading prepared by them. This is done on a take-it-or-leave-it basis, which might appear as a unilateral contract given that the shipper has little bargaining power and cannot negotiate the terms which are almost always boilerplate clauses.[13]

Therefore, the discussion contained in this chapter analyses *commercial arrangements* between *charterer* and *shipowner* for the payment of hire or freight, wherein a set of obligations pertaining to decarbonisation and performance can be agreed upon.[14] This chapter makes the argument that whilst shipping associations continue to produce appropriate clauses for tightening and expanding environmental regulations, which are effective in aligning contractual performance with the regulatory standard, a more comprehensive approach to greening charterparty agreements is needed to realise net-zero ambitions. Nevertheless, significant progress is underway with climate clauses that are presenting unique contract governance tools for the alignment of charterparties with the climate agenda. These tools are modernising existing ways of doing in English contract law to facilitate a modern set of objectives.

I. Environmental Compliance in Charterparties

As mentioned above, a number of duties exist within charterparties depending on the nature of the agreement, ie for a pre-determined adventure (voyage charter) or for a specified period of time (time charter). These duties are generally governed by the principles of English law, which recognise the importance of both express and implied terms. The ways in which terms may be implied into contracts are discussed in chapter one in relation to the importance of a green norm in maritime contracts more generally. However, it is not usually necessary to imply undertakings into charterparty agreements as, almost invariably, a charterparty will either incorporate or be based on a pre-printed standard charterparty form.[15]

Widely adopted standard forms are drafted by shipping associations with the benefit of substantial experience, on which shipowners and charterers rely in setting out their respective duties.[16] These forms may be altered or supplemented, but it is very unlikely that private parties would seek to modernise the printed form themselves – something which is usually left to the association itself or to its documentary drafting committee.[17] These standard forms are drafted in

[13] Melis Ozdel, 'Enforcement of arbitration clauses in bills of lading: where are we now?' (2016) 33 *Journal of international arbitration* (0255–8106) 151.

[14] Niche transportation contracts are not included in this discussion; however, green obligations could equally be inserted into such agreements.

[15] If a standard form is incorporated into the contract, the pre-printed form is a component of the physical document embodying the contract and is repeated in the contract. See *Aktieselskabet Ocean v B Harding & Sons Ltd (The Dagali)* [1928] 2 KB 371 at 393–394.

[16] *Summit Investment Inc v British Steel Corp (The Sounion)* [1987] 1 Lloyd's Rep 230.

[17] *Summit Investment* (n 16) 234 (Sir John Donaldson MR).

accordance with a high-level knowledge of English contract law and are aligned with the mercantile customs that comprise chartering practices.[18] They generally give effect to the common law allocations of responsibility between shipowner and charterer.[19] The common law allocations of responsibility may also be viewed as the result of implied terms or as the result of the true construction of the charterparty where the contract is silent or unclear.[20] Clear express terms would be required if the parties to a charterparty wish to depart from the recognised common law duties of owner and charterer.[21]

As standard forms are drafted with an understanding of a common law framework, section A.i below evaluates whether English common law recognises *any* environmental obligations in chartering. These implied undertakings or established customs, as recognised by the common law, also comprise the interpretive context for commonly used express provisions in charterparties.[22] As previously noted, standard forms enjoy a somewhat circular relationship with implied obligations (and contractual norms more widely construed) as the common law which interprets such obligations has been developed by judicial interpretation of the standard clauses themselves.[23]

Second, section A.ii below evaluates the express terms found in standard forms and the commonly used boilerplate clauses used to achieve the vessel's compliance with decarbonisation standards and to thereby avoid illegality of contract. This is important, because a charterparty which is illegal due to contravention of the law or because it is contrary to public policy will ordinarily be void.[24] A number of things could invalidate a charterparty on the basis of illegality: infringement of a state-administered licence; exceeding trading limits; importing or exporting in

[18] A custom has been described as 'in effect, the common law within that place to which it extends'. *Lockwood v Wood* (1844) 6 QB 50 at 64; *Anglo-Hellenic Steamship Co Ltd v Louis Dreyfus & Co* (1913) 108 LT 36.

[19] eg in a voyage charter, accidents which occurred on board the vessel would be the shipowner's responsibility and accidents which occurred on shore would be the charterer's responsibility – ie the ship's rail forms the geographical dividing line. See *CV Scheepvaartonderneming Flintermar v Sea Malta Co Ltd (The Flintermar)* [2005] EWCA Civ 17, [2005] 1 Lloyd's Rep 409, Rix LJ at [31].

[20] 'The Charterparty as a Contract: Parties, Formation and Interpretation' in Howard Bennett et al, *Carver on Charterparties*, 2nd edn (Sweet & Maxwell, 2020).

[21] *Pyrene Co Ltd v Scindia Steam Navigation Co Ltd* [1954] 2 QB 402 at 417–418; *GH Renton & Co Ltd v Palmyra Trading Corp* [1957] AC 149 at 169–170 (Lord Morton), 173 (Lord Cohen), 174 (Lord Somervell); *Societe de Distribution de Toutes Merchandises en Cote D'Ivoire v Continental Lines NV (The Sea Miror)* [2015] EWHC 1747 (Comm), [2015] 2 Lloyd's Rep. 395 at [7]–[9], [18]–[19].

[22] *Produce Brokers Co Ltd v Olympia Oil and Cake Co Ltd* [1917] 1 KB 320 at 328–331.

[23] Therefore, the Court may consider earlier authorities interpreting previous generations of the contractual clause under review, even where the evolution of such a clause presents materially different historical clauses. However, a court is never guaranteed to accept historical interpretations, especially where marked differences exist. See *Transgrain Shipping (Singapore) Pte Ltd v Yangtze Navigation (Hong Kong) Co Ltd* [2016] EWHC 3132 (Comm) at [24]; *Reardon Smith Line Ltd v Sanko Steamship Co Ltd (The Sanko Honour)* [1985] 1 Lloyd's Rep. 418 at 420–421.

[24] *Archbolds (Freightage) Ltd v S Spanglett Ltd* [1961] 1 QB 374 at 388. See also *Carver on Charterparties* (n 20) ch 2: The illegality of the contract will only render a severable part of the charterparty void or unenforceable, provided that the severance itself does not contravene prevailing law or public policy nor does it affect remaining clauses which would result in the re-writing of the contract in its entirety.

contravention of legislative provisions; carrying dangerous and prohibited goods; operating with sanctioned states; etc. However, as illustrated in the following sections, environmental compliance clauses need to be clearly and expressly drafted, particularly if they stand in opposition to traditionally understood common law obligations. As it presently stands, environmental regulatory interests must still fit within a common law regime prioritising purely commercial interests.

A. Implied Undertakings Recognising Environmental Matters

As charterparties are a traditionally recognised type or 'species' of contract covering a customary mercantile practice, there are a number of undertakings which may be implied by way of law or custom into such agreements. Terms can be implied on the basis of an established custom or usage particular to a relevant market or trade practice.[25] In addition to implication by way of custom, implication by law refers to those obligations attached to standardised contractual relationships of common occurrence, eg employment, sale of goods and construction contracts.[26] These obligations can be found in statute or the common law and may, in any event, already embody established customs. As such, many of the customs and usages found in charterparties are implied by way of the common law and the test for implication by way of custom or usage need not be revisited in relation to those commonly understood obligations.[27] Some of the main terms implied by the common law into charterparties include: seaworthiness, reasonable despatch, nominating a safe port, the duty to not carry dangerous goods, to not carry cargo on deck, and not to deviate from the agreed route.[28] The common law has also implied other certain terms into charterparties, such as the owner's indemnities against damages for decisions taken by the charterer.[29] Arbitration proceedings have similarly implied a term as to 'fitness for purpose', ordinarily applicable to sale and supply of goods and services by statute,[30] in respect of the bunkers supplied by the charterer.[31] To date, the common law does not recognise an implied duty pertaining to improving environmental performance, whilst

[25] *Hutton v Warren* (1836) 1 M & W 466; *Novorossisk Shipping Co v Neoptera Co Ltd* [1990] 1 Lloyd's Rep 425 at 431.

[26] *Société Générale, London Branch v Geys* [2012] UKSC 63.

[27] Effectively, a court will only imply a term by way of custom if there is in the particular trade or industry concerned a 'uniform … practice so well defined and recognised that contracting parties must be assumed to have had it in their minds when they contracted.' See *Vitol SA v Phibro Energy AG, The Mathraki* [1990] 2 Lloyd's Rep 84.

[28] Yvonne Baatz, 'Charterparties' in *Maritime Law* (Informa, 2017) 123.

[29] *Triad Shipping Co v Stellar Chartering & Brokerage Inc (The 'Island Archon')* [1993] 2 Lloyd's Rep 388; *Action Navigation Inc v Bottigliere Di Navigazione SpA (The'Kitsa')* [2005] EWHC 177 (Comm).

[30] Sale of Goods Act 1979; Sale and Supply of Goods and Services Act 1994.

[31] London arbitration 13/04: the charterers had paid for the bunkers but had failed to do so in an authorised manner, thus making the vessel susceptible to detention. Therefore, out of commercial necessity, a term would be implied into the Charter that bunkers supplied to the vessel during the charter should be lawfully purposed.

decarbonisation targets enjoy no judicial or statutory recognition in relation to charterparty characteristics. However, green matters may necessarily need to be considered in the fulfilment of mainstream common law duties in chartering.

Alongside this consideration of the common law duties imposed on shipowners and charterers in chartering agreements, the international rules governing contracts of carriage should also be given due attention. Although charterparties are expressly excluded from regimes such as the Hague-Visby Rules,[32] the Hamburg Rules,[33] and the Rotterdam Rules,[34] which all refer to those contracts covered by a bill of lading or equivalent document of title,[35] such rules may be expressly adopted by the parties in a clause paramount.[36] The English courts will give effect to a clause paramount provided that the charterparty, whether voyage or time, makes it clear that it is the parties' intention to incorporate a clause paramount into the agreement.[37] This may involve some creative interpretation and manipulation of the wording of the clause paramount, even it means that some of the rules referred to in the clause paramount should be ignored.[38] Therefore, despite the fact that the Hague-Visby Rules only apply to bills of lading, and the Hamburg Rules and Rotterdam Rules are not binding, these Rules will also be analysed where they may proffer interpretation of the inherent obligations in charterparties. The following subsections will evaluate the following implied duties to the extent that they make room for the consideration of green matters: i) seaworthiness, ii) due despatch, and iii) the duty not to deviate.

i. *Vessel Description and Seaworthiness*

There is an important initial obligation of the shipowner in both a voyage charter and a time charter as to the proper description of the vessel. In a voyage charter,

[32] A final amendment was made in 1979 by the Protocol Amending the International Convention for the Unification of Certain Rules of Law Relating to Bills of lading (adopted 21 December 1979; in force 14 February 1984). Many countries did not adopt the Hague–Visby Rules and stayed with the 1924 Hague Rules; whilst some countries which chose to upgrade to the Hague-Visby Rules subsequently failed to adopt the 1979 protocol.

[33] The UN Convention on the Carriage of Goods by Sea (adopted 31 March 1978, in force 1 November 1992) A/CONF.89/13.

[34] UNCITRAL Convention on Contracts for the International Carriage of Goods Wholly or Partly by Sea (New York, 2008).

[35] Art V of the Hague-Visby Rules also expressly state that, 'The provisions of these Rules shall not be applicable to charter parties, but if bills of lading are issued in the case of a ship under a charter party they shall comply with the terms of these Rules'.

[36] As a result, the expressly chosen regime would not amount to governing law, but the internal terms of the contract that govern party rights and duties. For an analysis of paramount clauses, see Jonatan Echebarria Fernández, 'Paramount Clause and Codification of International Shipping Law' (2019) 50 *Journal of Maritime Law and Commerce* 45.

[37] Yvonne Baatz, 'Clauses Paramount' in Bariş Soyer and Andrew Tettenborn (eds), *Charterparties: Law, Practice and Emerging Legal Issues* (Informa Law from Routledge, London, 2017) 258.

[38] *Anglo-Saxon Petroleum Co, Ltd v Adamastos Shipping Co, Ltd (The Saxon Star)* [1958] 1 Lloyd's L Rep 73 (HL); *The Satya Kailash*, [1984] 1 Lloyd's L Rep 588 (CA 1983).

the description of the vessel is less detailed than that included in a time charter.[39] This is because during a time charter period, the charterer hires the vessel with its associated services. It is thus important for the charterer to have accurate information regarding the vessel so as to form an opinion about its commercial value. Whilst describing the vessel, it is important that the shipowner makes truthful and accurate representations relating to the energy-efficiency of the vessel. If the shipowner makes a fraudulent representation during negotiations which induces the charterer to sign the charterparty, then the charterer may rescind the charter party and ask for damages. If, on the other hand, the shipowner makes an innocent representation, then the charterer will still be able to sue for damages unless it can be shown that the shipowner had reasonable grounds for believing that the facts presented were true at the time the contract was made.[40] In the context of vessel description, performance warranties and representations as to fuel-efficiency are often the subject of dispute. Given the IMO's EEXI and CII standards, these representations pertaining to the vessel will take on greater importance. An assessment of performance warranties and fuel efficiency representation will be explored in more detail later in section II of this chapter in the context of climate clauses.

There is also an implied undertaking that a ship will be seaworthy for that particular voyage (voyage charters) or that it will be delivered in a seaworthy condition and maintained in such order for the duration of the charter period (time charter). The undertaking of seaworthiness is both absolute and relative.[41] The standard which must be met is relative, but once it is defined in the contract, the shipowner's obligation to meet the standard is absolute.[42] It is not a valid excuse that the owner was unaware of the defect or that he undertook to ensure that the ship was fit for voyage.[43] Art III(1) and (2) of the Hague and Hague-Visby rules modify this aspect of common law doctrine, whereby the 'carrier'/owner shall exercise due diligence in making the ship seaworthy; properly manning, equipping and supplying the ship, exercise due diligence in making the ship seaworthy, and 'properly and carefully load, handle, stow, carry, keep, care for, and discharge the goods carried'.[44] The Hamburg Rules also indirectly refer to 'due diligence' under its liability provision, whereby damage or delay attributable to fault or neglect of the carrier will be actionable.[45] If the carrier is liable for any damage, loss or delay of the cargo when it receives the cargo into custody, it follows that the carrier has a duty to handle the goods with due care. Unfortunately, there is little scope to extend 'due

[39] Evi Plomaritou and Anthony Papadopoulos, *Shipbroking and Chartering Practice* 8th edn (Informa Law, 2017) 350.

[40] Evi Plomaritou, 'A Review of Shipowner's & Charterer's Obligations in Types of Charter' (2014) 4 *Journal of Shipping and Ocean Engineering* 307, 308.

[41] *Steel v State Line Steamship Co* (1877) 3 App Cas 72; see also Rogers, Chuah and Dockray (n 2) 73.

[42] *Steel v State Line Steamship* (n 41).

[43] *McFadden v Blue Star Line* [1905] 1 KB 697.

[44] An equal provision is found in the Rotterdam Rules, Art 14.

[45] Hamburg Rules, Art 5(7) and also Art 5(1) (carrier must take reasonable steps to avoid loss or damage to the goods transported).

diligence' to any environmental factor. This traditional approach is also reflected in the Rotterdam Rules, whereby the main obligation is constrained to delivering the goods to the consignee and to 'properly and carefully receive, load, handle, stow, carry, keep, care for, unload and deliver the goods'.[46] This view is maintained unless agreed otherwise between the contracting parties.[47] Furthermore, the Rotterdam Rules do not include any environmental obligation in organising a transport chain between one or more modes.[48] Therefore the 'due diligence' aspect of seaworthiness applicable to contracts of carriage, does not proffer much assistance in respect of green matters.

In a *voyage charter*, the seaworthiness undertaking is two-fold: 1) the vessel must be seaworthy at the time of sailing; and 2) the vessel must be fit to receive the specified type of cargo at the loading time.[49] The seaworthiness undertaking is not breached if a condition of unseaworthiness arises after the cargo has been shipped.[50] In *time charters*, it is not only important that the ship is delivered in seaworthy condition but that it will be kept in such a condition throughout the charterparty period. Generally, the shipowner is not obligated to ensure that the vessel is perfectly fit for purpose at all times under the contract and the obligation attaches only at the time of delivery of the vessel under the charterparty.[51] However, the seaworthiness undertaking is usually supplemented by a maintenance clause in which the shipowner would be expected to rectify defects and 'keep the vessel in a thoroughly efficient state in hull, machinery, and equipment for and during the service'.[52]

Seaworthiness must certainly consider external circumstances. Even on a traditional interpretation, seaworthiness requires that, 'a ship must have that degree of fitness which an ordinary careful and prudent owner would require his vessel to have at the commencement of her voyage having regard to all the probable circumstances of it'.[53] This can be extended to having the appropriate technology and equipment to adhere to prevailing environmental standards in order for the vessel to operate along certain routes without delays. Unseaworthiness can relate to a

[46] Rotterdam Rules, Art 11 and Art 13(1). See also Theodora Nikaki, 'The fundamental duties of the carrier under the Rotterdam Rules' (2008) 14 *Journal of International Maritime Law* 512.

[47] Rotterdam Rules, Art 13(2). Because of the multimodal application of the Rotterdam Rules, the primary obligation of the carrier is extended to an obligation to 'receive and deliver' as opposed to the mere 'load and discharge' obligation in the Hague-Visby Rules.

[48] Ellen Eftestøl-Wilhelmsson, *European Sustainable Carriage of Goods: The Role of Contract Law*, 1st edn (Routledge, 2015) 10.

[49] Channell J in *McFadden v Blue Star Line* (n 43) at 704; *Maxine Footwear Co Ltd v Canadian Government Merchant Marine* [1959] AC 589, 603.

[50] *McFadden v Blue Star Line* (n 43). In a voyage charter, ship owners are responsible for supplying fuel and factor the cost thereof into the freight rate, which is often referred to as a bunker adjustment factor (BAF). In an environmental compliance context, the same allocation of risk and responsibility is applicable to fuel type and sulphur content. Responsibility for compliance will almost always rest with the owner unless exceptional circumstances are proven.

[51] Simon Baughen, *Shipping Law*, 4th edn (Routledge Cavendish, 2009) 163.

[52] See NYPE 93 form, cl 6.

[53] *FC Bradley & Sons Ltd v Federal Steam Navigation Co* (1926) 24 Lloyd's LRep 446.

number of deficiencies or malfunctions relating to the vessel, competency of the crew or to the documentation carried.[54] These reasons can range from trivial to serious failings, but not every defect will necessarily make a vessel unseaworthy.[55] The classic 'ordinary careful and prudent owner' test is not the only test in deciding whether a ship is unseaworthy.[56] It can also be alternatively asked whether the ship, at the relevant moment, was 'reasonably fit to meet the perils of the voyage'.[57]

Practically, seaworthiness is evidenced by a number of documents. This becomes especially important where adequate documentation is necessary for the vessel to carry on her business without hindrance.[58] The shipowner must ensure that the ship has those documents relevant to the voyage as required by the ship's flag, classification society, and the domestic administrations at her ports of call.[59] In the case of *Golden Fleece Maritime Inc v ST Shipping and Transport (The Elli and The Frixos)*[60] it was specifically held that proof of compliance with MARPOL regulations would comprise those documents relating to seaworthiness.[61] Even where a charterparty spans a period of new regulations coming into force, contractual warranties as to vessel compliance with all relevant 'conventions, laws, regulations and ordinances of any international entity having jurisdiction, including but not limited to MARPOL 1973/1978 as amended and extended' shall require owners to refit vessels accordingly.[62] Where such retrofitting is problematic, the Court recognised that the doctrine of frustration is, in theory, available where such events render the performance of the contract radically different from what the parties contemplated at the outset.[63] It is against this backdrop that shipping associations have drafted various compliance clauses for MARPOL regulations in charterparties.

In respect of remedies for breach of the seaworthiness obligation, it is important to note that seaworthiness is considered an innominate term. Diplock LJ highlighted in *Hong Kong Fir Shipping Co v Kawasaki* that such an undertaking

[54] From a leaking hull: *Lyon v Mells* (1804) 5 East 428; to inadequate charts and navigation aids: *The Isla Fernandina* [2000] 2 Lloyd's Rep 15.

[55] *The Fjord Wind* [1999] 1 Lloyd's Rep 307, 319; *The Pride of Donegal* [2002] EWHC 24 (Comm), [2002] 1 Lloyd's Rep 659. The prudent shipowner might leave some defects to be rectified during the voyage or at a later day.

[56] The classic definition of seaworthiness is contained in the judgment of Lord Justice Scrutton in *FC Bradley & Sons Ltd v Federal Steam Navigation Co* (n 53) at 454: 'The ship must have that degree of fitness which an ordinary careful and prudent owner would require his vessel to have at the commencement of her voyage having regard to all the probable circumstances of it. To that extent the shipowner … undertakes absolutely that she is fit, and ignorance is no excuse. If the defect existed, the question to be put is, would a prudent owner have required that it should be made good before sending his ship to sea had he known of it? If he would, the ship was not seaworthy'.

[57] Rogers et al (n 2) 73.

[58] *Alfred C Toepfer v Tossa Marine (The Derby)* [1985] 2 Lloyd's Rep 325, CA.

[59] *Cheik Boutros Selim El-Khoury v Ceylon Shipping Lines Ltd (The Madeleine)* [1967] 2 Lloyd's Rep 224; *The Derby* (n 58).

[60] *The Elli and The Frixos* [2008] EWCA Civ 584, [2008] 2 Lloyd's Rep 119.

[61] ibid [19].

[62] ibid [27].

[63] *The Elli and The Frixos* (n 60).

'can be broken by the presence of trivial defects easily and rapidly remediable as well as by defects which must inevitably result in a total loss of the vessel'.[64] Therefore the breach of the obligation of the owner to deliver a seaworthy vessel could have variable results. Whilst damages are always available to the charterer for breach, repudiation would only be available where the breach deprived him 'of substantially the whole benefit which it was intended that he should obtain from the contract'.[65] Whether environmental performance could deprive the charterer of substantially the whole benefit of the contract would depend on the specific facts in question; however, the obligation is generally underpinned by commercial interests to deliver the cargo safely and without undue delay.[66] As such, seaworthiness does not embody any commitments as to the vessel's alignment with green objectives nor decarbonisations strategies and targets. It merely requires that the vessel be compliant with MARPOL and other applicable regional or national laws so that the vessel may complete its adventure without costly interruptions or delays.

ii. Reasonable Despatch and Delays

There is usually an express term in a charterparty providing that the owner must exercise reasonable despatch.[67] The obligation that the shipowner proceed with reasonable despatch applies to both the contracted (carrying) voyage and also to the approach voyage.[68] A voyage charterparty providing for such an obligation will also usually provide a date of arrival or readiness to load at the loading port. Where the charterparty does not provide a date, it will be implied by the common law that the obligation must be performed within a reasonable time.[69] Reasonable despatch obligations (implied if not express) also impact on lay/can clauses. These clauses allow a ship under a charterparty to be delivered for the charterer's use within a certain number of days, but the charterer is entitled to cancel the contract if the vessel has not arrived by the end of that period (the cancelling date).[70] The time permitted for loading and discharging operations by the charterer is called 'laytime', whilst 'demurrage' charges are essentially penalty charges payable to the owner which are applied after an allotted time for loading/discharge has run

[64] *Kawasaki* [1962] 2 QB 26.

[65] ibid.

[66] Oana Adăscăliței, 'An Overview on the Implied Obligations in a Contract of Affreightment' (2013) 92 *Procedia – Social and Behavioural Sciences* 7.

[67] Also known as 'all convenient despatch' (cl 1 of Asbatankvoy), 'utmost despatch' (cl 8 of NYPE 1946) or 'due despatch' (cl 8 of NYPE 1993 and cl 8(a) of NYPE 2015).

[68] *Freeman v Taylor* [1831] 8 Bing 124; *MacAndrew v Chapple* (1866) LR 1 CP 643. Also note, the approach voyage refers to the journey of the vessel to a nominated port for loading, whilst the carrying voyage refers to voyage that transports goods.

[69] *Wuhan Ocean Economic and Technical Cooperation Company Limited v Schiffahrts-Gesellschaft 'Hansa Murcia' MBH & Co KG* [2012] EWHC 3104 (Comm), [2013] 1 All ER (Comm) 1277.

[70] Hence, these days are often referred to as 'lay-can' days. If the vessel arrives before the first day of the laycan period, the charterers do not have to accept her until commencement of the agreed laydays. If she arrives after the final layday, the charterers are entitled to reject the vessel and cancel the charter.

out. In order for laytime to commence for either loading or discharging, the ship must: 1) have arrived at the port of loading/discharge named in the charterparty; 2) be ready for loading discharge (readiness); and 3) have received a valid notice of readiness.[71] The Court of Appeal has held that demurrage serves as a liquidated amount covering all damages arising from a charter's breach stemming from failure to complete cargo operations within the laytime and not merely some of them.[72] Therefore, shipowners can only seek additional damages arising from delay if there has been a breach of a separate obligation.

Once the cargo is loaded, the vessel proceeds with utmost despatch to the agreed discharge port. The inherent obligation of despatch may also require that the vessel proceeds with the shortest route at maximum speed where possible under ordinary navigation. However, in voyage charters, this is generally taken to mean that the vessel will embark on the voyage, load and discharge within a reasonable time or at the agreed time if stipulated.[73] The obligation to proceed with utmost despatch is considered as absolute. Hence, it is no defence that the delay was caused through no fault of the shipowner.[74] This is so even where the charterparty provides no estimated time of arrival at the loading port nor any date of expected readiness to load.[75] It is important to note that the duty to proceed with reasonable despatch is distinct and independent from the additional duty of the shipowner to deliver/offer the vessel ready to load at the agreed time.[76] An owner could therefore be liable for two different breaches: 1) failing to deliver the vessel for loading at the stipulated time; and 2) failure to commence with reasonable despatch. The charterer can exercise its cancellation rights in the case of the former, but a breach of the latter might have already occurred. As such, the charterer need not wait until the cancellation date if it becomes apparent the vessel did not proceed with despatch as there has already been a breach.[77] The implied due despatch obligation in the approach voyage is an innominate term, and will therefore provide the charterer with termination rights if the consequences are so serious as to 'frustrate the commercial purposes of the contract'.[78]

Delays can occur in either the approach voyage or carrying voyage. As it is the owner's obligation to proceed with utmost despatch, the general rule is that the owner bears the risk of such delay unless covered by an exception clause.[79] As such, a charterer may request a delay by agreement in return for remuneration

[71] Foxton D et al (n 3).

[72] *K line Pte Limited v Priminds Shipping (HK) Co Limited (the 'Eternal Bliss')* [2021] EWCA Civ 1712.

[73] ibid.

[74] *CSSA Chartering and Shipping Services SA v Mitsui OSK Lines Ltd (The 'Pacific Voyager')* [2017] EWHC 2579 (Comm).

[75] ibid; the only thing included in the charterparty was an estimated timetable relating to the previous voyage.

[76] *Universal Cargo Carriers Corp v Citati* [1957] 2 QB 401.

[77] *CSSA Chartering and Shipping Services SA. Mitsui OSK Lines Ltd (Pacific Voyager)* (n 74).

[78] *Universal Cargo Carriers Corp v Citati* (n 76) 190.

[79] Popplewell J considered the nature of the obligation of disponent owners under a voyage charterparty to proceed to the agreed loadport in *Pacific Voyager* (n 74).

(this could be beneficial for an owner provided that subsequent contracted voyages are not impacted).[80] It is important to note that the exceptions covered in charterparty, which would exempt an owner from delay, only apply to the approaching and contracted (or carrying) voyage, not to events prior.[81] Generally, exceptions to due despatch will be listed in the contract. For example, BIMCO BALTIME 1939 form (revised 2001) reads that:

> Owners shall only be responsible for delay in delivery of the Vessel or for delay during the currency of the Charter and for loss or damage to goods onboard, if such delay or loss has been caused by want to due diligence on the part of the Owners or their Manager in making the Vessel seaworthy and fitted for the voyage or any other personal act or omission or default of the Owners or their Manager. The Owners shall not be responsible in any other case or for damage or delay whatsoever and howsoever caused even if caused by the neglect of default of their servants.[82]

As such the owner in the above clause would only be liable for delays in either the approach voyage or the carrying voyage where there is *want for due diligence* in making the vessel seaworthy. This could apply to delays in relation to the owner obtaining environmental certification, as these documents comprise part of the seaworthiness package of obligations. However, if a vessel were to pose a risk to the marine environment if it were to proceed with reasonable despatch, the common law may not provide necessary protection. Article 17(3)(n) of the Rotterdam Rules may go further than the common law in relieving carriers from liability for loss of or damage to the goods, as well as for *delay* in delivery during its period of responsibility, if it can be proven that 'reasonable measures to avoid or attempt to avoid damage to the environment' caused or contributed to the damage or loss.[83] Damage to the environment is not defined in the Rotterdam Rules, but it seems that the purpose is to allow for commercial vessels to assist in salvage operations.[84] Article 1(d) of the 1989 Salvage Convention defines damage to the environment as 'substantial physical damage to human health or to marine life or resources in coastal or inland waters or areas adjacent thereto, caused by pollution, contamination, fire, explosion or similar major incidents.'

This is encouraging insofar as it will not deter a carrier from pursuing delays or alternative routes where there is a risk to the marine environment. However, it is unclear whether delays taken as a result of slow steaming would be seen to pose a risk to the marine environment under this definition. The clause does not seem to include ongoing endeavours such as global warming, but is limited to major incidents. Therefore, although the Rotterdam Rules do not impose environmental

[80] Foxton D et al (n 3).

[81] *Monroe Brothers Limited v Ryan* [1935] 2 KB 28.

[82] This clause was construed widely in *Gesellschaft Burgerlichen Rechts v Stockholms Rederi AB Svea (The Brabant)* [1967] 1 QB 588, where it was held that the shipowner was entitled to the exception under the clause when there was *personally* no want of due diligence on part of the shipowner.

[83] Rotterdam Rules, Art 17(1) read with Art 17(3)(n).

[84] Eftestøl-Wilhelmsson (n 48).

duties on carriers to make sustainable choices, they do make progress in respect of liability regimes which promote responsible environmental behaviour. This is significant because the UN Convention on Multimodal Transport of Goods 1980 is also silent on imposing environmental obligations on 'multimodal transport operators', despite governing a series of choices for the performing or procuring of transport which could reflect green preferences.[85] However, at present, there is little hope of the Rotterdam Rules being ratified as some countries still continue to show a preference for the Hague-Visby Rules.[86] Nevertheless, even though the Rotterdam exception for reasonable delays considers green matters more generally, it would not be suitable for decarbonisation decision-making.

iii. Deviations

The obligation not to deviate without justification is closely associated with the obligation to proceed with reasonable despatch.[87] Deviations may arise from the failure to proceed with despatch thus resulting in a commercially different voyage from that contemplated by the parties.[88] A charterparty may include a particular route to be followed, or in the case of a time charter, express instructions as to the route.[89] If no contractually agreed route is stipulated, then it is presumed that the vessel shall proceed along the most direct geographical route,[90] or a customary route where one exists,[91] alternatively along the most usual and reasonable route.[92]

This duty does not consider any environmental factors as it is premised on achieving commercial certainty. In order to justify a deviation for the protection of the marine environment, the charterparty would have to contain an exception or a carefully worded liberty clause. Charterparties often do include an express liberty to deviate, yet such a liberty clause will be interpreted restrictively against the owner.[93] Under the common law, only a narrow set of justifications exist for deviations:

(1) to save human life or to communicate with a ship in distress where there is a risk of loss of life (but not for the sole purpose of saving property);[94]

[85] The United Nations Convention on Multimodal Transport of Goods 1980 (Geneva) (never entered into force) Art 1.2.

[86] For example, Malaysia's The Carriage of Good by Sea (Amendment) Bill 2019 will incorporate the Hague-Visby Rules into domestic law.

[87] *Scaramanga v Stamp* (1880) 5 CPD 295; *Louis Dreyfus v Lauro* (1938) 60 l.loyd's L Rep 94; *Fyffes v Reefer Express (The Kriti Rex)* [1996] 2 Lloyd's Rep. 171 at 191; John F Wilson, 'Implied obligations in a contract of affreightment' in *Carriage of Goods by Sea*, 7th edn (Pearson Education Ltd, 2010) 15.

[88] *Deffell v Brocklebank* (1817) 4 Price 36; *Brandt v Liverpool NS Co* [1924] 1 KB 575 at 601.

[89] Baatz (n 28) 150.

[90] ibid 150–51.

[91] *Reardon Smith Line v Black Sea and Baltic General Insurance* [1939] AC 562.

[92] *Alianca Navegacao e Logistica Ltda v Ameropa SA (The Santa Isabella)* [2019] EWHC 3152 (Comm), [2020] Bus LR 360.

[93] *Glynn v Margetson* [1893] AC 351; *Stag Line v Foscolo, Mango & Co* [1932] AC 328.

[94] *Scaramanga v Stamp* (n 87), per Cockburn CJ at 304.

(2) to avoid a danger to the ship or its cargo, even where the cause of danger relates to the vessel being unseaworthy when she went to sea;[95]
(3) or where deviation is necessary due to the fault of the charterer.

A liberty clause may expand upon the common law reasons for justified delays, but this would need to be clearly and expressly worded. Article IV(4) of the Hague, or Hague-Visby, Rules recognises that in addition from attempting to save life or property, any reasonable deviation is also justified.[96] However, where the Rules apply, owners should be careful that wide liberty clauses are not interpreted as attempts to contract out of minimum obligations imposed by the Rules – something which is not permissible.[97] Article III(8) of the Rules states that:

> Any clause, covenant or agreement in a contract of carriage relieving the carrier or the ship from liability for loss or damage to, or in connection with, goods arising from negligence, fault or failure in the duties and obligations provided in this Article or lessening such liability otherwise than as provided in these Rules, shall be null and void and of no effect.

As such, a liberty clause would need to be interpreted as defining the scope of the owner's obligations and not to negate minimum obligations set forth in the Rules.[98] Nevertheless, what constitutes a reasonable deviation under the Rules appears to be broadly interpreted but does not yet make room for environmental factors. Lord Atkins in *Stag Line Ltd v Foscolo, Mango & Co Ltd* held that:[99]

> [D]eviation may be reasonable, though it is made solely in the interests of the ship, or solely in the interests of the cargo, or indeed in the direct interests of neither: as, for instance, where the presence of a passenger, or a member of the ship or crew, was urgently required, after the voyage had begun, on a matter of national importance. Or where some person on board was a fugitive from justice, and there were urgent reasons for his immediate appearance.

LJ Atkins held further that:[100]

> The true test seems to be what departure from the contract voyage might a prudent person controlling the voyage at the time make and maintain, having in mind all the relevant circumstances existing at the time, including the terms of the contract and the interests of all parties concerned, but without obligation to consider the interests of any one as conclusive.

[95] *Kish v Taylor* [1912] AC 604.
[96] *Stag Line v Foscolo, Mango & Co* (n 93); *Lyric Shipping Inc v Intermetals Ltd (The Al Taha)* [1990] 2 Lloyd's Rep 117; and *A v B (The Andreas)* [2018] EWHC 2310 (Comm).
[97] Art III(8) of the Hague and Hague-Visby Rules.
[98] The courts have been willing to respect freedom of contract in relation to express reallocation of responsibilities pertaining to loading and discharge. See *Pyrene v Scindia Navigation* [1954] 2 QB 402; *GH Renton & Co Ltd v Palmyra Trading Corporation of Panama* 1957 AC 149; *Jindal Iron & Steel Limited v Islamic Solidarity Shipping Co (The Jordan II)* [2005] 1 Lloyd's Rep 57.
[99] [1932] AC 328 at 350.
[100] Prof Simon Baughen has interpreted this test to include situations where a crew member requires treatment from contracting coronavirus, or where the crew are at risk from having an infected member

No precedent exists regarding delays caused for the avoidance of risk to the marine environment. As argued in chapter one, the recognition of an underpinning green norm would assist in determining reasonable behaviour in contract law. Whether it be the interpretation of a 'reasonable' delay or deviation, an implied green commitment illustrating a cooperative objective to promote marine protection (including decarbonisation agendas) would assist in protecting parties and act as an incentive to make environmentally prudent decisions. In contract law, the test of a reasonable person must represent both the legal and commercial externalities to the agreement.[101] Until such time as the notion of sustainable development and its sub-category of environmental sustainability (ie a principle of greenness) is recognised by English common law, it will be hard to interpret ideas of 'reasonableness' as including green decision-making. This is particularly so where implied undertakings or those incorporated from rules governing contracts of carriage, do not permit green considerations. As seen above, certain clauses encourage enhanced speed and might hinder the concept of 'slow-steaming' or a commitment to fuel reductions.[102] Laycan and demurrage clauses as well as the obligation to proceed with utmost despatch, would actually prevent fuel-efficiency measures where not expressly provided for in the charterparty agreement.[103] Even if slow-steaming or fuel-efficiency provisions are included, they will be interpreted against a commercial backdrop of cost-savings and not against a measure of what is best for the environment and the reduction of atmospheric emissions.

It is for this very reason that scholars such as Eftestøl-Wilhelmsson argue for a

> modern, harmonised liability regime that aims to enhance sustainable carriage of goods should cover rules on the environmental duties of transport integrators, the logistical service providers that procure and perform multimodal contracts of carriage, such as carriers and freight forwarders.[104]

The Norwegian Maritime Committee, in its proposal for an interpretation rule of the Rotterdam Rules, has similarly called for a deeper consideration of environmental factors in stating that, 'It should be assumed that the transport must be planned and implemented with due regard for the environment' (translation).[105]

on board. See Simon Baughen, *Contracts for the Carriage of Goods by See and Multimodal Transport: Key issues arising from the Covid-19 Pandemic* UNCTAD/DTL/TLB/INF/2022/1.

[101] Katarzyna Południak-Gierz, 'Eco-Reasonableness. Possibilities of Incorporating Green Principles Into General Private Law Clauses' in Mads Andenas and Maren Heidemann (eds), *Quo Vadis Commercial Contract?* (LCF Studies in Commercial and Financial Law, vol 1, Springer, 2023) 107–27.

[102] Art IV(4) of the Hague/Visby Rules.

[103] Wilson (n 87) 15.

[104] Eftestøl-Wilhelmsson (n 48) 130.

[105] Norge Offentlige Utredninger (NOU) 2012: 10 Gjennomføring av Rotterdamreglene I Sjøloven; translation and discussion provided by Eftestøl-Wilhelmsson (n 48).

B. Express Environmental Compliance Clauses

In respect of green matters more generally, charterparties have quite successfully dealt with matters of compliance. Template clauses have been consistently updated and published by shipping associations to deal with regulatory developments and transition periods. Key examples have included INTERTANKO's ballast water management clauses for time and voyage clauses,[106] BIMCO's 2020 Marine Fuel Sulphur Content Clause and its 2020 Fuel Transition Clause;[107] as well as INTERTANKO's 2020 Bunker Compliance clause for Time Charters.[108] These clauses have provided contractual enforcement techniques of environmental standards by providing a clear articulation of rights, responsibilities and consequent liabilities. Although the suggested clauses by shipping associations are very successful in providing suitable clauses for this purpose, it becomes apparent that they are very narrowly focused on party interests as bilateral commercial arrangements. In accordance with a contract governance approach, this view fails to acknowledge two major factors:

(1) There is an assumption that non-compliance will be attributed to the behaviour of either of the contracting parties. This fails to consider the interventions of third parties, such as equipment manufacturers or procedurally inaccurate port inspection schemes.
(2) These contractual clauses deal with issues of environmentalism as a regulatory hindrance, as opposed to a convergence of ideals. Traditional contractual enforcement provisions are an important part of governance, but they do not go far enough to influence real change and expectation.

It has been previously explained through contract governance theory why this traditional view of 'contract law in isolation' is becoming inadequate to deal with the complexities of contemporary global agendas.[109] The same holds true for the recognition of decarbonisation in chartering practices. Below, three clauses aimed at decarbonisation are evaluated: 1) EEXI clauses, 2) slow steaming clauses, and 3) emission trading scheme clauses. Although regulatory slow steaming has not

[106] INTERTANKO, 'Ballast Water Management Clauses' (2012), www.intertanko.com/info-centre/model-clauses-library/templateclausearticle/ballast-water-management-clauses.

[107] Both of these clauses were drafted for Time Charters as the charterer is responsible for supplying compliant fuel bunkers. BIMCO, '2020 Marine Fuel Sulphur Content Clause for Time Charter Parties' (2020), www.bimco.org/contracts-and-clauses/bimcoclauses/current/2020_marine_fuel_sulphur_content_clause_for_time_charter_parties; and BIMCO, '2020 Fuel Transition Clause for Time Charter Parties' (2020), www.bimco.org/contracts-and-clauses/bimco-clauses/current/2020_fuel_transition_clause_for_time_charter_parties.

[108] INTERTANKO, '2020 Bunker Clauses INTERTANKO Bunker Compliance Clause for Time Charterparties' (2018), www.intertanko.com/images/topics-issues/documentary/2018/Bunkers_Compliance_web_10_12.pdf.

[109] See ch 1, section V.A on a contract governance theoretical framework.

yet been imposed on the maritime sector, and nor is it likely to be, it is seen as an operational measure necessary for achieving the EEXI and CII requirements. The EU has also included slow steaming as an operational measure necessary as part of its 'Fit for 55' package, which will include FuelEU Maritime[110] – a proposal that seeks to limit the GHG intensity of energy used on-board by a ship, coupled with an obligation to use on-shore power.[111] Depending on a vessel's available technology and fuel selection, slow steaming may very well need to be included in charterparty obligations to achieve emission standards. Similarly, shipping's inclusion in the EU ETS comprises the other limb of the 'Fit for 55' legislative package. Again, slow steaming will be a useful operational measure in lowering carbon emissions under the EU ETS. EEXI, slow steaming and trading scheme allowance clauses undeniably impact on private actor behaviour in that they implement regulatory standards on a contractual level through the allocation of rights and responsibilities. However, it is clear that these compliance clauses have made little headway in achieving more aspirational behaviour.

i. EEXI Clauses

The workings of the EEXI and CII requirements have been explained in chapter one under the regulatory drivers of decarbonisation in green shipping. Airborne emission clauses have previously only focused on bunker compliance and sulphur dioxide limits. As such, there is not a wealth of clauses to draw from in respect of decarbonisation standards. This is probably why the Chancery Lane Project has provided a comprehensive set of climate clauses specially for charterparties. These will be discussed in section II.B of this chapter. BIMCO released an EEXI Transition clause for time charterparties in 2021,[112] yet much like its sulphur content transition clauses, the EEXI Transition clause is aimed at regulatory compliance. New regulations will require applicable ships to have their attained EEXI calculated and verified against the required EEXI for the ship.[113] Under the clause owners are required to effect any modifications to the vessel prior to the Effective Date – meaning the vessel's next annual, intermediate or renewal survey, whichever comes first, on or after 1 January 2023.[114] BIMCO notes that for most

[110] Proposal for a Regulation of the European Parliament and of the Council on the use of renewable and low-carbon fuels in maritime transport and amending Directive 2009/16/EC (COM(2021)562) final.

[111] The FuelEU maritime proposal used the European Parliament resolution of 27 April 2021 on technical and operational measures for more efficient and cleaner maritime transport (2019/2193(INI)) as a starting point. The 2019 resolution considers slow steaming as a key operational and propulsion measure.

[112] BIMCO, EEXI Transition Clause for Time Charter Parties 2021, www.bimco.org/contracts-and-clauses/bimco-clauses/current/2021_eexi_transition_clause#:~:text=Definitions,comply%20with%20the%20new%20regulations.

[113] Resolution MEPC.328(76) – amendments to MARPOL Annex VI (2021 revised MARPOL Annex VI) implementing EEXI and associated guidelines and/or any subsequent amendments.

[114] cl (b).

ships needing modifications, these will probably be in the form of either Engine Power Limitation (EPL) or Shaft Power Limitation (SHAPOLI). Essentially, an EPL comprises of adjusting the parameters within an engine's control system that enables a vessel to limit its engine power output when the pre-set limit is reached. Whether this requires additional software installation depends on whether the engine is mechanically controlled or electronically controlled. SHAPOLI operates similarly in that it enables a vessel to limit its shaft power output when the pre-set limit is reached. It works by limiting the output power of Controllable Pitch Propeller (CPP) shafts.

It is evident that BIMCO foresees these as the most practical and cost-effective ways to meet EEXI requirements as the clause is drafted almost entirely for this method that will be circumscribed by the obligations set forth in clause (c). For vessels not using these methods, all that is required is that:

(a) The Parties acknowledge and accept that the Vessel is required to comply with the EEXI Regulations from the Effective Date and that this may require EEXI Modifications.
(b) In the event that EEXI Modifications are required, these shall be completed by the Owners prior to the Effective Date.

and:

(d) EEXI Modifications other than or in addition to EPL or SHAPOLI shall be subject to the Charterers' prior agreement and approval, which shall not be unreasonably withheld or delayed by the Charterers.

The significance of these rather straightforward provisions for alternative methods of achieving EEXI standards is that BICMO's accumulated technical expertise does not foresee the EEXI standard revolutionising shipping technology. BIMCO also leaves it up to charterers and owners to negotiate alternative methods (other than or in addition to EPL or SHAPOLI) in more detail and how this will affect their agreements. It may be better for owners to simply provide notice regarding time and location of such modifications to have the necessary freedom to source available technologies without seeking the charterer's approval. There may also be a practical presumption that drastic technological changes will be for newer vessels that are not yet fixed on the market for chartered voyages.

In respect of clause (c), which applied to EPL and SHAPOLI only, owners should endeavour to make necessary modifications without loss of time to the charterer, yet have the right to take the Vessel out of service to effect necessary modifications. There will be a three-week notice period of the anticipated time-frame and location of such works. As per sub-clause (iv):

> The Owners shall be responsible for and bear the cost of such modifications including procurement, purchase, payment, installation and any trials associated therewith. Any actual loss of time to the Vessel (including bunkers consumed during such time) due to the installation and trials of such modifications (including deviation, if any) shall be for the Owners' account.

Thereafter, the owners will have to notify the charterers of the date from which the vessel's power is certified to be limited and from this date the new maximum speed and corresponding consumption figures shall replace those existing warranted maximum figures. New performance warranties and changes to vessel description will also be provided to the charterer.

In terms of overcoming the barrier of split incentives, the BIMCO EEXI Transition Clause does little to incentivise newer technologies entering the market. The owner will carry the cost of these new technologies whilst also being responsible for any time lost to the charterer. Split incentives are often amplified in the structure of environmental compliance clauses. The same is true of the Sulphur Compliance Clauses of 2020, whereby charterers bear the main responsibility of compliance under time charters and provide owners with wide indemnities for all losses arising from the failure to supply compliant fuel.[115] This outlook failed to take into account the monumental issues regarding third-party contracts with bunker suppliers. At the time, a number of off-spec fuels were being sold as compliant through no fault of the charterers in question, who were operating under the belief that the bunkers were fit for purpose.[116]

A similar situation would arise for owners under EEXI compliance clauses, whereby there is a dependency on third-party manufacturers and software providers. The costs of installations are also placed on the owner, when the charterer will ultimately benefit from fuel savings. These costs would be even greater to the owner who strives for more ambitious outcomes, such as zero-carbon tail emissions, as enabling technologies are not yet commonplace. Unfortunately, there is not much legal literature on overcoming the problem of split incentives for energy savings in chartering agreements. Although it is widely acknowledged that the problem has existed in shipping for some time now, it is predominantly economic research and financial product innovations that have focused on more cooperative ways of sharing the costs of green technologies or decarbonisation.[117]

ii. Slow Steaming Clauses

Slow steaming as a decarbonisation measure is not a new concept and many of the discussions pertaining to its legal implications were put to bed by BIMCO's

[115] See BIMCO, '2020 Marine Fuel Sulphur Content Clause for Time Charter Parties' (2020), www.bimco.org/contracts-and-clauses/bimco-clauses/current/2020_marine_fuel_sulphur_content_clause_for_time_charter_parties; and INTERTANKO, '2020 Bunker Clauses INTERTANKO Bunker Compliance Clause for Time Charterparties' (2018), www.intertanko.com/images/topics-issues/documentary/2018/Bunkers_Compliance_web_10_12.pdf.

[116] See UK Defence Club, 'Bunker contamination claims in the US Gulf' (August 2018), www.ukdefence.com/fileadmin/uploads/uk-defence/Documents/Soundings/2018/1111-UKDC-Soundings-Bunker-contamination-claims-v7.pdf; *Maersk Oil Trading Panama S.A. et al v Glencore Ltd.* (Case no: 1:2021cv01063).

[117] Nishatabbas Rehmatulla and Tristan Smith, 'The impact of split incentives on energy efficiency technology investments in maritime transport' (2020) 147 *Energy Policy* 111721; Hannes Johnson and Karin Andersson, 'Barriers to energy efficiency in shipping' (2016) 15 *World Maritime University Journal of Maritime Affairs* 79.

slow steaming clauses of 2011 and 2012. As a green measure, it was first brought to the attention of the IMO at MEPC 61 by the Clean Shipping Coalition in 2010 for its considerable scale for reducing emissions.[118] The MEPC concluded that no further investigation of speed-reduction measures as regulatory tools was necessary as such measures would be addressed indirectly through other instruments.[119] Therefore, slow steaming is not required by international environmental standards, yet it remains an important operational measure that can achieve other decarbonisation regulatory standards.

The most obvious implication for charterparties is that instructions to the Master of a vessel to reduce speed would be a contravention of the inherent obligation of due despatch (as discussed above in section II.A). If an activity such as slow steaming for fuel conservation is foreseeable or planned, it is important for the parties to include suitable express clauses in the charterparty to avoid any implied or express undertakings to proceed with reasonable despatch.

In 2011, BIMCO drafted a time charter clause for slow steaming and in 2012 it also published a naturally more simplistic clause applicable to voyage charters.[120] Under the Slow Steaming Clause for Time Charter Parties, the charterers may at their discretion provide, in writing to the master, instructions to reduce speed and/or adjust the vessel's speed to meet a specified time of arrival at a particular destination. It is important that both instructions for slow steaming[121] or ultra-slow steaming[122] (whichever applies) do not result in the vessel's engines and/or equipment operating outside the manufacturers' or designers' published recommendations. In the case of ultra-slow steaming, the Master shall not be obliged to comply with the instructions if design recommendations issued after the commencement of the charterparty require additional physical modifications to the engine or related equipment or require the purchase of additional spares or equipment.

The owner is instructed at all speeds to follow due diligence to ensure that the Vessel is operated in a manner which minimises fuel consumption taking into account, inter alia, warranties relating to the vessel's speed and consumption.[123] Importantly clause (e) states:

> (e) **For the avoidance of doubt, where the Vessel proceeds at a reduced speed or with reduced RPM pursuant to Sub-clause (a), then provided that the Master has

[118] MEPC 61/5/10 *Reduction of GHG Emissions from Ships: Speed Reduction – the key to the fast and efficient reduction of greenhouse gas emissions from ships*, submitted by the Clean Shipping Coalition (CSC).

[119] See Report of The Marine Environment Protection Committee on Its Sixty-First Session (MEPC 61/24) para 5.16.

[120] BIMCO, 'Slow Steaming Clause for Time Charter Parties' (2011), www.bimco.org/contracts-and-clauses/bimco-clauses/current/slow_steaming_clause_for_time_charter_2011; 'Slow Steaming Clause for Voyage Charter Parties' (2012), www.bimco.org/contracts-and-clauses/bimco-clauses/current/slow_steaming_clause_for_voyage_cp_2012.

[121] Where the vessel continues to operate above the cut-out point of its engine/s auxiliary blower/s (cl (a)(i)).

[122] Where the vessel operates either above or below the cut-out point of its engine/s and auxiliary blowers (cl a(ii)).

[123] cl (b).

> exercised due diligence to comply with such instructions, this shall constitute compliance with, and *there shall be no breach of, any obligation requiring the Vessel to proceed with utmost and/or due despatch (or any other such similar/equivalent expression).*

Negating the obligation to proceed with despatch is particularly important in the context of warranted performance. In the case of *Bulk Ship Union SA v Clipper Bulk Shipping Ltd (The 'Pearl C')*,[124] it was decided that even where performance is only warranted upon delivery, this performance warranty will be used as a yardstick for determining if there was underperformance (likely caused by deliberate slow steaming) thus breaching a duty to proceed with despatch. In this case, the owners chartered their vessel to the charterers on an amended NYPE time charter form. The charterparty contained a performance warranty of about 13 knots (in ballast and laden) in good weather conditions. That warranty applied only on delivery and was not a continuing warranty. The charterers withheld hire for alleged underperformance, arguing that the vessel had failed to proceed with the utmost despatch and that the charterers were entitled to deduct the time lost due to slow steaming under the first part of the off-hire clause. The tribunal held that there was no breach of the performance warranty, as this was on-delivery. However, in relation to the obligation of due despatch, the tribunal compared the vessel's actual speed with the warranted speed and found that there had been a breach of the due despatch clause a net loss claimable under the off-hire provision.

The owners appealed the decision of the tribunal under section 69 of the Arbitration Act 1996 on the basis that using the performance warranty as the benchmark for measuring utmost despatch loss of time was erroneous. The owners argued that in doing so, the tribunal had erroneously converted the performance warranty from one which applied at the time the vessel was delivered into a continuing performance warranty. The owners also contended that Article IV(2)(a) of the Hamburg Rules was not applied so as to exempt the owners from any liability. Judge Popplewell held that there had been no error by the tribunal in using the warranted speed as the benchmark against which to assess whether the vessel had proceeded with utmost despatch. He also rejected the owner's reliance on Article IV(2)(a) and stated that the tribunal had correctly referred to *The Hill Harmony* case.[125] The Article IV(2)(a) applies to a negligent error in the navigation or management of the ship concerning a matter of seamanship; and not to deliberate decisions not to proceed with utmost despatch. As such, *The Pearl C* illustrates the importance of expressly providing for slow steaming decisions, as owners will not be able to circumvent the due despatch rule by only providing on-delivery performance warranties.

[124] [2012] 2 Lloyd's Rep 533.
[125] *The 'Hill Harmony'* [2001] 1 Lloyd's Rep 147.

Under BIMCO's 'Slow Steaming Clause for Voyage Charter Parties' 2012, only the owners are allowed to give slow steaming instructions to the Master. As in the time charter clause for slow steaming, the owner in a voyage charter is not in breach of any obligation requiring the vessel to proceed with utmost and/or due despatch (or any other such similar/equivalent expression). From a sustainability perspective, it would be useful to have an obligation of environmental due diligence (ie a green principle) that could justify slow steaming decisions taken for the benefit of the marine environment, even where not expressly provided for. This could be interpreted for the purposes of slow steaming in one of two ways:

(1) striking a balance between the commercial objectives of despatch undertakings and green undertakings to achieve sustainable shipping; or
(2) viewing 'due' or 'reasonable' despatch as incorporating environmental considerations.

In the latter, what is 'reasonable' need not be the fastest route practically possible, but one that considers the impact of vessel performance in achieving decarbonisation goals.

Slow steaming implications for due despatch undertakings may equally apply to Just-In-Time (JIT) clauses, as JIT may require a vessel to deliberately slow down. The IMO has already noted in its JIT Arrival Guide that barriers for the implementation of JIT arrival exist at the contractual phase.[126] JIT arrivals have a number of benefits, including

> less congestion and traffic in the anchorage areas, reduced risk of accidents/collisions, reduced risk of attacks in areas prone to robbery or piracy (as these occur more frequently at anchorage than en route), [and] reduced hull fouling, especially in tropical waters.[127]

This all equates to less GHG emissions and reduced air pollution in ports as well as fuel savings and emission reductions from allowing the vessel to reduce its speed. The JIT Arrival Guide notes that with time charters, there is no problem as the charterer has the right to direct the ship to proceed at any speed whilst paying for all the bunkers, thus it directly benefits from the fuels savings.

However, in voyage charters, a due despatch clause obliges the ship's master to proceed to the next port with utmost despatch, regardless of whether or not a berth is available.[128] This is further complicated when the vessel is carrying goods belonging to multiple owners under numerous contractual agreements. Cargoes may also be traded many times between the load and discharge port, therefore contracts must be redrafted for each new owner. Even if a contractual solution is

[126] GEF-UNDP-IMO GloMEEP Project and members of the GIA, 'Just In Time Arrival Guide – Barriers and Potential Solutions', greenvoyage2050.imo.org/wp-content/uploads/2021/01/GIA-just-in-time-hires.pdf.

[127] ibid 5.

[128] *CSSA Chartering and Shipping Services SA v Mitsui OSK Lines Ltd (Pacific Voyager)* [2017] EWHC 2579 (Comm).

sought (such as the BIMCO Virtual Arrival Clause for Voyage Charter Parties),[129] the calculation of any costs/revenues from the implementation of JIT arrival can be difficult. JIT arrival would need to be incentivised by significant financial gains with a reduced demurrage rate for the delay period not providing sufficient incentive as the sales contract between charterer and the terminal often also includes a provision for demurrage, which allows the charterer to pass any demurrage costs down to the terminal (as the terminal is considered to cause the delay). Adaptations of charterparty agreements are often met with stakeholder reluctance where new and unfamiliar arrangements have to be made.[130] This strengthens arguments that certain environmentally friendlier practices should be incorporated into the overarching liability regime more generally or enforced by a port authority. Shipping associations therefore have a significant role to play, as those entrusted with the production of contractual terms, to include provisions that can realise environmental objectives between parties.

iii. Emissions Trading Allowance Clauses

The IMO is considering options for market-based measures (MBMs) 'as part of a basket of mid-term measures'.[131] Economic measures under consideration include levy and levy/feebate proposals, ETS and also IMRB/F[132] (as a short-term option). From a contractual perspective, it is possible that under broadly worded tax clauses, such levies could qualify as ordinary tax. However, state administrations would have to impose such a levy following the ratification of such a measure. A global standard would also require wide-scale uptake in order to effectively externalise the costs of CO_2 emissions from the entire sector. Until such time as the IMO decides upon a MBM, it is arguably better to start with regimes that are presently including shipping. The EU's Emission Trading Scheme can provide exemplar insights into how responsibility will be apportioned to shipping actors. Nevertheless, the EU's regional authority does not necessarily draw parallels with the IMO's mandate to adopt measures.

As discussed previously in chapter one (section I.B), the EU ETS works using a 'cap-and-trade' principle, whereby a cap (limit) is set on the total amount of greenhouse gas emissions that can be emitted by entities and parties are required to hand in allowances equal to their CO_2 emissions (1 allowance = 1 ton CO_2) at the end of each year.[133] Shipping was included in the EU ETS via amendments to the

[129] BIMCO 'Virtual Arrival Clause for Voyage Charter Parties' (2013), www.bimco.org/contracts-and-clauses/bimco-clauses/current/virtual_arrival_clause_for_voyage_charter_parties_2013.

[130] The IMO endorses a top-down approach whereby JIT Arrival is enforced through the port authority.

[131] Recent discussions took place in May 2022 at ISWG-GHG 12, which marks the third substantive discussion on mid-term measures (MTM), and the shift from phase 1 to phase 2 of the workplan adopted at MEPC76 in respect of decarbonisation.

[132] An International Maritime Research Fund.

[133] The price per allowance is not fixed as this will depend on market demand.

EU-ETS Directive (2003/87/EC),[134] as well as amendments to the MRV Regulation for updated changes to supporting reporting rules.[135] The relevant amendments pertain to Article 3, which states that the person responsible for compliance with the EU ETS remains the 'shipping company' defined as:[136]

> [T]he shipowner or any other organisation or person, such as the manager or the bareboat charterer, that has assumed the responsibility for the operation of the ship from the shipowner and that, on assuming such responsibility, has agreed to take over all the duties and responsibilities imposed by the International Management Code for the Safe Operation of Ships and for Pollution Prevention.

This definition also coincides with the with entities responsible under the MRV Regulations as amended by Regulation 2023/957, which also aligns the MRV Regulation with the ETS.[137] At first glance, this may appear that the responsible entity could be any charterer, but time charterers do not ordinarily take on responsibility for documentary compliance and the shipowner remains the technical operator of the vessel under the ISM Code. As such, Article 3gc of the Directive provides that where it is not the shipping company that is responsible for the purchase of fuel, or operation of the ship, or both, then the commercial operator shall reimburse the shipping company for the 'costs arising from the surrender' – this is in line with the principle of the 'polluter pays'. Member States should ensure that proper measures are in place for recovering such costs. It is evident from the Preamble (32) of the Directive that such a measure is a contractual one involving private law remedies for charterers failing to make such payments under the charterparty.

The owner is legally responsible for surrendering allowances – a process that will be administered by the Member State in which the owner/company is registered, or if registered in a third country, the Member State in which the owner/company had the highest estimated number of port calls in the two previous monitoring years.[138] Owners could simply pass down the costs of carbon pricing through negotiated prices per-ton basis, or as a lump sum. Another option would be for charterers to purchase allowances and transfer them to the shipping company

[134] Directive (EU) 2023/959 of the European Parliament and of the Council of 10 May 2023 amending Directive 2003/87/EC establishing a system for greenhouse gas emission allowance trading within the Union and Decision (EU) 2015/1814 concerning the establishment and operation of a market stability reserve for the Union greenhouse gas emission trading system.

[135] Regulation (EU) 2023/957 of the European Parliament and of the Council of 10 May 2023 amending Regulation (EU) 2015/757 in order to provide for the inclusion of maritime transport activities in the EU Emissions Trading System and for the monitoring, reporting and verification of emissions of additional greenhouse gases and emissions from additional ship types.

[136] Read Art 3gb with Art 3(w) of Directive 2003/87/EC.

[137] Regulation (EU) 2023/957 of the European Parliament and of the Council of 10 May 2023 amending Regulation (EU) 2015/757 in order to provide for the inclusion of maritime transport activities in the EU Emissions Trading System and for the monitoring, reporting and verification of emissions of additional greenhouse gases and emissions from additional ship types; this implemented the Proposal for amending Regulation (EU) 2015/757 in order to take appropriate account of the global data collection system for ship fuel oil consumption data, COM(2019) 38 final, 2019/0017 (COD).

[138] Art 3gf of the Directive (EU) 2023/959.

which will then surrender them to the Member State administration. Given that charterparties are usually governed by English law, whether an EU Directive can insert such a private law obligation poses some questions.[139] Nevertheless, owners would want to recover the costs to which they are entitled and would draft contractual clauses accordingly. As such, BIMCO has drafted clauses for both time charters and voyage charters needing to implement such arrangements.

a. ETS Clause for Time Charters

BIMCO has drafted an 'ETS – Emission Trading Scheme Allowances Clause For Time Charter Parties 2022' (hereafter 'ETS Clause') to assist owners and charterers navigate this arrangement. Subclause (c)(i) of the ETC Clause states: 'Throughout the Charter Party period the Charterers shall provide and pay for the Emission Allowances corresponding to the Vessel's emissions under the scope of the applicable Emission Scheme.'[140] Under the ETS Clause, the owners will notify the charterers of the quantity of Emission Allowances for a given month, whereafter the charterers shall transfer the quantity of Emission Allowances to the owner's account within seven days. As is aligned with the MRV Regulation, owners are responsible for monitoring and reporting the ship's emissions in order to calculate allowances. The clause works on the principle of transferring actual allowances as opposed to reimbursing the owners for the cost of allowances to avoid complications with price fluctuations.[141] As suggested by the Directive, this imposes a principle of the 'polluter pays' into commercial contracts, a norm not ordinarily recognised by contract law.

If the charterers fail to transfer the Emission Allowances, then per subclause (d):

> [T]he Owners shall, by giving the Charterers' five (5) days' notice, have the right to suspend the performance of any or all of their obligations under this Charter Party until such time as the Emission Allowances are received in full by the Owners. Throughout any period of suspended performance under this subclause, the Vessel shall remain on hire and the Owners shall have no responsibility whatsoever for any consequences arising out of the valid exercise of this right. The Owners' right to suspend performance under this Clause shall be without prejudice to any other rights or claims they may have against the Charterers under this Charter Party.

The main remedy for charterers failing to transfer Emission Allowances appears to be suspension only. Given that payment of hire does not always amount to a condition under English law, it is unclear whether issues surrounding the transfer of emission allowances will amount to a repudiatory breach.[142] However, the

[139] See Opportunity Green, 'Shipping ETS – Charterer Liability' (Analysis carried out for Transport & Environment, December 2021). This analysis also raises the question of whether such terms might be fair in terms of the Unfair Contracts Term Directive (93/13/EEC).

[140] For the full ETS Clause: www.bimco.org/contracts-and-clauses/bimco-clauses/current/etsa_clause.

[141] See BIMCO Guidance Notes beneath ETS time charter clause (n 140).

[142] *Spar Shipping AS v Grand China Logistics Holding (Group) Co Ltd* [2016] 2 Lloyd's Rep 447; but see the obiter remarks of Mr Justice Flaux in *Kuwait Rocks Co v AMN Bulkcarriers Inc (The MV 'Astra')*

charter's overall behaviour, including the non-payment of hire, could very well amount to a repudiatory breach. This principle could arguably be extended to the non-transfer of emissions allowances as a form of 'payment' under the contract. In the case of *Spar Shipping*, the following factors are relevant in determining whether conduct in relation to non-payment of hire can amount to a repudiatory breach:

(1) The amount of arrears accumulated as compared to the entire duration of the charter party.
(2) Failure to deliver a concrete payment plan to settle arrears.
(3) Failure to explain in proper detail why hire was unpaid.[143]

In respect of factor (1) above, the charterer in *Spar Shipping* had repeatedly failed to pay hire punctually. Almost all of the payments were unpaid when due; others were paid months late, and some were not paid at all. This situation stands in stark contrast to a situation where isolated instances of non-payment or a few consecutive late payments in a lengthy period.[144] In respect of factor (2) and (3), the charterers in Spar Shipping gave no concrete proposal for discharging its liabilities and it provided explanations for non-payments which illustrated that the problem was permanent or indefinitely continuing. Although the presence of certain factors alone may be insufficient to establish repudiatory breach, such factors may still constitute a renunciation of the contract 'as it would lead the reasonable observer to conclude that there was an intention not to perform in the future, and the past and threatened future breaches taken together would be repudiatory'.[145]

Failure to transfer emission allowances could be given similar weighting to payment hire of, yet it is important to bear in mind that the primary purpose of the charterparty is a commercial one for payment, not to comply with an EU-ETS regulatory scheme. It may therefore be less likely that cumulative renunciatory conduct regarding allowance transfers would amount to a repudiation as seen with non-payment. However, the consequences of an owner not complying with EU-ETS, through no fault of its own (ie because emission allowances are owed to it), would involve:

> In the event that a shipping company fails to comply with those requirements and any enforcement measures taken by the administering authority in respect of a shipping company have failed to ensure compliance, Member States should act in solidarity. As a last resort measure, Member States, except for the Member State whose flag the ship is flying, should be able to refuse entry to the ships under the responsibility of the shipping company concerned, and the Member State whose flag the ship is flying should be able to detain that ship.[146]

[2013] EWHC 865 (Comm) where punctual payment of hire in clause 5 of the NYPE 1946 form charter was considered a condition of contract.

[143] ibid [69].

[144] Simon Rainey QC, '"Interrupting the lifeblood": The Owner's remedies for non-payment of hire after Spar Shipping' in Bariş Soyer and Andrew Tettenborn, *Charterparties: law, practice, and emerging legal issues*, 1st edn (Informa Law, 2018) 10.

[145] Spar Shipping (n 142) [69].

[146] Recital 34 of Directive (EU) 2023/959.

Given the potential for differing port inspection schemes of Member States, as well as variable enforcement policies, the uncertainty for owners coupled with the potential of being denied entry into certain ports, could become commercially unviable. Thus far, the only solution put forth for shipping companies is through contractual mechanisms as enabled by Member States. There is therefore a huge onus on the owner to prove that a number of renunciatory actions have taken place evincing an intention to not transfer emission allowances in full, which would have regulatory consequences that would essentially deprive the owner of the whole benefit of the contract. Express clauses to allow for withdrawal of the vessel or termination of the contract might better protect the owner, but may present other impracticalities depending on the facts. However, the main remedy employed by BIMCO is suspension of performance to achieve enforcement.

Suspension is remedy that is quite different from withdrawal of service as it does not end the contract and allows hire to accrue for the suspension period.[147] Generally, suspension is used as a remedy where a charterer fails to pay hire, but such a right must be expressly stated in the contract.[148] This is because there is no common law right to suspension for breach of contract.[149] As stated by Staughton LJ in *Channel Group v Balfour Beatty Ltd*,[150] although for serious breaches of contract it is well established that the plaintiff may treat the contract as discharged, 'there is not yet any established doctrine of English law' permitting the plaintiff to merely suspend its performance. Given the use of this traditional remedy in relation to non-payment of hire, there are some noteworthy considerations regarding suspension. The first relates to whether notice is necessary to invoke the remedy of suspension, and second, what the practical implications are for third parties such as cargo interests and bunker suppliers.

Lessons from BIMCO's SUPPLYTIME 1989[151] form, a standard time charterparty for offshore service vessels, illustrate the importance of stipulating a notice period for the suspension of performance. In *Greatship (India) Ltd v Oceanografia SA DE CV*, the MV Greatship Dhriti was chartered under an amended BIMCO SUPPLYTIME 1989 form for a period of two years.[152] A dispute arose regarding clause 10(e) of the form which pertained to payment of hire. Point 4 of the clause stated:

> While payment remains due Owners shall be entitled to suspend the performance of any and all of their obligations hereunder and shall have no responsibility whatsoever

[147] *Steelwood Carriers Inc of Monrovia, Liberia v Evimeria Compania Naviera SA of Panama (The Agios Giorgis)* [1976] 2 Lloyd's Rep 192 at 202.

[148] *Aegnoussiotis Shipping Corp of Monrovia v Kristian Jebsens Rederi of Bergen AS (The Aegnoussiotis)* [1977] 1 Lloyd's Rep 268 at 276; *International Bulk Carriers (Beirut) SARL v Evlogia Shipping Co SA (The Mihalios Xilas)* [1978] 2 Lloyd's Rep 186 at 191.

[149] J Carter, 'Suspending Contract Performance for Breach' in *Good Faith and Fault in Contract Law* (Oxford University Press, 1997).

[150] [1993] 2 WLR 262.

[151] BIMCO, SUPPLYTIME 1989, www.bimco.org/contracts-and-clauses/bimco-contracts/supplytime-89#.

[152] *Greatship (India) Ltd* [2012] EWHC 3468.

> for any consequences thereof, in respect of which Charterers hereby indemnify Owners, and Hire shall continue to accrue and any extra expenses resulting from such suspension shall be for Charterers' account.

No notice period was stipulated, despite other points in the clause stating that a period of five banking days' grace would be permitted after payment is due before interest is charged and that owners may withdraw the vessel from service if following five banking days' notice, payment is not received. As such, the charterers successfully argued in arbitration proceedings that express notification of five banking days must be given in order for the owners to exercise the right to suspend performance. Mrs Justice Gloster in the English Commercial Court disagreed with these arguments, and it was held that on proper construction of clause 10(e), the owners were not required to give the charterers five banking days' notice of the suspension in order for the owner's right to withhold service under the charterparty to be validly exercised.[153] Emphasis was placed on the case of *Rainy Sky* at paragraphs 16–23, where the Supreme Court reiterated the principle of construction that, if the contract has used clear and unambiguous language, the court must apply it, however surprising or unreasonable the result might appear to be.[154] However, where there are two possible constructions, the court may reject the one that is commercially unreasonable and the one which flouts business common sense.[155] Furthermore, there was no need to imply the requirement of five banking days' notice as there was no business necessity to justify doing so.[156]

A similar outcome was reached in London Arbitration 17/4 where the charterer in the dispute argued that the right to suspend performance arose only after the expiry of as stipulated grace period and furthermore that the grace period provision did not apply to deliberate non-payment of hire (as was the case here), therefore the owners had no right to suspend.[157] The owners also argued that the grace period did not apply here and that they therefore had the right to suspend performance at any time, provided always that hire was still outstanding. The tribunal found in favour of the owners and that it was uncommercial and unlikely that, in the case of charterer's deliberate failure to pay hire in accordance with their charterparty obligations, that owners would be deprived of the option to suspend performance and be left only with the right to withdraw the vessel from the charterers' service. It was also commented that withdrawal is not a practical option where the ship had cargo on board and particularly where she was arrived at or off her discharge port.

The BIMCO ETS clause seems to overcome any potential confusion by explicitly stating that five days' notice must be given. Furthermore, it does not differentiate

[153] *Greatship (India) Ltd* (n 152) [42].

[154] ibid [17] interpreting *Rainy Sky SA v Kookmin Bank* [2011] 1 WLR 2900.

[155] ibid [17] citing Hoffmann LJ (as he then was) in *Co-operative Wholesale Society Ltd v National Westminster Bank plc* [1995] 1 EGLR 97 at 99, after quoting a passage from the speech of Lord Diplock in *The Antaios* [1985] AC 191, 201.

[156] ibid [42].

[157] London 17/14, Lloyd's Maritime Law Newsletter (October 2014).

between deliberate or non-deliberate transfer of allowances. Charterers may therefore want to amend the clause to include reasons for which allowance transfers may be late or withheld through no fault of their own, however negligence or mismanagement will unlikely suffice and such a clause will need to stipulate reasons that are permissible to both parties.[158] It is clear that the clause weighs quite heavily in the owner's favour as it is the owner who will face administrative sanctions from Member States if they are unable to surrender sufficient allowances per voyage.

The second point to consider regarding suspension of performance is that it also involves a suspension of discharge/delivery of cargo. This may potentially place the vessel at risk of a ship arrest in certain jurisdictions for two reasons: 1) cargo owners exercising a lien on cargo; and 2) if the charterer can no longer pay bunker suppliers due to the financial consequences it faces from suspension. In relation to the first situation, in some jurisdictions the cargo receivers may simply arrest the vessel if the owners withhold the discharge or delivery of the cargo.[159] Under an NYPE form,[160] owners in fact have a lien over cargo for unpaid hire, but it is a contractual lien and may place the owner in breach of the bill of lading (if subject to English law).[161] Owners may try to exercise a lien under a bill of lading instead of the charterparty,[162] as holders of the bill are bound to a liens clause where one is present. However, some jurisdictions do not enforce such a lien clause.[163] With regards to the second situation, most common law jurisdiction such as England and Wales, Hong Kong and Singapore, whereby a claim in respect of goods or materials supplied to a ship for her operation or maintenance (including bunkers), does in principle come under the admiralty jurisdiction.[164] However, it is possible under certain circumstances to arrest a vessel for unpaid bunkers in the USA, Australia, Italy, South Africa, Belgium, the People's Republic of China and Japan.[165]

[158] The ordinary rules of frustration may apply here or perhaps such situations would be covered by a clause.

[159] In the People's Republic of China, ship arrest is a method of preservation of claim that applies to only a limited number of claims including cargo. See Arts 21 and 22 of the Special Maritime Procedure Law.

[160] Under the NYPE 1946 Form clause 18: 'the Owners shall have a lien upon all cargoes … for any amounts due under this Charter.'

[161] The shipowner's lien over cargo is only a possessory lien, see *Castle Insurance Co v Hong Kong Islands Shipping Co (The 'Potoi Chau')* [1984] AC 226. For academic commentary on shipowner's liens, see Aiden Lerch, Luke Zadkovich and Edward Floyd 'International Uniformity and Maritime Liens over Cargo: An Ocean Not Easily Navigated', (2020) 44 *Tulane Maritime Law Journal* (1048-3748) 251.

[162] As seen with clauses in Gencon 94 into a Congenbill bill.

[163] Many jurisdictions – China, for example – do not recognise the right to lien cargo, unless it is owned by the debtor, so unless the cargo is owned by charterers, owners cannot lien the cargo.

[164] Maritime liens giving rise to admiralty jurisdiction can be found in s 20 of the Senior Courts Act 1981 (England & Wales), s 12A(2) of The High Court Ordinance (Hong Kong), and s 3 of the High Court (Admiralty Jurisdiction) Act (Singapore).

[165] A comparative analysis of each jurisdiction is provided in The Swedish Club, 'The Risk of Ship Arrest for unpaid Bunkers arising from the OW Bunker group collapse' (Member Alert, 23 February 2016), www.swedishclub.com/news/member-alert/ow-bunker-2?query=RISK+OF+SHIP+ARREST.

The issues surrounding the availability of suspension as a remedy or insufficient alternative remedies where transfer of allowances does not take place from charterer to shipowner might be resolved by strengthening the 'polluter pays' norm underlying the construction of the clause. Although it has been noted that charterparties are only intended to serve commercial purposes, the BICMO ETS mechanism transposes a regulatory requirement into commercial arrangements that must be considered within the factual matrix of interpreting the clause. Although it is unlikely that parties would want to terminate the contract based on the failure to transfer allowances, the consequences imposed by EU Member States for non-compliance with the EU ETS remains to be seen as shipping actors will test the waters of this new scheme. The surrender of allowances is indeed a mandatory entitlement, to be ensured by national law, with serious implications for competition in the internal market.[166] As such, it cannot be avoided through contractual shortcomings.

b. ETS Clauses for Voyage Charters

On the other hand, the remedy available under a voyage charter is much more straightforward. BIMCO released three options for voyage charters depending on the needs of its members in late 2023.[167] The most comparable of the three options to BIMCO's ETS clause for time charters, is the 2023 ETS – Emission Scheme Transfer of Allowances Clause for Voyage Charter Parties.[168] Under this clause, the owners will notify the charterers in writing of the estimated quantity of Emission Allowances corresponding to the voyage and charterers shall transfer the estimated quantity of allowances into the owners' nominated Emission Scheme account by the date on which freight or any other initial freight payment falls due. Any discrepancy between the estimated quantity and actual quantity of Emission Allowances shall either be transferred by the charterers to the owners' nominated Emission Scheme account (where actual quantity is higher than estimated quantity) or reimbursed to the charterer by the owner (where actual quantity is lower than estimated quantity).[169] Failure on behalf of the charterer to transfer emission allowances is deemed as non-payment of freight.

[166] Lia I Athanassiou, 'Shipping Operators' Obligations and Liabilities Under the International and EU Emission Reduction Strategy' in Barış Soyer (ed), *Damages Recoveries and Remedies in Shipping Law*, 1st edn (Informa Law, 2023).

[167] BIMCO, ETS – Emission Scheme Freight Clause for Voyage Charter Parties 2023 (2023); Emission Scheme Surcharge Clause for Voyage Charter Parties (2023); BIMCO, ETS – Emission Scheme Transfer of Allowances Clause for Voyage Charter Parties (2023), www.bimco.org/contracts-and-clauses/bimco-clauses/current/ets-emission-scheme-transfer-of-allowances-clause-for-voyage-charter-parties.

[168] BIMCO, ETS – Emission Scheme Transfer of Allowances Clause for Voyage Charter Parties (ibid).

[169] cl b(iv) of BIMCO, ETS – Emission Scheme Transfer of Allowances Clause (n 167).

Treating the non-surrender of allowances as non-payment of freight is a powerful enforcement mechanism for the shipowner. The ordinary remedy for non-payment of freight is to apply for summary judgment or to invoke arbitration if such a dispute resolution mechanism is enabled by the contract.[170] There are also self-help remedies available to the shipowner such as a liens on cargo,[171] or sub-freights.[172] This clause also reflects that, similar to time charters, it remains the owner's responsibility to comply with the applicable Emission Scheme. As such, the clause may seem weighted in favour of owners as it does not mention remedies available to charterers where allowances are not reimbursed following a calculation that actual emissions were lower than estimated emissions.

The same available remedies are also available under BIMCO's two other voyage charter clauses for ETS compliance. Under the ETS Emission Scheme Surcharge Clause for Voyage Charter Parties (2023), the owner will charge the charterer a fixed 'Emission Scheme Surcharge'. The clause also provides an optional price adjustment clause to allow for variations in the market conditions, which is similar to a bunker adjustment clause.[173] On the other hand, BIMCO's ETS – Emission Scheme Freight Clause for Voyage Charter Parties (2023) simply includes the cost of emission allowances in the freight rate itself. In accordance with clause (a):

> The freight due under this Charter Party is inclusive of all costs arising from the surrender of Emission Allowances corresponding to the Vessel's emissions under the scope of the applicable Emission Scheme for the voyage(s) performed under the Charter Party.

Voyage charters therefore have an easier time of including the responsibility of compliance with the EU ETS for the obvious reason that the owner is vested with fuel costs and commercial operation of the vessel. Yet the notion of 'payment of freight' is being pushed beyond the ordinary commercial costs associated with the calculation of freight rates. In this way, the decarbonisation mandate and the commercial viability of the voyage charter are perfectly aligned. The 'polluter pays' principle is effectively contractualised as a shipowner faces immense uncertainty where it cannot comply with the requirements of the ETS.

Finally, it is important to note that the BIMCO ETS clause is essentially a contractual mechanism to implement a market-based measure. It cannot overcome any problems associated with the measure itself. In respect of overcoming the problem of split incentives for installing green technologies, the inclusion of shipping in an ETS does not go much further in imposing a 'polluter pays' principle into contracts that former environmental regulatory requirements

[170] Simon Baughen, 'Voyage Charterparties – Payment of Freight' in *Shipping Law*, 8th edn (Routledge, 2023).

[171] Under the NYPE 1946 Form, cl 18.

[172] Baughen (n 170).

[173] See BIMCO's Guidance notes for its ETS – Emission Scheme Surcharge Clause for Voyage Charter Parties (2023).

have. It has also been argued that an ETS, generally speaking, poses high administrative burdens with low practical feasibility.[174] Although these clauses do little to challenge existing charterparty architecture as ETS requirements are easily factored into traditional payment of hire/freight obligations, these clauses still require a high level of collaboration, information sharing, and proactiveness. The effectiveness of such a clause actually stands in contrast to the EU ETS itself, which is a reactionary measure seeking reimbursement from the actual polluter.[175]

II. Climate Clauses in Charterparties

In the absence of a cooperative normative framework for green chartering, decarbonisation commitments will predominantly stem from voluntary initiatives. However, maximising the benefits of competitive energy savings and sharing accurate and reliable data serves to benefit all parties in chartering agreements whether they have signed up for voluntary commitments or not. This section will evaluate key clauses adopted by private actors to promote net-zero targets in chartering and implement voluntary efforts that go beyond regulatory compliance. These should necessarily include fleets financed in accordance with the Poseidon Principles framework which are required to report carbon intensity data to help the lender ascertain whether their portfolios fall in line with climate goals – ie reducing total annual emissions from shipping by at least 50 per cent by 2050.[176] This begs the question of how fleets financed by other green finance schemes must be chartered – ie the 'knock-on-effects' of green finance for subsequent transactions. This question is addressed in chapter two on green finance frameworks. Whilst chartering is not yet mentioned in green finance taxonomies, these frameworks inevitably prescribe operational parameters for chartering in respect of carbon emissions. The owners will therefore be responsible for ensuring that the charterer complies with the framework during voyages in order to not breach its contractual obligations with the financier.

Chartering's most notable global development in this regard has been the Sea Cargo Charter, which sets a 'benchmark for what it means to be a responsible charterer' through four principles: assessment, accountability, enforcement and transparency.[177] Signatories will enforce a commitment to climate alignment through the use of a Sea Cargo Charter Clause as a recommended charterparty clause. A fundamental purpose of the Sea Cargo Charter is to extend the green

[174] Harilaos N Psaraftis, Thalis Zis and Sotiria Lagouvardou, 'A comparative evaluation of market based measures for shipping decarbonization' (2021) 2 *Maritime Transport Research* 100019, 13.

[175] Athanassiou (n 166).

[176] The measurement used is called the Annual Efficiency Ratio (AER) which is reported in grams of CO_2 per deadweight ton-nautical mile (gCO_2/dwt-nm).

[177] Sea Cargo Charter, www.seacargocharter.org.

values of the Poseidon Principles applicable to vessel financing, to the subsequent endeavour of chartering. By committing to this framework, private actors recognise a green soft norm commitment to decarbonisation, yet this decarbonisation norm is hardened when given contractual effect through standard terms.[178] The Chancery Lane Project has also published four climate clauses for the shipping sector as part of its Net Zero Toolkit – all are applicable to voyage and time charters.[179] These clauses are key tools in setting out how parties are to cooperate to achieve decarbonisation in chartering. However, some additional third-party transactions may need further consideration to enhance their effectiveness. Here, shipping associations are key actors in utilising the full power of the 'law of standard agreements' to include contractual provisions in charterparty forms that can elevate new business norms centred on green behaviour.[180] As such, BIMCO has also drafted a progressive CII Operations Clause for Time Charter Parties (2022) which embeds many of the climate drafting techniques that are emerging from climate clauses more generally. This is important because, as pointed out in chapter one, standard form clauses are, 'generally speaking, the most important instrument nowadays for norm creation in business'.[181] Although climate clauses, including BIMCO's latest CII clause, are sometimes considered vague and unworkable, contract law and the standard forms that govern shipping require this push towards a modernised agenda.

A. Sea Cargo Charter Standard Covenant Clause

On 7 October 2020, the Sea Cargo Charter was launched during the Global Maritime Forum Virtual High-Level Meeting.[182] The Sea Cargo Charter is the equivalent of the Poseidon Principles framework for charterers – it contains the same four core principles, but the framework employs different metrics. Signatories are to abide by the following principle:

> We will ensure ongoing compliance with the Sea Cargo Charter for new chartering activities through contractual means by using the Sea Cargo Charter Clause in charter parties. We will contribute to the update and addition of the Sea Cargo Charter Clause through the annual review process.[183]

[178] Publication of the first Sea Cargo Charter Annual Disclosure Report (15 June 2022), www.seacargocharter.org/wp-content/uploads/2022/06/Sea-Cargo-Charter-Annual-Disclosure-Report-2022.pdf.
[179] TCLP, *Climate Clauses: Transport*, chancerylaneproject.org/climate-action-pathways/.
[180] The creation of such norms is discussed in ch 1 (section III).
[181] Ulf Bernitz, 'Commercial Norms and Soft Law' (2013) 58 *Scandinavian Studies in Law* 29.
[182] Sea Cargo Charter, 'How did we get here', www.seacargocharter.org/about/how-did-we-get-there. The Sea Cargo Charter was developed by a group of cargo owners – Anglo American, Cargill, Dow, Total, Trafigura – and shipowners – Euronav, Norden, Stena Bulk – in collaboration with Stephenson Harwood (expert support provided by the Global Maritime Forum, UMAS and Smart Freight Centre).
[183] ibid.

To enforce this principle, a Sea Cargo Charter Clause is recommended for voyage data reporting, along with a data reporting template.[184] It contains the following obligations to be inserted into charterparty agreements:

(a) The head owner or disponent owner (as appropriate) shall provide a duly completed fuel emission report in the format appearing in the table below within seven (7) days after completion of the voyage. Such a report shall be sent by email to: (to be completed by the Signatory)
(b) Nothing in the aforementioned provision shall affect any other rights or obligations under the relevant contract.
(c) In the event of a conflict with any other contractual provisions, such other provisions shall prevail.

In order to fully understand the responsibilities of signatories, one needs to look at the terms and definitions set out in the Membership Agreement relating to the Sea Cargo Charter Association.[185] 'Signatory' means a 'Relevant Entity' that is a signatory to the Charter, the membership agreement and governance rules. Relevant entities can comprise a charterer:

> (a) who has interest in the cargo on board; or (b) who simply charter out the vessels they charter in; or (c) who is a disponent owner; or (d) is a charterer in a charterparty chain; and (e) which carries out any Business Activity (f) entities involving the commercial employment of ships in pools, regardless of the legal structure of the pool.[186]

In order to fulfil the signatory charterer's package of obligations, data must be sourced from the owner in accordance with the above clause and the Data Collection Templates provided on the Sea Cargo Charter website. Signatories are expected to already have all the necessary data for time charters, therefore sourcing data will likely only be necessary from owners in voyage charters.[187] Once data is sourced (Step One), it is preferred that a third party calculates the voyage level carbon intensity and climate alignment (known as a Preferred Pathway Track). However, under an Allowed Pathway Track, it is permissible that the signatory calculates the carbon intensity of the voyages – this is essentially and EEOI calculation (Step Two). The next step is for signatories to calculate the vessel category climate alignment and the total annual activity climate alignment using the voyage climate alignment data (Step 3). Under a Preferred Pathway Track the calculation is either performed by a third party or by the signatory itself, with the data and methodology being verified by a third party. On an Allowed Pathway Track the signatory can do this all internally. The final and fourth step (Step Four) involves

[184] 'Sea Cargo Charter Clause' (2021), www.seacargocharter.org/wp-content/uploads/2020/10/Sea-Cargo-Charter-Clause.pdf.
[185] The Sea Cargo Charter Association Membership Agreement (updated 10 March 2022), www.seacargocharter.org/wp-content/uploads/2021/01/The-Sea-Cargo-Charter-Association-%E2%80%93-Membership-Agreement.pdf.
[186] ibid 3.
[187] Sea Cargo Charter Technical Guidance Version 3.0 (February 2024), www.seacargocharter.org/wp-content/uploads/2020/10/SCC-Brochure-V09.pdf.

the signatory preparing disclosures and submitting them to the Secretariat. This step involves certain disclosure requirements which serve as a 'quality control mechanism'.[188] The information flow pathway tracks are illustrated in the following diagram provided by the Sea Cargo Charter Technical Guidance Version 3.0.[189]

Figure 4.1 Information flow pathway tracks

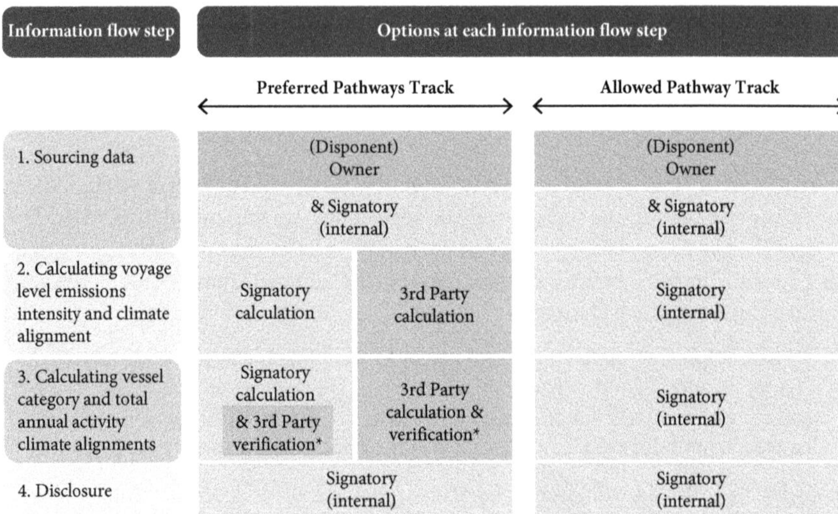

*E.g. using the Indicative Verification Guidelines provided by the signatory.

Climate alignment is defined as 'the degree to which voyage carbon intensity of a vessel category is in line with a decarbonization trajectory that meets the IMO ambition of reducing total annual GHG emissions by at least 50% by 2050 based on 2008 levels'. In order to calculate this, the most important information to be furnished by owners to signatories is information pertaining to the carbon intensity of a certain voyage. Climate alignment will then be calculated as a 'percentage difference between the carbon intensity and the decarbonisation trajectory at any point in time'. Essentially, the carbon trajectory comprises a representation of the permissible grams of CO_2 that can be emitted to move one tonne of goods one nautical mile (gCO_2/tnm) over a time horizon. The total CO_2 shipping emissions permitted is in accordance with the IMO's 2050 target and also relies on projected transport demand for various shipping sectors.[190] Carbon intensity information per voyage is thus crucial to a signatory's annual reporting obligations. These are coupled with transparency requirements which involve that the signatory publicly

[188] ibid 37.
[189] Diagram from page 29.
[190] Sea Cargo Charter Technical Guidance Version 3.0 (n 187) 22.

acknowledges that it is a signatory, and that it provides the secretariat with reported submissions as published in its relevant institutional reports. The secretariat will use such submissions to publish all vessel category climate alignment scores and total annual activity climate alignment scores of the signatory on the website.

Despite the importance of sourcing information from ship owners regarding energy intensity, the standard covenant clause is fairly weak as a term and proffers no suggested remedy. However, this is merely a recommended charterparty clause combined with a number of Data Collection Templates. The Technical Guidance states that the clause is:[191]

> [D]esigned to be generic and broad in its nature (so as to be consistent with any charter party form or type of trade) and non-prescriptive (so as to reduce the impulse for amendment from contractual counterparties).It is hoped that this approach will maximize the appeal and widen the future endorsement of a charter party clause linked to the Sea Cargo Charter.

This is aligned with the intention of the Sea Cargo Charter to maintain flexibility and to not impose too heavy a burden on parties. Parties are expected to take reasonable commercial measures to include appropriate wording in negotiated charterparty documentation and the secretariat will continue to work with 'those organizations to whom the market has entrusted the production of contractual terms with a view to including the wording of this recommended charter party clause as part of the recognized industry standard terms'.[192] Although it may appear that the Sea Cargo Charter does not do much in the way of expecting anything more from owners and charterers than what is already required under MEPC.278(70) in respect of data collection, the power of the Sea Cargo Charter lies in its normative function which steers parties towards cooperation for greener performance. It also guides signatory charterers in the selection of vessels/shipowners, as charterers would want the vessel to achieve climate alignment to improve their disclosure submissions thus elevating their green credentials to cargo interests and consumers. From a contractual perspective, the inclusion of the standard covenant clause is helpful in that it achieves:

(1) Normative principles: As the charterer has publicly published its membership as signatory to the Sea Cargo Charter and included appropriate contractual clauses for data collection, the climate alignment objectives of the Sea Cargo Charter may assist in the interpretation of other contractual obligations.[193] This is because the charterer and owner have effectively committed themselves to a set of principles and must work together to achieve climate alignment.

[191] ibid 38 (section 3.4).

[192] ibid.

[193] The relevant question is what a reasonable person in the position of the parties would understand the instrument to mean, and that question is answered by reference to the text in its context. See *Sirius International Insurance Co v FAI General Insurance Ltd* [2004] 1 WLR 3251 [18] (Lord Steyn, with whom Lord Nicholls and Lord Walker agreed).

(2) Evolution of standard forms: Through increasing membership, the Sea Cargo Charter intends that its standard covenant clause will be adopted as part of recognised standard industry terms. This will harden the soft norm purport of the Sea Cargo Charter and allow the 'law of standard agreements' to elevate climate alignment to a contractual principle more generally.

(3) Strengthening climate provisions: The standard covenant clause provides a starting point for cooperation between owner and charterer to achieve decarbonisation. Charterers may wish to go further if they have a wider interest in decarbonisation efforts. They can utilise a number of additional contractual methods to implement a set of conditions, innominate terms, and warranties to ensure that vessel selection aligns with their business management goals.

In respect of point (3) above, the same contractual tools would be available as discussed in chapter two relating to the Poseidon Principles standard covenant clause. Although charterparties do not include events of default or conditions precedent as seen in loan agreements, a charterer may want to include additional performance warranties and fuel consumption clauses to reflect the level of energy efficiency that the vessel *must* achieve. If a commitment to the Sea Cargo Charter is stated in a guiding Preamble, there may even be scope for elevating energy efficiency to a condition or innominate term, the breach of which could result in repudiatory breach.[194] It would be fundamental to a green charterer that the vessel achieves a certain percentage (or within a certain range) of carbon alignment. Chartering efforts to elevate climate commitments in charterparties may depend on the bargaining power between owner and charterer. However, owners enjoy a number of incentives from climate alignment, including improved charter rates, fulfilment of their own obligations under green credit facilities, and other commercial interests including reputation and climate risk management.

B. The Chancery Lane Project Climate Clauses

The Chancery Lane Project (TCLP) has been referred to throughout this book and its clauses have been discussed in the context of green loans and even the construction sector in previous chapters.[195] In respect of chartering, the TCLP has drafted four clauses:[196]

(1) Otto's Clause: a contractual duty between owner and charterer to take all reasonable steps to maximise energy efficiency.[197]

[194] Arguing that energy efficiency is a condition of the contract may not yet be possible given the attitude of English courts in confirming their status as a warranty. However, normative green values may eventually enable the elevation of such terms. See section II.B.iii below.

[195] The Chancery Lane Project (2022), chancerylaneproject.org/about.

[196] At the time of publication of this Book, The Chancery Lane Project (TCLP) was in the process of updating its website and shipping clauses. These clauses may therefore not be available at the time of publication, but direct requests can be made to TCLP.

[197] TCLP, Energy Efficiency in Shipping – Otto's Clause (published 1 April 2021 and updated 3 November 2021), chancerylaneproject.org/climate-clauses/energy-efficiency-in-shipping.

(2) Ariel's Clause: encourages energy efficiency upgrades through cost sharing between charterer and owner.[198]
(3) Aiden's Clause: imposes a duty on parties to use the greenest fuel available to the vessel and report the fuel type and other data.[199]
(4) Bradleigh's Clause: charterers and owners agree to use best reasonable endeavours to minimise ballast voyages undertaken by the vessel and to maximise the laden ratio of the vessel for each voyage.[200]

There is also an additional clause governing the relationship between shipper and carrier called Levi's Clause, which enables customers to terminate a long-term contract for the transportation of goods for a greener carrier or shipper.[201] All these clauses are drafted in accordance with the laws of England and Wales, take a comprehensive contractual approach and suggest both recitals and add-on clauses for parties who wish to adopt greater ambitions. These climate clauses serve a primary function in addition to the prescriptive elements of each clause: they expand the purpose of the contract beyond commercial efficacy and achieve a cooperative framework for decarbonisation. The following features and methods employed by the clauses are noteworthy.

i. Recitals and Definitions

Recitals or 'background provisions' illustrate the commercial context of an agreement and assist with the reading and interpretation of contractual obligations therein. The TCLP provides 'Eddie's Recital' which can be inserted into agreements to 'frame a contract and the intentions of the parties in terms that are aligned with achieving net-zero or net negative emissions and Paris Agreement goals'.[202] BIMCO's use of a Preamble in the RECYCLECON to ensure that a vessel is sold exclusively for recycling a vessel in 'a safe and environmentally sound manner consistent with the international and national law and relevant guidelines', uses the same technique (discussed in detail in section II of chapter three). The case of *Blackpool FC (Properties) Ltd v JSC Baltic International Bank* illustrates how recitals provide evidence of the relevant 'factual matrix' at the date of execution.[203] It is well established that the factual matrix is one of the factors in contractual interpretation.

[198] TCLP, Incentivising Fuel Efficiency Investments In Time Chartered Vessels – Ariel's Clause (published 8 November 2021), chancerylaneproject.org/climate-clauses/incentivising-fuel-efficiency-investments-in-time-chartered-vessels-new.
[199] TCLP, Fuel Reporting Clause for Shipping Charterparties – Aiden's Clause (published 5 November 2021), chancerylaneproject.org/climate-clauses/fuel-reporting-clause-for-shipping-charterparties-new.
[200] TCLP, Maximising the Laden Ratio of Vessels in Shipping Charterparties – Bradleigh's Clause (published 8 November 2021).
[201] TCLP, Green Fuel Requirement and Termination for Greener Carrier or Shipper (Maritime) – Levi's Clause (published 15 August 2022).
[202] TCLP, Eddie's Recital (updated 29 September 2021), chancerylaneproject.org/climate-clauses/climate-recitals.
[203] *Blackpool FC (Properties) Ltd v JSC Baltic International Bank* [2018] EWCA Civ 732.

Blackpool FC (Properties) Ltd v JSC Baltic International Bank concerned an investment agreement between the appellant and the respondent which set out the terms for a construction project at the football ground Blackpool FC Ltd. The project was set out in three phases and the contract employed a number of recitals to set out the nature of each phase. The problem arose with a recital pertaining to the third phase of the project that envisioned that the cost of the intended third phase would be borrowed from a third party on terms acceptable to the both the appellant and respondent. A clause in the contract allowed both parties to deduct certain expenditure (including such borrowed money) before the profits were distributed to each party. Unforeseeably, Blackpool FC was promoted to the Premier League and the appellant could now borrow money for the third phase directly from its subsidiary. This borrowing was not approved by the respondent as required by the contract, and the appellant attempted to deduct the sums borrowed from its subsidiary from the amounts it owed to the respondent. The court held that the clause had to be read in the context of the contract as a whole, including its recitals, so as to be consistent with a protective scheme intended to prevent the profits of the development being encumbered by unauthorised borrowing or intra-borrowing between groups. In relation to the legal status of recitals, the court said that although only a recital, it provides evidence of the 'factual matrix' of the contract.[204]

The TCLP also recognises that definitions are important to include into charterparty agreements. A court is unlikely to consider definitions set out in published documents unless they are incorporated into the charterparty.[205] As such, the climate clauses for charterparties provides key terminology such as EEOI, fuel efficiency, the scope of GHG emissions, the gases included in an understanding of GHG emissions and residual emissions.

ii. Energy Efficiency as a Negotiated Term

In proposing a workable contractual mechanism, economic research using game theory has been done to propose an Energy Efficiency Investment Sharing Scheme (EEISS).[206] This mechanism, as supported by the findings of Psarros, is summarised here. The EEISS essentially aims to achieve the optimum reward for energy efficiency which determines a fair payment and resolves the level of contribution between the contracting parties. In ordinary negotiations, an initial bid from the shipowner would include certain details about the vessel, its capacity and date of readiness, as well as the owner's reservation. On the other side, the charterer would state the size and type of cargo, readiness and laycan dates and the charterer's reservation price (expected market price). Once a match is found between a

[204] ibid [26].
[205] *Navalmar UK Ltd v Kale Maden Hammaddeler Sanayi Ve Ticaret AS (The MV Arundel Castle)* [2017] EWHC 116 (Comm) at [25]–[31].
[206] ibid.

vessel and the cargo, the shipowner (the seller) can estimate the costs of the voyage and negotiations become increasingly detailed. Obviously, the rate is subject to market behaviour and vessel availability, and it is possible that the rate may change by the end of this process. Negotiating a sharing scheme for energy efficiency investments can also be included in this negotiation process. Both parties may not be fully aware of the vessel's energy efficiency performance. The seller is in a better position to know the energy efficiency details of the ship in question. Parties can thus enhance their position through disclosing optimal information. Clauses are included to reflect the parties' asymmetric information of a variety of issues including costs, performance and environmental attributes. Thus, an owner who has an honest reputation of disclosing accurate information of high levels of energy efficiency offers a competitive advantage and might have a higher reservation price. Thus, it also becomes important to specify fiduciary obligations in the sharing scheme.

Although supported by economic theory and not necessarily one of contract governance, Psarros indirectly recognises ways of promoting sustainability through the way in which contracts can govern commercial relationships in a cooperative way. He proposes a workable contractual solution to include energy efficiency as a negotiated term from the inception stages of the chartering process as providing an incentive for environmental commitment from both parties.[207] Additionally, it provides a means for distributing energy efficiency costs and rewards as well as providing clarity on the rights and responsibilities of the parties.[208] Negotiating such a clause can be instrumental in empowering parties with differing interests to share a common green objective. It would also stimulate continued improvement of the vessel's energy efficiency which encourages continued investment on green technology upgrades. Such a clause could also help parties determine the legal status of the obligation to comply with emission regulations.[209] There is also a strong argument that the inclusion of design energy efficiency clauses as a legally operative rider clause could more clearly demarcate duties and responsibilities in the event of civil lawsuits for environmental pollution and damage, as seen with oil pollution cases, especially given the increase in climate change litigation over recent years.[210]

Furthermore, due diligence should be exercised so as not to conflict with other provisions of the contract.[211] Contracting parties will also have to establish the basis of measurements, what constitutes breach, remedies for violations, and other protection mechanisms. The most important aspect of this EEISS is that it will unify the objectives of both parties to achieve greater levels of energy efficiency and

[207] George Adamantios Psarros, *Energy Efficiency Clauses in Charter Party Agreements: Legal and Economic Perspectives and Their Application to Ocean Grain Transport* (Springer ProQuest, 2016).
[208] Key findings of economic research conducted by George Adamantios Psarros (n 207).
[209] Psarros (n 207).
[210] ibid 36–38.
[211] ibid 64.

environmental protection. This solution offered by Psarros firmly recognises that current available technologies impose huge capital costs on owners with imperfect data on certainty of performance. In order to pay back their loans for financing green technology, owners would have to increase freight rates and justify this to charterers. Thus, to give owners a competitive advantage, external factors other than a costs equilibrium between capital investment and fuel savings have been included in the calculation. An owner's transparency, goodwill and disclosure of information can also act as a *nudge* for better environmental performance.[212]

Other specific cost-sharing schemes include those which more directly integrate financial incentives into chartering. Examples of these initiatives include Save as You Sail (SAYS),[213] developed by the finance workstream of the Sustainable Shipping Initiative (SSI) together with Deloitte, Holman Fenwick Willan (HFW) and University College London, and the Self-Financing Fuel-Saving Mechanism (SFFSM),[214] developed by stakeholders, including the Carbon War Room, PwC and University College London. Under the SAYS scheme, the owner of a vessel takes out a loan with the finance provider and agrees to a regular fixed SAYS fee with the time charterer on top of their charter rates. The owner is thus apportioned some of the cost savings made by the charterer, which can be used to offset loan payments for the retrofitting. The SFFSM essentially works as a tripartite contractual agreement between the financier, the technology partners and the fuel payer. This financial model has two important features: 1) a guarantee of fuel savings from the technology vendors; and 2) a refined data collection methodology which continuously monitors equipment to accurately quantify and verify fuel savings.

SAYS and SFFSM models therefore overcome split incentives to afford more innovative cost-sharing schemes. In addition, they can overcome the problem of uncertainty surrounding the performance data of green technologies as the technology provider must be able to guarantee that their technologies will deliver a certain percentage of fuel savings, and the owner must accurately verify those savings to charterers. Cost-sharing schemes also achieve a stronger convergence of objectives between owner and charterer which must be aligned with the terms of the underlying finance agreement for the retrofitting of the vessel. This alignment will necessarily see the norms and commitments of the applicable green finance agreement being strongly carried over into the chartering agreement. In fact, as seen with SAYS and SSFSM, the charterer can also be bound to the terms set forth by the financier.

[212] Ellen Eftestøl-Wilhelmsson and Suvi Sankari, 'Nudging a behavioural change in maritime carriage of goods – the role of information' in Jason Chuah (ed), *Research Handbook on Maritime Law and Regulation* (Edward Elgar Publishing, 2019) 170.

[213] Sustainable Shipping Initiative, *Save As You Sail*, www.ssi2040.org/news/call-for-ship-owners-to-join-pilot-of-innovative-save-as-you-sail-technology-financing-model.

[214] Victoria Stulgis et al, *Hidden treasure: Financial models for retrofits* (The Carbon War Room / UCL Energy Institute, 2014) 32–33.

Ariel's Clause by the TCLP similarly attempts to overcome the problem of split incentives by recovering the costs of energy savings from the charterer which assists the owner in recuperating the investments costs of any installed energy device. The clause gives charterers the options to expressly agree to share the costs through a cost-sharing mechanism. Sub-clause 1.5 best explains the main obligation contained in Ariel's Clause:

> If Costs-Sharing was accepted by the Charterer pursuant to clause [1.3], at redelivery of the Vessel, the Charterer shall pay to the Owner [[•]% of the market value of the volume of fuel saved as a result of each Energy Saving Device installed with the Charterer's prior written agreement to Costs-Sharing pursuant to clause [1.3] above] [OR] [an increased freight rate/ daily hire rate of [$][•]].

Fuel savings are to be calculated by a third party and parties are required to disclose to each other for all information required to calculate the fuel efficiency [and EEOI] for any relevant period required by this charterparty. This clause goes a long way to include energy efficiency as a negotiated term in time charters, but there are some additional considerations needed to fully overcome the problem of split incentives. First, passing down 100 per cent of the market value of fuel energy savings to the charterer as a stipulated provision would simply reallocate costs in a way that is seemingly too preferable to the owner. The owner should thus carefully consider how much of the technology costs it wants to recover within the charter period. An increased freight rate would be the most simple solution, but charterers would likely want the vessel's fuel efficiency to be guaranteed to offset the increased freight rate with fuel savings made in the voyage. Furthermore, nothing in the clause obliges the charterer to accept the cost-sharing. After receiving an Energy Saving Notice from the owner, the options for the charterer are as follows:[215]

> (i) accepting the Costs-Sharing;
> (ii) requesting further information;
> (iii) rejecting the Costs-Sharing (explaining, in reasonable detail and in good faith, the grounds for such rejection); or (iv) where the Energy Saving Notice details the installation of more than one device, a combination of (i), (ii) and (iii) as relevant.

The clause appears to assume that the energy-saving technology will be installed during a contracted voyage, and the owner will not require the charterer's consent to proceed to install any such device. As noted in the *Essential Notes and Guidance on Ariel's Clause*, it remains a barrier to the uptake of the clause if the vessel is unavailable for employment outside of agreed maintenance intervals while upgrades are carried out. It is unclear how sub-clause 1.10 will overcome this by stating that the owner must take all reasonable steps to ensure that the installation of any energy saving device takes place at a time and location that does not [materially] interrupt the charterer's use of the vessel. Although there will always

[215] cl 1.3.

be an initial installation of an energy-saving device, it would make more sense for an owner to retrofit a vessel between fixtures if practically possible. Owners should not be fettered by charterer acceptance or non-acceptance, and may want to employ more comprehensive approaches.

It is a matter of common sense that it is in the best interests of sellers (owners), who bear the cost of installing innovative technology, when providing a level of efficiency beyond the minimum to alert buyers (charterers) to the fact that they have done so. Thus, when bargaining the energy-efficiency sharing scheme, it must be stipulated that evidence shall be provided with respect to the vessel's performance taking into account available data on the vessel's condition and monitoring systems.[216] Contractual provisions will also have to take into account how slow steaming influences the operation of the installed energy efficiency equipment and safety of the vessel. The barriers to slow steaming and virtual arrival can thus be eliminated where a clear and legitimate environmental agenda is pursued, and the obligations of the parties are clarified and agreed upon.

iii. Overcoming Problems Surrounding Performance Warranties

Time charters have for a long time included fuel consumption and performance warranties. However, these warranties are yet to make any sort of provision for environmental interests and have been the source of frequent disputes between owner and charterer. Most standard forms include a clause whereby the owner will warrant the vessel's speed and fuel consumption. Clause 24(a) of the standard form charter known as SHELLTIME 4, states that the 'Owners guarantee that the speed and consumption of the vessel shall be as follows', as seen in the diagram extract of such form below.

Figure 4.2 Clause 24(a) of SHELLTIME 4

Detailed	24. (a)	Owners guarantee that the speed and consumption of the vessel shall be as follows:-		
Description		Average speed	Maximum average bunker consumption per day	
and		in knots	main propulsion	auxiliaries
Performance			fuel oil/ diesel oil	fuel oil/diesel oil
		Laden	tonnes	tonnes
		____	___/___	___/___
		____	___/___	___/___
		____	___/___	___/___
		Ballast		
		____	___/___	___/___
		____	___/___	___/___
			/	/

The foregoing bunker consumptions are for all purposes except cargo heating and tank cleaning and shall be pro-rated between the speeds shown.

This document is a computer generated SHELLTIME 4 form printed by authority of BIMCO. Any insertion or deletion to the form must be clearly visible. In event of any modification being made to the pre printed text of this document which is not clearly visible, the text of the original BIMCO approved document shall apply. BIMCO assumes no responsibility for any loss, damage or expense caused as a result of discrepancies between the original BIMCO approved document and this computer generated document.

[216] Psarros (n 207) 36–38.

If the vessel fails to achieve the performance guaranteed, then deduction from hire may be made according to an adjusted performance calculation. Charterers frequently claim against owners for underperformance or overconsumption – meaning that the vessel is either not complying with the speed specifications described or the vessel is using more fuel per day than specified in the charterparty.[217] Owners therefore require accurate and comprehensive data to determine the speed and consumption of the vessel. This presents a major issue when such data is inaccurate, and the charterer and owner dispute the vessel's actual performance. The disputes surrounding these clauses are also helpful in construing how energy efficiency clauses can avoid such disputes where an environmental objective represents a convergence of interests. This is especially important given the far-reaching losses envisioned by Otto's Clause. A recent Appeal Court decision illustrates the difficulties with traditional performance and fuel consumption warranties.

In *SK Shipping Europe PLC v (3) Capital VLCC 3 Corp (5) Capital Maritime and Trading Corp (The C Challenger)*,[218] the charterer purported to rescind a long-term time charter on the basis that the owner had fraudulently misrepresented the ship's fuel consumption.[219] Alternatively, the charterers alleged that the owners had made the statements negligently, or without reasonable grounds for believing them to be true as per section 2(1) of the Misrepresentation Act 1967.[220] The owner in this case, SK Shipping Europe, did not ordinarily charter its vessels under time charters as it had been in the business of chartering out its vessels on the spot market through consecutive voyage charters. Under the long-period time charter, the owner was required to offer warranties as to speed and performance – something it had never previously done. An agreement was concluded and after delivery of the vessel, it became clear that the vessel consumed bunkers in excess of the warranted consumption and that the information circulated in the negotiation stages pertaining to the vessel's fuel performance was inaccurate. The charterer, being aware of the over-consumption, threatened to terminate the charterparty, but continued to employ the ship under a 'reservation of rights'. Later that year, the charterer purported to rescind the charterparty on the basis of misrepresentation or to terminate it for repudiatory breach. The charterer stated that the 'negotiations for the "C CHALLENGER" which included the Owner's representations … formed part of the inducement for the Charterer's to ultimately contract on the terms of the Charterparty'.[221] The charterer also said that the 'Owners' guaranteed speed and consumption of the vessel were false and negligently made and as a result the Charterers are entitled to rescind the Charterparty'.[222]

[217] For speed performance, it is generally accepted that owners are given a 0.5 knot margin. This 'rule' is generally applied in London arbitrations, but is not actually mandated by law. Legally, the margin' must be tailored to the ship's configuration, size, draft and trim etc' (*The Al Bida* [1987] 1 LLR 124).

[218] *The C Challenger* [2020] EWHC 3448 (Comm).

[219] ibid [111].

[220] ibid.

[221] ibid [101].

[222] ibid.

Therefore, the main argument put forward by the charterers was that the circulated details of the vessel's consumption constituted a representation of fact that was substantially inaccurate. Justice Foxton held that when the owner offered a continuing speed and consumption warranty in a charterparty, it could not be assumed to make an implicit representation as to the vessel's current or recent performance.[223] He clarified a few principles on such a warranty, that the 'language of an undertaking, a warranty is inherently promissory, and is expressed in relation to the future (performance during the chartered service)'; implying such a representation gives difficulty in determining the date at which any level of performance is said to be represented; speed consumption warranties are subject to a degree of margin – this is not the case involving representations as to the vessel's actual consumption; and the warranty given is not so much a warranty given as the vessel's capability at any particular point, but as to its average performance over a longer period.[224] Yet, the charterers also argued that the owners had sent a letter containing the historical speed and consumption data which was not reasonably consistent with the average performance of the vessel over its last three voyages and was therefore untrue. Mr Justice Foxton in the commercial court was willing to accept that the statement based on the three recent voyages amounted to material representation, but there was no inducement and therefore no right to rescind.[225] If SK Shipping had made the same warranty, but made no representation as the vessel's historic or recent performance, the same charterparty would have been concluded on the same terms.

Despite the charterers 'reserving rights' pertaining to the misconduct of the owners, they proceeded to fix a voyage with a sub-charterer expecting the owners to execute this voyage, bringing the owner into contractual relations with third parties under which the owner would be liable for cargo claims.[226] Justice Foxton held that these actions of the charterers were not consistent with an attempt to reserve rights to rescind the charterparty and set it aside *ab initio* for misrepresentation.[227] The charterers also argued that the owners had breached a number of clauses pertaining to obligations as to the condition of the vessel on delivery, as to maintaining the vessel, consistent breach of the consumption warranty, as well as unjustified demands for payment of hire and refusing to make deductions of hire, and asserting that the charterer was in breach.[228] However, although Foxton J accepted that these were breaches of the contract, the terms breached were deemed to be innominate terms. The cumulative breaches complained of had not substantially deprived the charterers of the whole benefit that they intended to receive under the charterparty for payment of hire, nor did they 'go to the root of

[223] ibid [129].
[224] ibid.
[225] ibid [191].
[226] ibid [221].
[227] ibid [222].
[228] ibid [273].

the contract' of the charterparty.[229] Therefore, the charterers were not entitled to terminate the charterparty and their communication to that effect was a renunciation in and of itself, thus entitling the owners to damages.[230]

The charterers appealed this decision on the grounds that there was a misrepresentation as to the vessel's current or recent performance which was warranted by the charterparty within a five knott and that this representation was repeated on several occasions.[231] That there was indeed inducement as the charterers would not have entered into the same agreement or have concluded an agreement at all if the representations had not been made. The charterer argued that they did not affirm the charterparty; in fact, it expressly reserved its rights because the owner was itself saying that more data was needed and that the position should be reviewed. They also argued that the judge could not deny a rescission of contract as this is dependent upon the actions of the representee, not a court order. Furthermore it would be wrong to hold the contract as subsisting when this would render the representee liable for damages. Finally, the judge should have awarded damages putting the charterer in the same position as it would have been in had rescission been granted.

Given the focus on performance warranties, it is only necessary to address what the Appeal Court said on this point. It was held that performance warranties are only a representation that the owner expected the vessel to achieve substantially the same performance in the future, or at any rate that it had no reason to believe that the vessel would not do so. Lord Justice Males found that a prospective charterer would have understood the owner to be saying 'this is how my vessel has performed on its most recent voyages and these are the warranties which I am prepared to give', and nothing more.[232] This would be enough for the prospective charterer to decide whether to pursue the negotiations. Furthermore, as is the case in here and clause 24 of Shelltime 4, there is no warranty as to any individual voyage, but only as to performance over a period (the standard clause provides for annual reviews; here six monthly reviews were agreed). There was, therefore, an 'element of swings and roundabouts built into any warranty of future performance, with the possibility that over-consumption in the early period might be compensated later on, for example by arranging for the hull to be cleaned'.[233]

The C Challenger therefore illustrates that such warranties are promissory in nature and would not allow for remedies stemming from misrepresentation. One way to overcome any prejudice to a charterer as result of this, as suggested by the economic literature in the previous section, is to calculate energy efficiency and consequent energy savings through a commitment to data sharing. However, data sharing in this context is an ongoing and collaborative process as opposed

[229] ibid [305].
[230] ibid [311].
[231] *The C Challenger*, Appeal decision: [2022] EWCA Civ 231.
[232] ibid [36].
[233] ibid [37].

to the once-off delivery of documents in the negotiating phases of the contract. Calculations can take place periodically or at the end of the voyage and would be dependent on the collection of real time data throughout the voyage. It may therefore not be necessary to warrant performance, but warranties as to the accuracy of data would still be necessary. Ariel's Clause aims to overcome such disputes by using the services of a third party for monitoring and verifying fuel savings. Calculating energy savings is thus arguably better than an owner simply factoring the benefit of green technologies into the freight rates, as a higher rate would almost certainly need to be accompanied by fuel efficiency warranties to maintain competitive in the market. There may be issues pertaining to a calculating energy savings where an owner misrepresents what the ordinary performance of the vessel would be in comparison to performance with an energy-saving device. However, this could be easily addressed by making comparisons to a vessel of the same category as opposed to the specific past performance of that particular vessel. As such, the owner could benefit from all design improvements both previously and very recently installed.

Otto's Clause employs similar cooperation between owner and charterer, but with an aim of maximising energy efficiency through operational measures, not to share the costs of energy-saving installations. For the purposes of this clause, fuel efficiency shall be measured by reference to the energy efficiency operational indicator as set out in the Energy Efficiency Operational Indicator (EEOI) Guidelines. The EEOI was developed by the IMO and is the total carbon emissions in a given time period per unit of revenue ton-miles. Variations in the index are mainly caused by three factors: the technical efficiency of the ship, the amount of cargo transported per unit of time, and variations in speed.[234]

In order to calculate this, the shipowner must disclose information required to calculate the EEOI for the requested period. Hence, some sort of performance warranty should either be expressly stated in the charterparty or technical performance data should be represented in negotiations or upon request. If the owner breaches these obligations or misrepresents technical performance data, an all-encompassing fuel efficiency fee may be paid for:

> [L]osses that are wide-ranging in nature and difficult to quantify with precision, including losses related to damage to the climate and the environment, consequential breaches of environmental laws, diminished standing with states, governments and regulators, and/or damage to that party's reputation.[235]

This operates as a liquidated damages fee to incentivise accurate data-sharing. Failure to pay the stated fee can result in termination rights under clause 2.4. These are far more serious consequences for owners than under ordinary charterparties containing fuel consumption. It would also be more difficult to employ

[234] See ch 1 for a full explanation of how EEOI is calculated.
[235] cl 2.1 of Otto's Clause (n 197).

the reasoning of *The C Challenger* to protect the owner in saying that there is an element of 'swings and roundabouts' providing the owner with some leeway in reporting performance data as Otto's Clause, along with Eddie's Recital, clearly frames the contract as one premised on cooperation for accurate data sharing to achieve energy efficiency. The liquidated damages fee also contextualises the parties' intentions so that performance warranties should not be interpreted as having margins for inaccuracy. Where owners innocently misrepresent data, there are notice periods allowing them to correct contractual performance. Parties may also wish to rely on agreed third-party monitoring services and exclude the application of the penalty fee if any inaccurate data sharing arises from the fault of a third party.

iv. *Overcoming Problems Surrounding Bunker Supply*

Aiden's Clause raises an old question that usually arises in the context of fuel sulphur content: the problems of bunker supply agreements with third parties and misrepresentations as to fuel quality. A major concern leading up to the IMO's 1 March 2020 carriage ban on high sulphur fuels (ie those not meeting the new 0.5 per cent m/m standard) was the issue pertaining to low-sulphur fuels and resultant operational problems. Between 24 February and 6 May 2020, BIMCO, ICS, INTERCARGO and INTERTANKO conducted an industry survey aimed at ascertaining how the industry has experienced the transition to low-sulphur fuel oil from 1 January.[236] The survey found that shipowners were experiencing a number of problems such as 'increased sludge discharge, clogging of fuel pipes, preheaters, fuel separators and fuel filters, fuel pumps getting stuck, problems with fuel injection and poor ignition of fuel oil'.[237] The survey also highlighted other issues such as wax appearance, increased wear and tear of cylinder liners, propulsion problems, and/or blackout.[238] Commercial testing of fuel samples after bunkering also revealed that sulphur content is the most frequent parameter to be off-specification.[239]

The problem pertaining to off-spec fuels was predominantly related to engine damage. Charterers and owners alike, depending on whether a charter agreement is a voyage charter or time charter, therefore need to consider *another*

[236] BIMCO, '2020 Fuel Oil Quality and Safety Survey' (2020), www.bimco.org/news/priority-news/20200819-industry-survey.

[237] ibid; BIMCO media summary of Survey.

[238] An engine-damage claim similarly arose in 2021, wherein Maersk filed a suit in the Southern District of New York to hold commodities trader Glencore liable for supplying off-spec fuel to the company's vessels. See *Maersk Oil Trading Panama SA et al v Glencore Ltd* (Case no: 1:2021cv01063).

[239] Off-spec fuels have previously caused major problems, most notably in the US Gulf region in what became known as the 'Houston Problem'. Contaminated fuels provided a serious problem for shipowners as engines were severely damaged and the safety of the ship was therefore compromised, see 'Contaminated bunkers: "the Houston problem"' *Hellenic Shipping News* (26 September 2018), www.hellenicshippingnews.com/contaminated-bunkers-the-houston-problem-2.

contractual relationship with third parties very carefully: *bunker supply contracts*. Under English law, the sale of bunkers is governed by the Sales of Goods Act 1979. Section 14(3) provides that 'there is an implied condition that the goods supplied under the contract are reasonably fit for that purpose'. Owners could also argue that charterers are therefore under an implied obligation to source bunkers which are 'fit for the purpose intended'.[240] In an unreported arbitration case, 'fit for purpose' was considered in the context of bunkers which were provided within specification by DNV, but were found to have poor ignition qualities.[241] The tribunal found that there was an implied term in the charterparty that bunkers had to be fit for the purpose intended, and that due to the engine damage caused, the bunkers could not have been fit for purpose. A legal questions arises in whether 'fit for purpose' be extended to the parties intentions to reduce carbon emissions? Aiden's Clause for time and voyage charterparties provides an easy solution to fulfilling the 'fit for purpose' criteria by stating that:[242]

> During the performance of this charter owners and charterers shall use [[best/ reasonable] endeavours to] [cooperate with a view to using]* bunker fuel with the lowest available CO_2 Emissions Factor compliant with the Vessel's bunkering infrastructure and operational requirements.

If a party to the agreement elects to use bunker fuel with a CO_2 Emissions Factor of higher than what is agreed to, when a fuel type with a lower CO_2 Emissions Factor is available, that party shall pay a Climate Remediation Fee to selected charity organisation which focuses on tackling climate change or reducing emissions from shipping.

A major barrier to the uptake of this clause, as similarly noted in the Drafting Guidance,[243] are the historical pressures exerted by bunker suppliers in markets of constrained availability. Although this chapter does not permit an extensive discussion of Bunker Supply Agreements, they are extremely relevant to the operational phase of ship's lifespan. The bunker supplier may try to insert terms and conditions that are heavily weighted in its favour. Many of these agreements take place on the supplier's standard forms, which may make the supplier's sample testing of the fuel binding. They may also seek to place very limited time bars for notification of claims (usually seven days), whilst limiting their liability for any losses caused by the fuel.[244] BIMCO has tried to balance the interests of buyer and seller more

[240] Clyde & Co, 'Bunker Quality Claims in 2020 – Issues to Consider' (2 January 2020), www.clydeco.com/en/insights/2020/01/bunker-quality-claims-in-2020-issues-to-consider.

[241] UK Defence Club, 'Bunker contamination claims in the US Gulf' (August 2018), www.ukdefence.com/fileadmin/uploads/uk-defence/Documents/Soundings/2018/1111-UKDC-Soundings-Bunker-contamination-claims-v7.pdf.

[242] cl 1 of Aiden's Clause (n 199).

[243] Aiden's Clause – Essential notes and guidance (5 November 2021), chancerylaneproject.org/climate-clauses/fuel-reporting-clause-for-shipping-charterparties-new.

[244] Other considerations for an owner may be that the owner may be exposed to an arrest where a charterer fails to pay for the bunkers; see *Forsythe International (UK) Ltd v Silver Shipping Co Ltd and Petroglobe International Ltd. (The 'Saetta')* [1993] 2 Lloyds Rep 268.

evenly in its standard BIMCO Bunker Terms 2018 form.[245] Clause 4 of the form allows buyers or their representatives an opportunity to have the sampling carried out in their presence at an agreed point. Clause 6 also allows the master of the vessel to make appropriate remarks or issue a letter of protest following delivery.

Aiden's Clause may have very real consequences for bunker supply contracts, the terms of which should be carefully thought through. Charterers and owners may be afforded more guidance under the Fuel EU Maritime Initiative, which intends to set a maximum limit on the greenhouse gas content of energy used by ships.[246] This may see fuel suppliers having to guarantee that their bunkers meet this requirement. Parties to a Charterparty may then be able to indemnify themselves where suppliers breach such guarantees and reclaim their losses from the supplier.

C. BIMCO's CII Clause

BIMCO's CII Clause marks a noticeable difference from previous environmental compliance clauses.[247] For shipping, the CII will be based entirely on data reported by the vessel under the IMO Data Collection System (DCS) and is only achievable with extensive cooperation between owner and charter. As such, it reflects many of the norms and mechanisms prevalent throughout the TCLP climate clauses for charterparties, such as the cooperative norm of 'working together in good faith' (clause (a)).[248] Although a doctrine of 'good faith' is not recognised by English contract law, it is accepted that good faith should from a basic principle of all contractual negotiations.[249] It is also questionable whether good faith is included in the seven principles of EU civil law,[250] yet 'good faith and fair dealing' is a fundamental principle of the UNIDROIT Principles of International Commercial Contracts (UNIDROIT Principles).[251] It is a logical corollary of cooperation for a shared goal that the parties act in good faith.

This is not dissimilar to Eddie's Recital, which requires the parties to acknowledge their 'common intention' to achieve net-zero targets, align themselves with

[245] BIMCO, 'Bunker Terms' (2018), www.bimco.org/contracts-and-clauses/bimco-contracts/bimco-bunker-terms-2018#.

[246] COM(2021) 562 final, Proposal for a Regulation of the European Parliament and of the Council on the use of renewable and low-carbon fuels in maritime transport and amending Directive 2009/16/EC.

[247] Pia Rebelo, 'BIMCO's Carbon Intensity Indicator Clause (CII) for time charters: towards a new era of climate drafting' (2022) 28 *Journal of International Maritime Law* 240.

[248] BIMCO, CII Operations Clause for Time Charter Parties (2022), www.bimco.org/contracts-and-clauses/bimco-clauses/current/cii-operations-clause-2022.

[249] William Tetley, 'Good Faith in Contract: Particularly in the Contracts of Arbitration and Chartering' (2004) 35 *Journal of Maritime Law & Commerce* 561.

[250] Norbert Reich, *General Principles of EU Civil Law*, 1st edn (Intersentia, 2014).

[251] Article 1.7 of UNIDROIT Principles states: '(1) Each party must act in accordance with good faith and fair dealing in international trade. (2) The parties may not exclude or limit this duty'. UNIDROIT, 'Model Clauses for the Use of the UNIDROIT Principles of International Commercial Contracts' (2019), www.unidroit.org/instruments/commercial-contracts/upicc-model-clauses.

the UNFCCC Paris Agreement, and to promote a just transition to a low carbon economy.[252] Cooperation between contracting parties and third parties is also a persistent theme in TCLP's Otto's Clause for energy efficiency in chartering.[253] Remarkably, TCLP notes the binary opposition of interests and split incentives in BIMCO's former energy efficiency clauses, namely the BIMCO Slow Steaming and Virtual Arrival clauses. It notes in its Essential Guidance on Otto's Clause that these BIMCO clauses tend 'to be drafted primarily with a view to enable cost savings and to confer rights on the party paying for bunkers only as a result'.[254] As previously noted, Aiden's Clause for Fuel Reporting in Charterparties is also premised on cooperation, whereby, 'owners and charterers shall use [[best/ reasonable] endeavours to] [cooperate with a view to using]* bunker fuel with the lowest available CO_2 Emissions Factor'.[255]

Despite the principle of cooperation underpinning the CII clause, there are still some issues that the BIMCO CII Clause is yet to completely overcome. The first problem which seems difficult to resolve is that of performance warranties (see section II.B.iii). The owner will not be in breach of its performance warranties where owners have validly invoked subclause (g) to bring the vessel into compliance with the Agreed CII. Charterers cannot therefore rely on any performance warranties to try to avoid meeting their obligations under the CII Clause.[256] This is contrary to the idea of the vessel affording a competitive advantage and benefiting the charterer. Nevertheless, any 'existing warranties as to despatch, speed and consumption or to maintain the Vessel's description provided for elsewhere in the Charter Party shall continue to apply to the Charter Party'.[257]

To make a fixture more attractive, performance warranties should be represented in a reliable manner, which can be difficult with newer technologies or energy saving operational measures where data is incomplete.[258] To overcome this, TCLP's Otto's Clause for energy efficiency affords the charterer greater protection in the form of an all-encompassing fuel efficiency fee, as stated above in section II.B.iii.[259] Ultimately, the BIMCO CII Clause needs to find ways to become more attractive to charterers who have responded 'disappointingly'.[260]

[252] TCLP, Eddie's Recital (n 202).
[253] TCLP, Otto's Clause (n 197).
[254] Otto's Clause – Essential Notes and Guidance (2021), https://docs.google.com/document/d/1dYynisoHsLpDJv0QJrxLG1hCHFQvs_xFsJvZGEeE8ds/edit#.
[255] TCLP, Aiden's Clause (n 199).
[256] cl (c)(ii) BIMCO CII Clause.
[257] cl (c)(ii) BIMCO CII Clause.
[258] See Josefin Borg and Hannes von Knorring, 'Inter-organizational collaboration for energy efficiency in the maritime sector: the case of a database project' (2019) 12 *Energy Efficiency* 2201–2213.
[259] cl 2.1 of Otto's Clause.
[260] Nigel Lowry, 'Charterers face rebuke for 'disappointing' CII clause pushback' (Lloyd's List, 13 December 2022), lloydslist.maritimeintelligence.informa.com/LL1143329/Charterers-face-rebuke-for-disappointing-CII-clause-pushback#:~:text=CHARTERERS%20have%20reacted%20%E2%80%9Cdisappointingly%E2%80%9D%20to,according%20to%20some%20shipowning%20sources.

Despite this shortcoming, there are still some noteworthy innovations in BIMCO's CII clause which either mirror or improve upon some the TCLP techniques.

i. Cooperation in Good Faith

BIMCO's CII clause shares this notion of 'collaboration' that marks a pronounced theme in modern climate drafting for shipping. BIMCO's CII Clause contains a duty (subclause (b)) premised on good faith for parties to work together to:

> (i) share any findings and best practices that they may identify on potential improvements to the Vessel's energy efficiency; and
> (ii) collect, share and report on a daily basis any relevant data that may assist the monitoring and assessment of the Vessel's compliance …

This obligation is repeated where the charterer's written plan for the vessel's next voyage would fail to meet CII standards, thereby requiring the plan to be adjusted. The idea of cooperative data-sharing formed the basis of the above discussion on energy efficiency as a negotiated term (section II.B.ii).

Including energy efficiency as a negotiated term from the inception stages of the chartering process can distribute energy efficiency costs and rewards as well as provide clarity on the rights and responsibilities of the parties.[261] Overcoming the problem of split incentives requires exchanging complete information and emphasises factors such as the owner's transparency, goodwill and accurate disclosure of information.[262]

ii. Advance Warning

Most notably, BIMCO's CII Clause also makes use of an advance warning mechanism. From an environmental perspective, this new mechanism is extremely proactive as pollution cases depend on predicting future contractual breaches. Prevention is always preferable to rehabilitation and remediation in accordance with international law's 'precautionary principle'.[263] However, a prospective approach to contractual breaches is not easily reconciled with the English law doctrines on anticipatory breach. Under English law, a promisee may anticipate a promisor's breach where the promisor, 'by words or conduct, evinces an intention not to perform, or expressly declares that he is or will be unable to perform his obligations under the contract in some essential respect'.[264] Such conduct can

[261] Psarros (n 207).
[262] ibid 53.
[263] Jose Felix Pinto-Bazurco, *Brief #4: The Precautionary Principle* (International Institute for Sustainable Development Bulletin, October 2020).
[264] *Mersey Steel and Iron Co Ltd v Naylor, Benzon & Co* (1884) LR 9 App Cas 434; *Bradley v H Newsom Sons & Co* [1919] AC 16; *Brinkibon v Stahag Stahl und Stahlwarenhandels GmbH* [1980] 2 Lloyd's Rep 556 (CA).

include previous behaviour by the promisor which would allow the promisee, on a balance of probabilities, to draw an inference that the promisor is likely to commit a breach when the time arrives to perform an obligation under the contract.[265] This leaves the promisee with two choices: 1) affirm the contract and seek an order of specific performance; or 2) accept the renunciation, after which the contract will be terminated, obligations will be discharged, damages can be sought immediately,[266] and the duty to mitigate will be brought forward to the time at which the anticipatory breach was accepted.[267]

Neither remedy would be suitable in the context of energy efficiency, where the owner needs to maintain tight control over voyage emissions as the owner is ultimately responsible for compliance despite passing many of duties in respect of the vessel's CII performance to the charterer. BIMCO's 'Advance Warning' mechanism is therefore an effective way to deal with potential deviations from agreed CII performance. Under subclause (g): 'If, at any time, based on the data shared in accordance with this Clause, the trajectory of the C/P Attained CII is deviating from the Agreed CII, the Owners shall give the Charterers advance warning of this.'

If a such a deviation continues or the charterer indicates a 'reasonable likelihood' of being able to meet their CII obligations, then the owners shall request from the charterers a written plan detailing the charterer's commercial operation of the vessel upon which the owners can assess whether the agreed CII standard will be met.[268] Parties may then agree to an adjusted written plan, whilst owners are entitled to take necessary action until such time. These actions include adjusting the vessel's speed and where speed reduction would be insufficient, to require the charter to instruct the vessel in a manner that would align it with the Agreed CII.[269] Such actions will not be deemed breaches of the owner's obligations under the charterparty. Similar problems arising from anticipatory breach may still impact on how an owner proves a 'reasonable likelihood' of the charterer not meeting the CII standard.[270] Anticipatory breach provides a high standard for the justification of a 'firm inference' of breach along with the risk of early notice of termination.[271] However, as the remedy here is not one giving rise to termination rights, the causal link should not be construed strictly and should rather be interpreted as a convergence of interests in meeting the Agreed CII. Providing the charterer of notice of potential failings to meet the Agreed CII also serves to benefit the charterer.

[265] *Johnstone v Milling* (1886) 16 QBD 460 (CA) 467.

[266] *Synge v Synge* [1894] 1 QB 466; *Lep Air Services Ltd v Rolloswin Investments Ltd* [1973] AC 331, 356.

[267] *Hochster v De la Tour* (1853) 2 E & B 678.

[268] cl (g)(i)-(ii).

[269] cl (g)(iii).

[270] *Chilean Nitrate Sales Corp v Pansuiza Cie de Navigacion SA (The Hermosa)* [1982] 1 Lloyd's Rep 570, 580.

[271] ibid; *Gulf Agri Trade FZCO v Aston Agro Industrial AG* [2008] EWHC 1252 (Comm) [5].

These contractual measures are useful in innovatively projecting the likelihood of breach, and then taking corrective action so that both parties can still honour their requisite obligations. Although not recognised by English law, BIMCO's CII clause shows compatibility with the doctrine of adequate assurance, explained by Beheshti:

> Adequate assurance is a logical corollary of the doctrine of anticipatory breach of contract. Because the latter doctrine is utilised only when a purported repudiation occurs with utmost clarity, it is difficult for the promisee to meet this requirement in situations where promisors exhibit inconsistent conduct. In such situations, the doctrine of adequate assurance can be applied to determine with sufficient certainty whether the promisor intends and is able to perform the contract.[272]

The doctrine of adequate assurance is accepted by the American Uniform Commercial Code (UCC) § 2-609. Llewellyn, the legal realist who led the drafting of the UCC, was a strong proponent of designing rules which could deal with commercial parties in troubled times and believed that the law is an instrument to achieve social ends.[273] He aimed to place prevailing norms at the centre of legal rules that are 'clear, sane and safe'.[274] Therefore in order for the law to attain net-zero targets and the 'social end' of sustainability, contractual mechanisms aimed at preventing future breach are not only better for the environment but also more commercially viable for the parties concerned.

iii. Third Parties

The BIMCO CII clause also considers that charterparties operate within a chain of contracts. Customers and cargo interests with green supply chain credentials or labelling standards would serve to benefit from the CII rating associated with the transportation of cargo. This could offer a competitive advantage to shipowners and operators who could benefit from increased freight rates or simply being the carrier of choice. Developments in various sectors are showing that business customers and consumers are increasingly interested in sustainability and are even willing to pay a premium for greener services.[275] Hence TCLP drafted Levi's Clause which would allow 'a customer to exit a shipping transportation agreement without incurring exit-related liability, unless the incumbent carrier/shipper can match the "green" improvements of a competitor'.[276] Levi's Clause is drafted with

[272] Reza Beheshti, 'Anticipatory breach of contract and the necessity of adequate assurance under English law and the Uniform Commercial Code' (2018) 2 *Lloyd's Maritime and Commercial Law Quarterly* (0306–2945) 276.
[273] K Llewellyn, 'Some Realism about Realism-Responding to Dean Pound' (1931) 44 *Harvard Law Review* 1222.
[274] State of New York Law Revision Committee Report, Hearing on the Uniform Commercial Code (1954) 113.
[275] Simon Kucher & Partners, *Global Sustainability Study 2021*, www.simon-kucher.com/sites/default/files/studies/Simon-Kucher_Global_Sustainability_Study_2021.pdf.
[276] TCLP, Levi's Clause (n 201).

the intention to drive green competition and to incentivise carriers or shippers to improve their green performance. Within the clause, 'Carrier' and 'Shipper' are used interchangeably to represent the party responsible for transporting the goods and can extend to carriers, shipowners or charterers depending on the agreement entered into. This includes bills of lading as a 'contract which wholly or partially contemplates the transportation of goods by sea'.[277] Levi's Clause is in fact recommended in the drafting notes to give effect to the CII Regulation.[278]

To protect owners, there is a duty for charterers to ensure that bills of lading, waybills or other documents evidencing contracts of carriage issued by or on behalf of the owners do not impose liability on the owner as a result of CII standards. The CII clause provides for an indemnity provision in this regard.[279] A shipowner under a time charter is usually entitled, either by implication of law or by express agreement, to be indemnified by the charterer against losses arising from the owner's act of complying with the charterer's instructions.[280] In the case of the owner not following the charterer's order to bring the vessel in line with the CII standard, the owner is thus also protected under this clause from ordinary duties under the bill of lading to proceed with utmost dispatch or not to deviate.[281] Although the CII indemnity provisions for contracts of carriage offer protection to owners, this clause is premised entirely on commercial notions that customers (ie holders of a bill of lading) are only interested in speed of delivery. Incorporating the CII into a bill of lading and making the customer aware of the CII rating of the vessel could further enhance the competitive advantage underpinning Levi's Clause and would align subsequent contractual arrangements with the purpose of the CII regulation – to link the GHG emissions to the amount of cargo carried over distance travelled.

III. Conclusion

Climate clauses in charterparties are marking a green shift away from traditional common law customs to more fully embrace new climate mandates. Contrary to formalistic ideas of the preservation of freedom of contract, it is indeed freedom of contract that is advancing green norms in commercial settings. Drafting associations are therefore key contract governance actors as newly proposed climate clauses are crucial platforms for business norm creation. The TCLP has provided invaluable assistance in seeking out the contractual tools that will enable shipping actors to realise the commercial benefits of decarbonisation efforts. Specific

[277] Levi's Clause – Essential Notes and Guidance, docs.google.com/document/d/1uPstCsjKzZLDi_9FM4dAGBfNLY2qslv2I1JaywuK0gA/edit#.

[278] ibid.

[279] cl (i) of BIMCO CII Clause.

[280] *Telfair Shipping Corp v Intersea Carriers SA (The Caroline P)* [1984] 2 Lloyd's Rep 466.

[281] cl (i) of BIMCO CII Clause. BIMCO has not yet released CII clauses for incorporation of the CII standard and into bills of lading.

to shipping, industry heavyweights such as BIMCO are also key pluralistic governance actors that can contribute to full integration of net-zero targets into private transactions. Whilst BIMCO's previous environmental compliance clauses have been restricted by the traditional common law duties in charterparties, which are cemented by the prominent industry choice of standard forms, it is showing a surprising openness to the new era of climate drafting.[282] These climate clauses are pushing the envelope in respect of new cooperative norms, data-sharing schemes, preventative tools in avoiding breach, liquidated damages such as a fuel efficiency fee, and a much deeper integration of net-zero targets throughout all aspects of a contract.

Principled arguments for the recognition of implied green norms require significant evidence of the parties' intention and their interests within the factual matrix. Contract governance theory allows for a much deeper cognisance of the role of contracts, how they operate within a global decarbonisation mandate, and that contractual agreements should be interpreted accordingly – implication of green commitments *by way of law* could soon be possible if sustainability becomes customary.

[282] Rebelo (n 247).

5

Decarbonisation and Future Transactions

This book has been concerned predominantly with contractual approaches to facilitating green shipping objectives. It has focused on specific transactional relationships which characterise key sites for private law climate governance tools in commercial shipping, ie ship finance, ship building and chartering. In doing so, it applied a contract governance approach to contract theory that comprises a comprehensive and holistic approach to a diverse range of issues which impact on contract law.[1] This theoretical framework was appropriate in recognising that contract law does not exist in a vacuum, but interacts and intersects with *normative* objectives and can achieve a number of governance goals – here the divide between public and private law is viewed as artificial as private interests and public interests should not be viewed in opposition.[2] An emphasis on market transactions also goes beyond views of private authority or private regulation, as it permits a broader enquiry into how to *implement* and *enhance* the effectiveness of voluntary efforts.[3] As a specific transaction has been presented in each chapter, and conclusions drawn, it is not necessary to repeat the findings. Therefore, the main focus of this final chapter is to identify key pervasive findings for the greening of shipping contracts; and to set out future areas for contract law discourse in the green shipping mandate.

While the focus of this book is on key primary contractual relationships between a shipowner and other shipping actors to enable green shipping, there are many other transactions that will be impacted by decarbonisation standards within shipping and supply chains. Much work is still to be done in the areas of marine insurance, alternative financing schemes and smart contracts. At the moment, these areas remain open for exploration from a contract governance perspective as much remains uncertain about the risks and opportunities for such business activities.

[1] Stefan Grundmann, Florian Möslein and Karl Riesenhuber, 'Contract Governance: Dimensions in Law and Interdisciplinary Research' in *Contract Governance: Dimensions in Law and Interdisciplinary Research* (Oxford University Press, 2015) ch 1.

[2] ibid.

[3] For private environmental governance, see Michael P Vandenbergh, 'Private Environmental Governance' (2013) 99 *Cornell Law Review* 129; Martin Herberg, 'Private authority, global governance, and the law' in Gerd Winter (ed), *Multilevel Governance of Global Environmental Change: Perspectives from Science, Sociology and the Law* (Cambridge University Press, 2006) 149–78.

I. Pervasive Findings of a Contract Governance Approach to Decarbonisation

As discussed in chapter one, contracts are a useful and often neglected governance tool for the achievement of sustainable development or net-zero targets. This is particularly true of shipping, which enjoys a formalistic and well-defined set of commercial customs that are now embodied in recognised standard forms. Yet, despite the conservative nature of dry shipping, contracts require immediate recognition as a climate governance tool. As a transnational sector, international shipping cannot rely on a patchwork quilt of varying domestic standards and efforts. Furthermore, the 2023 IMO GHG Strategy is a culmination of compromises between stakeholders consisting of non-governmental bodies representing industry views and governmental delegates who are often more concerned with trade than a wider sustainable development mandate. As Tsimplis noted, albeit prior to the latest amendments to MARPOL, an IMO-compliant ship is not necessarily a non-polluting one.[4] Nevertheless, the latest MARPOL amendments also reflect the technical nature of the regulatory regime, which does not allow all actors to participate effectively, nor does it promote ratification where such rules are deemed complicated and overly restrictive. The IMO has only started to consider financial incentivisation for regulatory compliance through the CII standard which can afford ships a competitive advantage despite not having any sanctions. It is also considering market-based measures whereas the EU has already included shipping in its Emissions Trading Scheme. Yet these incentives will rely heavily on expressions of private authority and forms of self-regulation. The tools for such self-regulation are contracts and the control mechanisms that they entail. As elucidated by this book, traditional contractual mechanisms are too often isolated from external norms and struggle with the achievement of cooperative and aspirational behaviours. There are thus two major arguments put forward by this book: 1) the private agreements underpinning commercial shipping require a *normative framework* for environmental sustainability in the sector; and 2) the uptake of innovative *climate clauses* is necessary to overcome the problems associated with contractual formalism.

In respect of the first argument, private actors can also implement directional frameworks where the IMO has failed to set clear targets or has not expeditiously aligned the sector with the Paris Climate Change Agreement. This has taken place through a diversification of private ESG standards and CSR soft law policies, particularly in the area of green finance.[5] Although a common language for green shipping is desirable, various framework efforts are nevertheless helpful in enhancing the pervasiveness of 'sunstainable development' or 'net-zero' (traditionally

[4] Michael Tsimplis, 'Governance for sustainable Development' in *Environmental Norms in Maritime Law* (Edward Elgar Publishing, 2021) ch 11, 296.

[5] See ch 2 for the Green Finance Landscape for Shipping.

considered exclusively public law principles) as directional norms in the private law. In shipping, private frameworks such as the Poseidon Principles, Sea Cargo Charter, and Getting to Zero Coalition, are laying the groundwork for a shift in priorities as a matter of principle. To effectively implement these frameworks and to overcome the risks that they purport to manage, new contractual architecture is required to enforce what are often considered vague ambitions. Green terms or climate clauses should seek to achieve a desired outcome in respect of environmental behaviour and energy-efficiency.

The contractualisation of environmental principles into commercial agreements requires deep integration of green terms throughout a transaction to manage the risks associate with green transitions. Express terms provide commercial certainty, allocate obligations and achieve desired levels of enforcement to effectively reap the benefits of green financial incentives. Where express terms are ambiguous or lacking, an underpinning normative framework serves as an interpretive guide as to the green intentions of the parties. *Implied terms* for environmental sustainability, as well as trade usages or customs, should form part of the civil liability regimes governing shipping contracts. Although contract law requires greater intersection with sustainability principles more generally, the transactions that characterise shipping should eventually introduce their own set terms *implied by law* with a stronger recognition of 'types' or 'categories' of contracts that can tailor the meaning of sustainability to a particular context.[6]

The English principles of contract law which are dominant throughout shipping transactions require *modernisation* and creativity to implement a climate-aligned mandate in shipping. Although not entirely unique to English contract law, a libertarian view of the law of private obligations existing on a separate plane to principles of public environmental law can no longer prevail.[7] Present standardised forms for shipping transactions perpetuate the status quo by viewing environmental concerns purely from the perspective of allocating the responsibility for regulatory compliance. Environmental sustainability needs to be elevated to a legitimate intention which may push the boundaries of the types of contractual mechanisms and remedies traditionally available to parties.[8]

This dilemma is not unique to shipping contracts as the contractualisation of environmental sustainability is yet to be given adequate consideration in all market transactions.[9] The lack of guiding norms, customs and trade usages, which

[6] The civilian law approach is stronger than the common law at placing agreements 'within a context of certain (default) rules applicable to the pertinent "type" of transaction'; Helge Dedek, 'Art 6:102: Implied Terms' in Nils Jansen and Reinhard Zimmermann (eds), *Commentaries on European Contract Laws* (Oxford University Press, 2017) 806–07.

[7] Chs 2 and 4 discuss how new mechanisms and norms should be established in finance and chartering agreements respectively.

[8] Contractual mechanisms in this book propose potential solutions not recognised by English law, eg the doctrine of assurance and green damages.

[9] See also Cristina Poncibò, 'The Contractualisation of Environmental Sustainability' (2016) 12 *European Review of Contract Law* 339.

translate global mandates pertaining to climate change into contractual obligations are lacking, despite an English law regime which permits implication by law as well as civil law regimes which more deeply integrate a system of norms into 'types' and categories of relationships.[10] This is understandable, given traditionalist views of laissez-faire capitalism and classical contract law. Chapter one of this book noted that despite the early cognisance of the role of contract-governed financial instruments and transactions in the 'pre-crisis speed-up of securitization markets', laissez-faire contract law has remained very resilient to any attempt at embedding it a wider socio-political context.[11] This book acknowledges why the shipping sector specifically needs contract governance solutions as international shipping is an inherently transnational enterprise, yet the same contract law strategies can be applied to a number of economic sectors. Indeed, The Chancery Lane Project has developed an entire bank of sector-specific climate clauses for facilitating net-zero goals.[12]

Contract governance perspectives allow for a wide range of contractual innovations which can obtain and converge both public objectives and private intentions. There are emerging avenues of research for all types of contractual relationships to integrate sustainability norms, despite possible infringement into the comfort zones of common law jurists.[13] This is supported by a growing number of environmental risk-management strategies and the growing threat of environmental litigation. Constitutional developments are heralding a 'rights-turn' in private climate litigation,[14] meaning that human rights are enjoying increasing application in climate-related cases.[15] The horizontal application of environmental rights to private actors is opening up new doors in the Global South where post-colonial constitutions have embedded special recognition of the right to a healthy environment.[16] Shipping firms, as well as other industrial sectors, should similarly prepare for the litigation risks that fossil fuel companies are presently navigating; advances in attribution science are overcoming problems of causation and remoteness in determining the extent to which the 'polluter pays'.[17]

[10] See section 1.3.1.

[11] James 'Jay' Varellas, 'Contract law, securitization and the pre-crisis transformation of banking' (2016) in Bertram Lomfeld, Alessandro Somma and Peer Zumbansen (eds), *Reshaping Markets: Economic Governance, the Global Financial Crisis and Liberal Utopia* (Cambridge University Press, 2016) 130–31.

[12] The Chancery Lane Project, chancerylaneproject.org.

[13] Kateřina Peterková Mitkidis, 'Using Private Contracts for Climate Change Mitigation' (2018) 2 *Groningen Journal of International Law* 54.

[14] Pia Rebelo and Xavier Rebelo, 'Rights-Based Climate Change Litigation Against Private Actors' in Kim Bouwer et al (eds), *Climate Litigation and Justice in Africa* (Bristol University Press, 2024) 187–219.

[15] Geetanjali Ganguly, Joana Setzer and Veerle Heyvaert, 'If at First you don't Succeed: Suing Corporations for Climate Change' (2018) 38 *Oxford Journal of Legal Studies* 841.

[16] Joana Setzer and Rebecca Byrnes, *Global trends in climate change litigation: 2023 snapshot* (Grantham Research Institute on Climate Change and the Environment and Centre for Climate Change Economics and Policy, London School of Economics and Political Science).

[17] Mary Kathryn Nagle, 'Tracing the Origins of Fairly Traceable: The Black Hole of Private Climate Change Litigation' (2010) 85 *Tulsa Law Review* 477.

There are also mounting pressures from a corporate governance perspective as commitments to economic, social and environmental values are requiring express terms whilst more parties are recognising mutually observed trade usages.[18] It is therefore arguable that existing regimes governing commercial contracts (not just the Hague-Visby Rules or the Rotterdam Rules where applicable) should be revisited for the establishment of recognised implied terms, customs or trade usages involving aspects of sustainable development. This could include critiques of the UNIDROIT Principles, the Convention on Contracts for the International Sale of Goods,[19] international law customs more generally and domestic regimes.

Consumer preference and pressure has been noted by Eftestøl-Wilhelmsson and Sankari, who have applied the concept of 'nudging' to carriage of goods by sea.[20] These authors argue that information is key to changing behaviour and increasing pro-environmental choices, but choice architecture or labelling standards are yet to account for the maritime transport emission costs that contribute to a product's overall 'greenness'. Adequate mechanisms are not yet in place to ensure that transport emission data reaches the buyers of transport services and the consumers of products, which could ultimately breach consumer rights and affect transactional decisions. Effective nudging requires the implementation of disclosure requirements for the achievement of transparency and a consumer's right to such information. One suggestion is that an information requirement be integrated into a proposed EU electronic transport document, whilst protecting a consumer's right to such information could fall under the Unfair Commercial Practices Directive (UCPD).[21]

II. Marine Insurance

A socio-techno regime change within the shipping sector comes with a number of risks that have been the focus of green finance taxonomy initiatives.[22] Financial frameworks, whether regulatory or voluntary, are largely concerned with the risks surrounding greenwashing, non-compliance and expanding avenues for climate litigation. Yet, green finance frameworks cannot account for all climate risks and the liability accruing to such risks will become the endeavour of marine insurers. Marine insurance is entirely concerned with liability arising from marine losses, ie 'the losses incident to the marine adventure'.[23] Generally, these have been

[18] See OECD Guidelines for Multinational Enterprises (2011); UN Global Compact Office and Business for Social Responsibility, Supply Chain Sustainability: A Practical Guide for Continuous Improvement (2010); Mitkidis (n 13).

[19] Vienna, 11 April 1980.

[20] Ellen Eftestøl-Wilhelmsson and Suvi Sankari, 'Nudging a behavioural change in maritime carriage of goods – the role of information' in Jason Chuah (ed), *Research Handbook on Maritime Law and Regulation* (Edward Elgar Publishing, 2019) 170.

[21] ibid 183.

[22] These are expanded upon in ch 2.

[23] Marine Insurance Act 1906 (MIA 1906), s 1.

restricted to an understanding of 'maritime perils' which is required to calculate the 'premium' of the marine insurance policy, as underwriters will have to estimate the degree of risk a vessel faces taking into account the amount of indemnity that will need to be paid out if that risk materialises.[24] New fuels and technologies present a number of risks for which there is presently very limited data. Thus far, insurers are exploring private governance tools to collect necessary data and pave a way forward on managing the risks associated with a green transition.

A. Poseidon Principles for Marine Insurance

To help collect data and an understanding of the risks associated with decarbonising shipping, the Poseidon Principles for Marine Insurance (PPMI) were launched in December 2021, 18 months after the release of the equivalent Poseidon Principles for Financial Institutions (PPFI).[25] Not dissimilar to the original PPFI, the PPMI follow a system of assessment and disclosure for assurance providers with hull and machinery (H&M) shipping. Signatories will annually measure carbon intensity and assess climate alignment of their H&N portfolio using appropriate methodologies established by the PPMI. There are four principles of the PPMI, each requiring certain things from signatories:[26]

(1) Assessment of Climate Alignment: Climate alignment is framed within the existing IMO regulatory framework and targets with the same methodology employed by the CII measure. This is the Annual Efficiency Ratio (AER),[27] based on available and existing data from the IMO DCS. Climate alignment is the degree to which a vessel, H&M policy or portfolio is aligned with one of the two trajectories: 1) IMO trajectory: 50 per cent CO_2 reduction in absolute carbon emissions by 2050; and 2) Paris Agreement trajectory: 100 per cent CO_2 reduction in absolute carbon emissions by 2050.[28] The IMO trajectory provided by the PPMI still reflects the 2018 GHG Reduction Strategy as this technical guidance was released just two months prior to the IMO's 2023 Revised GHG Strategy.

(2) Accountability: There are specific accountability requirements for relevant data sources and service providers. It is preferred that data is collected from and that calculations are made by recognised organisations (preferred pathway), although it is allowed that data is collected from the shipowner itself and calculated by the signatory (allowed pathway).[29]

[24] Christopher Kingston, 'Marine Insurance in Britain and America, 1720–1844: A Comparative Institutional Analysis' (2007) 67 *The Journal of Economic History* 379, 383.

[25] Poseidon Principles for Marine Insurance (PPMI), www.poseidonprinciples.org/insurance/#about.

[26] PPMI, Technical Guidance (Version 1.1, May 2023), www.poseidonprinciples.org/insurance/wp-content/uploads/2021/12/Poseidon-Principles-for-Marine-Insurance-Technical-Guidance.pdf.

[27] As discussed in ch 2, this uses the parameters of fuel consumption, distance travelled and deadweight at maximum summer draught (DWT).

[28] PPMI Technical Guidance (n 26) 18–31.

[29] ibid 35.

(3) Enforcement: This is done through contractual enforcement in all business activities using standardised covenant clauses.[30]
(4) Transparency: This requires the signatory to declare publicly that it is a signatory to the PPMI; to report annual climate alignment of its H&M portfolio to the secretariat of the PPMI; to publish the overall climate alignment of its H&M portfolio in relevant institutional reports.[31]

Detailed technical guidance is provided for each principle, and like the PPFI, the PPMI will likely improve over time as enforcement is tightened. An increased attention on enforcement will be necessary as the first PPMI annual report published in January of 2023 (using data collected in 2021) showed that, on average, signatories' H&M emissions were 12.7 per cent higher than the IMO-aligned trajectory target and 20.8 per cent higher than a Paris Agreement-aligned trajectory.[32] At present the main contractual enforcement mechanism is the PPMI standard covenant clause, that provides:[33]

> It is a requirement that any and all Assured(s) hereon shall supply or procure, without undue delay, the supply to the Claims Leader the data and/or information require to comply with its obligations under the PPMI in respect of any/all Ship(s) insured by this policy on 01 October each year.

This is coupled with obligations on the part of the signatory to restrict the use of such data to compliance with the PPMI and its own business purposes; as well as to not publish PPMI Data or derivatives in a way that 'makes either ships or clients identifiable'. The signatory is authorised to share PPMI data with calculation providers and other insurers subscribing to the policy who are also signatories to the PPMI.

As far as private governance tools are concerned, this is a step in the right direction towards achieving decarbonisation but much remains unclear about the effectiveness of the contractual mechanism employed. If the assured fails to provide such data, a remedy is not provided. Would the assured choose to treat this as a breach of condition or the right to avoid insurance for material non-disclosure or misrepresentation? There are also commercial remedies such as choosing to not renew a policy. The possibility of avoiding insurance for material non-disclosure or misrepresentation arose in *Drake Insurance plc v Provident Insurance plc*[34] where the Court of First Instance found that an insurer could avoid a policy if grounds

[30] ibid 46.
[31] ibid 48–49.
[32] PPMI Annual Disclosure Report 2022 (January 2023), www.poseidonprinciples.org/insurance/wp-content/uploads/2023/01/Poseidon-Principles-for-Marine-Insurance-Annual-Disclosure-Report-2022.pdf; see also Neil Henderson, 'Keeping a hand on the tiller: the Poseidon Principles for Marine Insurance' (23 May 2023) Maritime Risk International (© Maritime Insights & Intelligence Limited).
[33] PPMI Standard Covenant Clause (updated October 2023), www.poseidonprinciples.org/insurance/wp-content/uploads/2023/10/PPMI-Standard-clause_October-23_v2.pdf.
[34] *Drake Insurance plc v.Provident Insurance plc* [2003] EWCA Civ 1934.

exist to do so and such a right is effective immediately upon communication to the assured.[35] The two main questions for the court of appeal were:

(i) Whether the assured was entitled to avoid the policy irrespective of any argument that could be raised as a matter of good faith.
(ii) Whether the right to avoid the policy was limited by the doctrine of good faith.

In respect of the first issue, it was accepted that there was a material non-disclosure on the part of the assured, yet the Court still had to consider whether knowledge of the information withheld would have induced the actual underwriter to act differently.[36] On the facts, it was found that there was no such inducement in entering into the contract or at its renewal. The burden of proof was on the insurer alleging misrepresentation to show that they would have acted differently if they knew about the disclosure.[37] On the second issue, the majority of the Appeal Court (Lord Justices Rix and Clarke) did not wish to make a decision as it did not matter on the outcome of the first issue.[38] However, if the insurer does have the right to avoid the contract on the basis of a material non-disclosure, then such a right is indeed limited by the doctrine of good faith.[39]

This is hard to reconcile with the outcome of *Brotherton v Aseguradora Colseguros SA*[40] whereby Lord Justice Mance stated that, 'rescission in the general law of contract … is not generally subject to any requirement of good faith or conscionability'. Green refers to this as the 'no-hindsight' approach that involves looking at the circumstances when the risk was accepted.[41] The insurer is not precluded from maintaining its exercise of right to avoid by receiving subsequent information. *Brotherton* was dismissive of the alternative approach raised by *The Grecia Express*[42] that Green refers to as the 'hindsight test – reopening avoidance'.[43] This refers to the outcome that avoidance would be unjust and unconscionable if the insured were allowed to maintain the right to avoid if it is later proved that the disclosure would have made no difference to the insured. However, it is important to keep in mind that *Brotherton* was decided on different facts, where the insurers sought to rely on matters that occurred after the contract of reinsurance and such information was not available at the time of contracting. In *Drake Insurance*, the Court of Appeal was prepared to allow an insured to show, subsequent to avoidance being invoked, that the non-disclosure was not material and did not induce the insurers.

[35] [2003] Lloyd's Rep LR 781, Mr Justice Moore-Bick at 788.
[36] Relying on *Pan Atlantic Insurance Co Ltd v Pine Top Insurance Co Ltd* (1995) IAC 501.
[37] *Drake Insurance* (n 34) [64] (Lord Justice Rix).
[38] ibid [79].
[39] ibid [85].
[40] [2003] Lloyd's Rep LR 746.
[41] Alison Green, 'Drake Insurance Plc v. Provident Insurance Plc' (British Insurance Law Association), bila.org.uk/wp-content/uploads/old/4ff4163e752fd1.62779926.pdf.
[42] *Strive Shipping Corporation v Hellenic Mutual War Risks Association, (The Grecia Express)* [2002] 2 Lloyd's Rep 88.
[43] Green (n 41).

What this means for PPMI signatories is that non-disclosure by clients does not automatically sustain the right to avoid under English common law. This is particularly true when a signatory cannot present evidence of inducement. At this early stage in the PPMI's uptake by the wider industry, it seems unlikely that carbon data would significantly impact the underwriter's decisions in insuring a shipowner or setting a premium. This may change as insurers adopt tightening ESG standards and sustainability mandates.

B. The Nordic Marine Insurance Plan

A clear indication that decarbonisation is now a factor in marine insurance is the latest amendment to the Nordic Marine Insurance Plan 2013, version 2023.[44] Rules governing the assured's choice of repair yard in Chapter 12 of the Plan have been amended to include disqualification of shipyard if it has poor performance in environmental and social governance.[45] There is also a built-in incentive for the assured to choose a yard with low CO_2 emissions, as the assured can recover the costs of taking such a decision if that specific yard does not offer the lowest adjusted tender but has advantageous emissions savings.[46] The use of express clauses that mention CO_2 emissions data and decarbonisation performance, such as the PPMI's standard covenant clause and the Nordic Plan's Clause 12-12 respectively, do indeed help to recognise decarbonisation targets as part of the objective intentions of the parties concerned. In particular, the PPMI offers a significant normative vision for the sector to meet decarbonisation trajectories. Whether this will impact on the construction of other duties in insurance policies remains to be seen.

The idea that the PPMI holds weight in interpreting other duties, was not considered when Gard Marine & Energy Limited as well as several underinsurance companies, were successful in arguing that an assured is obliged to apply for dispensation from emission regulations where it would keep the cost of repairs down. This was despite Gard Marine & Energy being proud publishers of their commitment to the PPMI, albeit they were not signatories at the time the dispute arose.[47] In *Champion Express*, a landmark case by the Norwegian Supreme Court, the Court ruled that the contractual duty of loyalty applies to marine insurance.[48] As such, the shipowners were obliged to make wholehearted efforts to obtain flag state waivers from regulations which would make repairs more costly and therefore increase the insurance cover. Following the breakdown of the Champion Express tanker due to significant engine failure in the Indian Ocean in 2018, a

[44] The Nordic Association of Marine Insurers, The Nordic Marine Insurance Plan of 2013, Version 2023, www.nordicplan.org/The-Plan.

[45] cl 12-12(3), see extended commentary.

[46] cl 12-12(2).

[47] Gard, 'Gard signs Poseidon Principles for Marine Insurance' (12 January 2022), www.gard.no/web/news/article?p_document_id=32803930.

[48] LA-2021-97236-4 *Champion Express*.

significant claim for repairs arose. There were two proposed methods of repair: 1) replacing the parts; or 2) installing a new engine. The problem with the latter was that a replacement engine would only fulfil the IMO's Tier II requirements for NOx emissions and not Tier III requirements for new vessels. A marine diesel engine that is installed on a ship constructed on or after certain dates and operating specific ECAs shall comply with the Tier III NOx standard.[49]

In accordance with the Nordic Plan 2013, Clause 11-3, the assured may claim for Constructive Total Loss (CTL), ie condemnation, if repair costs will amount to at least 80 per cent of the insurable value according to hull insurance, or the value of the vessel after repairs if the latter is higher than the insurable value according to the hull insurance. The installation of a new engine would require compliance with Tier III NOx standards, which can be met through the installation of a NOx scrubber.[50] The owners of Champion Express argued that the installation of a NOx scrubber would increase costs beyond the 80 per cent of the insurable value of the vessel. However, the insurer argued that the owner should have applied to the flag state authority for dispensation from the relevant NOx regulations as part of its duty of loyalty to mitigate its losses. The Court of Appeal found that the contractual duty of loyalty obliges the assured to make wholehearted efforts to obtain such waivers from public regulations, particularly where such waivers are decisive to calculating CTL. The Court was not satisfied that the owner had done so and upon discovery, found that: 'The correspondence with the [flag state] clearly indicates that the owners wanted it to appear as if they had applied, whilst in reality, they wanted the application to be dismissed.'[51]

Although nitrous oxides do not garner as much attention as CO_2 emissions, they are a significant greenhouse gas. The contractual duty of loyalty was therefore interpreted as one of purely financial considerations and the mitigation of costs. This stands in stark contrast to the insurer's outspoken commitments to a decarbonisation trajectory. It is also reflective of the larger inadequacies of contract law in recognising anything other than commercial efficacy norms.

C. Environmental Principles for Marine Insurance in English Law

The approach of English law to environmental consideration for repairs in calculating CTL is illustrated in the *Renos* case.[52] Here, the vessel was damaged by fire

[49] Reg 13 of MARPOL, NOx Technical Code 2008 (resolution MEPC.177(58) as amended by resolution MEPC.251.(66)).

[50] Reg 13.2.2 of MARPOL, requirements adopted at MEPC.230(65).

[51] Anders W Færden, Halvard Saue and Oskar Otterstrøm, 'Insurers prevail in landmark – Nordic Plan CTL judgment' (Wikborg Rein, Newsletter 31 May 2023), www.wr.no/en/news/insurers-prevail-in-landmark-nordic-plan-ctl-judgment.

[52] *Sveriges Angfartygs Assurans Forening (The Swedish Club) and others v Connect Shipping Inc and another* ('*Renos*') [2019] UKSC 29.

off the Red Sea coast on 23 August 2012, resulting in the vessel losing main engine power and requiring salvage assistance. Salvors were appointed under a Lloyd's Open Form (LOF) with Special Compensation P&I Clause (SCOPIC). SCOPIC is an optional clause under the LOF which, if invoked, provides remuneration that is only payable insofar as it exceeds the conventional salvage award (ie the Article 13 H&M Risk cover).[53] Having received estimates for the cost of repairs, salvage costs including SCOPIC charges, the assured claimed a CTL. The insurers argued that SCOPIC costs are not included in repair costs for the purposes of calculating CTL. Both the High Court and the Court of Appeal found that the vessel was a CTL, on the basis that SCOPIC costs were included, therefore it was unnecessary to make findings as to the other alleged costs of recovery and repair. However, the Supreme Court found that SCOPIC costs were not included in the CTL calculation. The UK Supreme Court made some significant remarks on the purpose of salvage and the inclusion of certain items in 'costs of repairing the damage' under section 60(2)(ii) of the Marine Insurance Act (MIA).[54]

The Supreme Court found that SCOPIC clauses are P&I clauses aimed at preventing environmental damage.[55] Lord Sumption opined at [25]:

> The objective purpose of SCOPIC charges was different. It was not to enable the ship to be repaired, but to protect an entirely distinct interest of the shipowner, namely his potential liability for environmental pollution. That purpose has nothing to do with the subject-matter insured, namely the hull. It was no part of the measure of the damage to the ship, and had nothing to do with the possibility of repairing her. The point may be tested by asking what the position would have been if the shipowner, instead of making a single agreement with salvors to salve the ship and prevent or minimise environmental damage, had contracted with one enterprise to salve the ship and another to put floating booms around her with a view to preventing or minimising environmental damage.

The Supreme Court was not willing to accept the argument of the assured that a prudent owner would have contracted for both H&M liability and P&I liability and that protecting the environment is a natural corollary of the salvage endeavour. The Supreme Court found that the two types of coverage are distinctive and followed the precedent of the *Angel* that section 6(2)(ii) of the MIA assumes that the prudent shipowner is only interested in the comparison between the cost of repair and the repaired value.[56] The problem with the Supreme Court's stark declaration that protection of the environment should not be considered as 'repair costs', is somewhat artificial in respect of the commercial realities of salvage. The fairness of this outcome to owners seems dubious as SCOPIC is commonly employed and owners would surely expect SCOPIC compensation to be included in a reckoning of whether the vessel is 'financially worth saving'.[57]

[53] See Art 13 of the Salvage Convention 1989.
[54] *Renos* (n 52) [23].
[55] ibid [25].
[56] ibid [26], applying *Angel v Merchants' Marine Insurance Co* [1903] 1 KB 811.
[57] Jeffrey Thomson, 'Constructive Total Loss – The Diminishing Importance of the Prudent Uninsured Owner' (2019) *Lloyd's Maritime and Commercial Law Quarterly* 489, 496.

Given the Supreme Court's ruling, it is clear why the court in the Norwegian case of the *Champion Express* would cite *Renos* in arriving at the inference that the contractual duty of loyalty is underpinned by commercial efficacy and should not be motivated by environmental considerations and emissions regulations. *Renos* has made it quite clear that English law would not permit environmental costs to be factored into a CTL calculation. From the insurer's perspective, if an assured wants a cleaner vessel for commercial reasons, it is unlikely that the insurer would want to lay the cost of achieving this because, fortuitously, the ship has suffered some insured damage. Interestingly, in the *Champion Express*, this was not the line of argument. It was never contested that a NOx scrubber should form part of the reasonable repairs, rather that the assured had a duty to apply for dispensation from MARPOL requirements to keep costs of repair lower where possible.

The fact that a contractual duty can be interpreted as requiring evasion of environmental law is deeply problematic from a sustainability perspective. In *Champion Express*, the contractual duty of loyalty on the part of the assured arguably requires a modernised construction. Given that an insurer has published its commitment to the PPMI, the decarbonisation mandate should be considered as part of the 'factual matrix' in which such a duty is placed, at least for matters arising following the publication of such a commitment.[58] In *Bank of Credit and Commerce International SA v Ali*,[59] Lord Hoffmann considered the factual matrix as 'anything which a reasonable man would have regarded as relevant'. This could also include relevant background facts and the state of the law. As the PPMI gain prominence and widescale acceptance, H&M insurers may have to 'green' their understanding and interpretation of contractual duties and to provide for appropriate mechanisms where necessary. This is not only to further decarbonisation trajectory commitments, but to also protect themselves from the mounting risk of greenwashing their own portfolios. More stringent contractual remedies for non-disclosure on emissions data would be a first step in avoiding greenwashing exposure. This is something that the PPMI standard covenant clause does not yet achieve, while *Drake Insurance* illustrates that the threshold for 'inducement' would have to be met in proving contractual misrepresentation.

D. Artic Shipping and Insurance

Arctic shipping is starting to emerge as a key research area given the noticeable impacts of climate change. September sea ice has diminished by 43 per cent from 1971 to 2019 while sea ice thickness decreased by two metres at the end of the melt

[58] *Investors Compensation Scheme Ltd v West Bromwich Building Society* [1998] 1 WLR 896 at 912–913 per Lord Hoffmann; *Marley v Rawlings* [2014] UKSC 2.

[59] [2001] UKHL 8, [2002] 1 AC 251 [39].

season from 1958 to 2018.[60] Diminishing ice shelves are allowing for new navigable passages which will facilitate increasing plans for natural resource exploitation,[61] including fishing, mining and hydrocarbon exploration.[62] While there are clearly strong climatological and sustainable development arguments against increasing offshore oil and gas extraction in the polar region,[63] the war between Russia and Ukraine has reinvigorated the appeal of fossil fuels as a matter of European energy security.[64] Setting aside the moral appropriateness of granting gas and oil exploration licences, it remains a reality that the ice is melting and new arctic shipping routes will be utilised to provide connections between major world economies and for shorter and more cost-effective voyages.[65] Although arctic shipping still accounts for a relatively insignificant percentage of maritime trade flows, risk governance of arctic shipping remains a major issue.[66] To assist with risk management, the marine insurance sector was instrumental in the development of the International Code for Ships Operating in Polar Waters (Polar Code) which came into force on 1 January 2017.[67]

The Polar Code was necessitated by the need for a risk-based and holistic approach to mitigating the risks of polar shipping to acceptable levels, to provide uniformity between differing national and regional regulations governing polar shipping,[68] and to supplement the already mandatory conventions.[69] Prior to its enactment, safety and environmental discharges were dealt with under the International Convention for Safety of Life at Sea (SOLAS);[70] the International

[60] Ronald Kwok, 'Arctic sea ice thickness, volume, and multiyear ice coverage: losses and coupled variability (1958–2018)' (2018) 13 *Environmental Research Letters* 105005.

[61] Proshanto K Mukherjee and Huiru Liu, 'Legal Regime of Marine Insurance in Arctic Shipping: Safety and Environmental Implications' in Lawrence P Hildebrand et al (eds), *Sustainable Shipping in a Changing Arctic* (Springer, 2018) 192.

[62] Ingvild Ulrikke Jakobsen and Elise Johansen, 'Efforts of the Arctic Council to Protect Sensitive Arctic High Sea Areas from the Impact of Shipping' (2016) *Scandinavian Institute of Maritime Law* MarIus number 471, 7.

[63] Floris Goerlandt and Ronald Pelot, 'An Exploratory Application of the International Risk Governance Council's Risk Governance Framework to Shipping Risks in the Canadian Arctic' in Aldo Chircop et al (eds), *Governance of Arctic Shipping: Rethinking Risk, Human Impacts and Regulation* (Springer Polar, 2020) 16.

[64] Kari Lundgren, 'Arctic Oil drilling plans revived in Norway as priorities change' (Bloomberg, May 2023), www.bloomberg.com/news/articles/2023-05-03/arctic-oil-drilling-plans-revived-in-norway-as-priorities-change?leadSource=uverify%20wall.

[65] Frédéric Lasserre et al, 'Polar seaways? Maritime transport in the Arctic: An analysis of shipowners' intentions' (2016) 57 *Journal of Transport Geography* 105.

[66] Aldo Chircop et al (eds), *Governance of Arctic Shipping: Rethinking Risk, Human Impacts and Regulation* (Springer Polar, 2020).

[67] International Code for Ships Operating in Polar Waters (Polar Code), (Safety-related provisions) (21 November 2014), IMO Resolution MSC.385 (94) (Environment-related provisions) (15 May 2015), IMO Resolution MEPC. 264(68).

[68] Anish Arvind Hebbar et al 'The IMO Regulatory Framework for Arctic Shipping: Risk Perspectives and Goal-Based Pathways' in Aldo Chircop et al (eds), *Governance of Arctic Shipping: Rethinking Risk, Human Impacts and Regulation* (Springer Polar, 2021) 235.

[69] Polar Code, preamble 2.

[70] International Convention for the Safety of Life at Sea (adopted, 1 November 1974, entered into force 25 May 1980) 1184 UNTS 2.

Convention on Standards of Training, Certification and Watchkeeping for Seafarers (STCW);[71] and the International Convention for the Prevention of Pollution from Ships 73/78 (MARPOL), respectively.[72] The Polar code amended the SOLAS by the addition of new chapter XIV, amended Annexes I, II, IV and V of MARPOL, and Chapter V regulation 4 of the STCW Convention and STCW Code.[73]

The Polar Code is divided into two parts: the first part deals with safety issues while the second deals with pollution issues[74] – both seek to address risks inherent in arctic waters that are not adequately mitigated by other conventions of the IMO.[75] Pollution matters have been integrated into MARPOL in five chapters covering pollution by oil, pollution by noxious liquid substances in bulk, pollution by sewage, pollution by harmful substances carried by sea in packaged form, and pollution by garbage from ships. While chapters one and two apply a 'zero-tolerance approach'[76] with respect to pollution by oil and noxious liquid substances in bulk, chapters four and five do not. Discharge of sewage and garbage are permissible when in accordance with relevant MARPOL regulations and further requirements of the Code. Harmful substances carried by sea in packaged form do not have any additional requirements under the Code, the rationale being that in relation to pollution from packaged harmful substances, the pollution impacts are the same in arctic waters as they are in normal waters.[77]

The problem with the Polar Code in relation to decarbonisation is that it does not cover airborne emissions. Although the ordinary EEXI and CII provisions would apply to all applicable ships, there is no complete ban on HFOs in the Arctic region. While Regulation 43 of MARPOL Annex I has banned the carriage of HFO as cargo, ballast or carriage and use as fuel in the Antarctic since 2011, there is no equivalent ban in the Arctic. The hazards posed by HFO in the Arctic region have not been resolved by the Polar Code and black carbon remains a major hindrance to global decarbonisation efforts. Black carbon and other short-lived climate pollutants such as methane, fluorinated gases including hydrofluorocarbons are far more potent for their global warming potential than CO_2.[78] Black carbon absorbs heat and also falls out of the sky in a matter of weeks, settling on the snow, heating the ice surface and further hampering the reflective capacity of

[71] International Convention on Standards of Training, Certification and Watchkeeping for Seafarers (adopted, 7 July 1978, entered into force 28 April 1984) 1361 UNTS 2.

[72] International Convention for the Prevention of Pollution from Ships (adopted, 2 November 1973, entered into force 2 October 1983) 1340 UNTS 184.

[73] Aldo Chircop, 'Canada and the Polar Code: Balancing Unilateralism and Multilateralism in the Regulation of Arctic Shipping' (2018) 51 *Revue Belge de Droit International* 380, 392–93.

[74] Polar Code, introduction 1.

[75] ibid.

[76] Jiayu Bai, 'The IMO Polar Code: The Emerging Rules of Arctic Shipping Governance' (2015) 30 *The International Journal of Marine and Coastal Law* 674, 682.

[77] ibid 683.

[78] Steven Messner, 'Future arctic shipping, black carbon emissions, and climate change' in Adolf KY Ng, Jason Monios and Changmin Jiang (eds), *Maritime Transport and Regional Sustainability* (Elsevier Inc, 2020) 195.

the ice. On the other hand, some may argue that the shortened routes enabled by arctic shipping could decrease emissions,[79] yet this argument does not account for the fact that opening up new trade routes will inevitably increase economic activity overall.

At present, climate risks are not dealt with by the Polar Code and the insurance sector does not have many tools for projecting the future implications of underwriting ships with voyages in the arctic region. For H&M insurers, the Polar Code approaches risk management by focusing on technical parameters and crew training.[80] A vessel engaging in arctic shipping must comply with the Code's structural and other documentation requirements. The Polar Ship Certificate serves as prima facie evidence of such compliance and sets limitations for the operation of the ship in accordance with the class of the ship. Mandatory training and certification for crew is set out through the amendments to the STCW Convention and Code.[81] For P&I insurance, although covering different risks, obtaining full H&M cover is a condition precedent to obtaining a P&I cover for arctic shipping.[82] Neither H&M nor P&I risk management tools are adequate to allow insurers to underwrite arctic maritime transport at present. Given the very recent prospect of arctic shipping, P&I clubs are still grappling with traditional risks occurring in the sensitive arctic waters such as oil spillage,[83] toxic missions, habitat destruction, biofouling, noise pollution, and ecosystem disruption.[84] Third-party claims can also involve disturbances to local fishing trade and hunting practices, the preservation of natural environments and archaeological sites, as well as the additional pressure placed on local infrastructure due to the increased presence of other people.[85]

Increased shipping in the arctic region is arguably not consistent with the Paris Accords without drastic technological overhauls to vessels and shipping infrastructure. Marine insurers with commitments to the PPMI should be extra-cautious in considering whether their policies will permit arctic voyages. It is hard to develop contractual tools for risk mitigation when so much remains uncertain about arctic shipping risks. Contract governance approaches will benefit from the

[79] Dimitrios Theocharis et al, 'Arctic shipping: A systematic literature review of comparative studies' (2018) 69 *Journal of Transport Geography* 112–28.

[80] Laurent Fedi, Olivier Faury and Daria Gritsenko, 'The impact of the Polar Code on risk mitigation in Arctic waters: a "toolbox" for underwriters?' (2018) 45 *Maritime Policy & Management* 478, 485.

[81] Guidance on methodologies for assessing operational capabilities and limitations in ice, IMO Doc. MSC.1/Circ.1519 (6 June), Appendix: Polar Operational Limit Assessment Risk Indexing System (POLARIS).

[82] Diana L Torrens, 'Marine Insurance for the Northern Sea Route: Pilot Study' *INSROP Working Paper* IV.3.3, NO 1-1994, 133.

[83] Jiayu Bai and Aldo Chircop, 'The Regulation of Heavy Fuel Oil in Arctic Shipping: Interests, Measures, and Impacts' in Aldo Chircop et al (eds), *Governance of Arctic Shipping: Rethinking Risk, Human Impacts and Regulation* (Springer Polar, 2020) 275.

[84] Lambert Joseph et al, 'A techno-economic environmental cost model for Arctic shipping' (2021) 151 Transportation Research Part A 28–51.

[85] Henry Huntington et al, 'Effects of Arctic commercial shipping on environments and communities: context, governance, priorities' (2023) 118 Transportation Research Part D: Transport and Environment 103731.

sector's experience of the risks managed by green finance frameworks and energy efficiency regulatory requirements. However, contract governance mandates the cooperation of all actors in effectively providing for a pluralistic solution that balances sustainability agendas.

III. Non-traditional Ship Financing

Chapter two of this book discussed how ship finance is generally governed by traditional ship loan agreements – an arrangement whereby finance is advanced from the bank to the shipowner, usually with an undertaking to register a first priority mortgage over the vessel in favour of the lender/bank.[86] As such, LMA forms have become popular standardised agreements for ship finance and green shipping will likely make increased use of LMA green loan and sustainability-linked loan documentation. However, there remain a plethora of alternative financing mechanisms that also require green contractual mechanisms to safeguard similar interests. In particular, sale-and-leaseback arrangements have increased in popularity. This is an agreement whereby the original shipowning company sells a vessel to another company, and then leases it back from them. The original shipowner then becomes a lessee and the new buyer a lessor with the benefit that the shipowning company has raised cash and freed up liquidity.[87] Whilst loan agreements are easy to standardise as most loans contain similar mechanisms, leases generally vary from one lease to another. Given the shipping sector's preference for standardisation, the rise of ship leases has corresponded with an uptake of Japanese Operating Leases with Call Option (JOLCO) transactions, which were historically used for the aviation sector.[88] To assist the industry, BIMCO has produced a standardised term sheet called the SHIPLEASE 2020[89] based on its earlier loan term sheets (SHIPTERM and SHIPTERM S).

The SHIPLEASE term sheet defines the lease-back transaction as: 'The Seller to sell the Vessel to the Lessor and the Lessor to purchase the Vessel from the Seller, and the Charterer to charter the Vessel from the Lessor'.[90] The nature of the charter agreement is a bareboat charter on an 'as is where is' basis and on the terms and conditions set out in the Bareboat Charter for which hire shall be paid on a 'hell or high water' basis.[91] The charterer also has a purchase option to repurchase the vessel from the lessor.[92] There are no environmental covenants within the term

[86] *Citibank NA v Hobbs, Savill & Co (The Panglobal Friendship)* [1978] 1 Lloyd's Rep 368, 371.

[87] Guy Cooper and Jacari Brimmer-Landy, 'Alternative Financing in the Shipping Industry' (Conveyers, September 2021), www.conyers.com/publications/view/alternative-financing-in-the-shipping-industry.

[88] ibid.

[89] BIMCO, SHIPLEASE 2020, www.bimco.org/contracts-and-clauses/bimco-contracts/shiplease.

[90] Part II, cl 1 of SHIPLEASE.

[91] Part II, cls 5 and 6 of SHIPLEASE.

[92] Part II, cl 10 of SHIPLEASE.

sheet, yet the Bareboat Charter could present a site for ordinary environmental compliance provisions. Bareboat charters have not been considered fully in this book as chapter three deals exclusively with voyage charters and time charters. However, a bareboat charter is quite straightforward and the charterer would assume the responsibilities of the owner in respect of compliance, and 'structural changes or new equipment becoming necessary for the continued operation of the Vessel by reason of new class requirements or by compulsory legislation … shall be for the Charterers' account'.[93] Owners retain the right to inspect the vessel at any time after giving reasonable notice, including inspection of class records, log books, certificates, maintenance and other records.[94] Under the SHIPLEASE, it is the responsibility of the charterer to keep the vessel insured in terms of H&M, P&I and war risks including blocking and trapping.[95]

The charterer and the lessor would have to consider their own respective interests in meeting any decarbonisation targets that either apply from a regulatory perspective or from a voluntary commitment. The charterer would have to ensure that both the IMO's EEXI and CII standard is met, as well as any regional requirements such as the EU ETS. Under EU law, the bareboat charterer can be responsible for compliance with both the ETS and MRV in respect of a vessel if it has accepted to assume ISM Code responsibilities in respect of that vessel.[96] Parties may want to make explicit mention of relevant IMO and regional regulations that apply to the vessel with clear indications that the responsibility rests with the Charter, yet further consideration would involve whether the lessor has a more ambitious decarbonisation mandate and what sort of activities the vessel can be used for. It is also important to know that the lessor could very well have obtained green finance for the purchase of the vessel and both the shiplease form and accompanying bareboat charter should correspond to any environmental obligations in the green loan agreement.

Alternative financing mechanisms are also emerging from new digital innovation. Sustainable Supply Chains (SSCs) have shown how digital platforms can increase sustainability performance. These platforms have been leveraged in certain ways to manage the economic, social and environmental impacts of companies (state or non-state) in a way which holistically considers the lifecycle of goods and services.[97] Smart contracts are being widely used in supply chains to solve these critical issues and enhance trust between parties.[98] New approaches

[93] cl 13(b)(ii) of the BARECON 2017 Standard Bareboat Charter Party.
[94] cl 14 of the BARECON 2017.
[95] Part II, cl 15 of the SHIPLEASE.
[96] Read Art 3(gb) with Art 3(w) of Directive 2003/87/EC; see ch 4, section I.B.iii.
[97] Pia Rebelo, 'Sustainable Supply Chain Finance: The Incorporation of Green Principles into SCF Agreements' (2020) 4 *International Trade Law Review* 260.
[98] Wolfram Groschopf et al, 'Smart Contracts for Sustainable Supply Chain Management: Conceptual Frameworks for Supply Chain Maturity Evaluation and Smart Contract Sustainability Assessment' (2021) *Frontiers in Blockchain* 4.

such as blockchain and the internet of things are allowing for tracking and tracing of products, supplier identity, and reputation along the supply chain.[99] No universal definition of smart contracts exist, but smart contracts are generally arrived at through a decentralised consensus using data inputted by the parties, and is self-executed on the performance of certain contingencies.[100] Similar processes are available to enhance the greenness of shipping transactions and implement climate commitments. A major feature of climate clauses is mutual cooperation and data-sharing. The prevention of greenwashing also relies on heightened transparency and information-sharing.

Smart contracts can employ distributed ledger technology (DLT) and blockchain to provide 'a distributed database organized as an ordered list of blocks in which the submitted blocks are immutable'.[101] This distributed record database can be used to verify and permanently record transactions between participants which ensures traceability and security.[102] Cheng and others identify how smart contracts can be used at different stages for sustainability:[103]

(1) The design stage: 'sustainable design analysis and optimization, information management, thus reducing negative environmental impacts and improving overall project efficiency and performance.'
(2) The construction stage:' formulate new and automatic approaches in contract management, information management and stakeholder management, thus improving the relationship between project partners, cost savings, materials efficiency, and overall health and safety.'
(3) The operation stage: 'providing real-time monitoring and facilities management.'

The same sorts of benefits are prevalent for financiers and banks. Products are already underway for managing the transparency of the environmental outcome of the asset or activities funded by the proceeds of a green bond.[104] Unlike lengthy and manual assessment, reporting and verification, investors can track environmental impact in real time. Although the benefits of blockchain have the potential to significantly aid sustainability, facilitate the trading of carbon credits and emission allowances, as well as improve transactional optimisation overall, there are

[99] Horst Treiblmaier, 'The impact of the blockchain on the supply chain: a theorybased research framework and a call for action' (2018) 23 *Supply Chain Management* 545.
[100] Treiblmaier (ibid) explores the different academic definitions of smart contracts.
[101] Fran Casino, Thomas K Dasaklis and Constantinos Patsakis, 'A systematic literature review of blockchain-based applications: Current status, classification and open issues' (2019) 36 *Telematics Informatics* 55.
[102] Mengyuan Cheng, Heap-Yih Chong and Yongshun Xu, 'Blockchain-smart contracts for sustainable project performance: bibliometric and content analyses' (2023) 2 *Environment, Development, and Sustainability* 1.
[103] ibid.
[104] Hong Kong Monetary Authority, *Project Genesis 2.0: Smart Contract-based Carbon Credits attached to Green Bonds* (October 2022), www.bis.org/publ/othp58.pdf.

still a number of hurdles that exist in respect of implementation and adoption of this technology. Further research is necessary on how to best leverage the benefits of the technology.[105] Similarly, the development of climate clauses for a much wider range of financial transactions is necessary to effectively manage green obligations and ambitions.

IV. Concluding Remarks

From an academic standpoint, climate change and broader environmental sustainability has not yet been the focus of contract governance approaches. Contract governance allows for the identification of 'weak spots' within the scheme of collaboration between law-makers and the actors who express environmental behaviours and preferences.[106] Sustainable Development is already a pervasive principle within public international law – one which needs to more strongly permeate commercial dealings. This book has sought to contribute to a growing cognisance that market transactions *cannot* be viewed as isolated bilateral agreements. The artificial divide between public and private actors serves no purpose when the law must serve a set of unified goals. This book has attempted to contribute a unique perspective on environmental obligations in private contracts which calls for the modernisation of contract law to recognise and implement an urgent climate change mandate.

From a judicial interpretation perspective, this book calls for presiding officers (judges, arbitrators, tribunal members) to constructively interpret contractual obligations through a prism of environmental rights (and other related SDGs). English law already has the tools for the construction of terms where necessitated by the external milieu.[107] A horizontal application of the sustainable development public law mandate between private actors is necessary to provide a set of business norms that may guide decision-making in times of uncertainty. Where contractual rights and obligations have effects on the quality of the surrounding environment (atmospheric, marine or land) – the utmost level of environmental protection should be implicated in such an obligation. It is arguable that other competing interests also deserve consideration in giving effect to commercial obligations, the most obvious being profitability and economic efficiency. However, the urgency of the climate change mandate and the resultant harms posed to humans makes the justification of environmental norms easy to contemplate and apply. More specifically, in a shipping context, this book calls for judicial bodies to give effect to more than mere IMO standard setting, but to uphold its underlying

[105] Mohammed Ali Alqarni et al, 'Use of Blockchain-Based Smart Contracts in Logistics and Supply Chains' (2023) 12 *Electronics* 1340.
[106] Grundmann, Möslein and Riesenhuber (n 1) ch 1.
[107] *Prenn v Simmonds* [1971] 3 All ER 237 (HL) at 241.

long-term vision and goals for decarbonisation. This requires an understanding that international state-bodies can only achieve so much in the context of cross-jurisdictional transactions and agreed conduct in the high seas. The same principles of international environmental law which bind state bodies, should equally apply to all actors along the value chain. Commercial interests and climate risk mitigation are becoming increasingly conflated; the distinction between the two as perpetuated by the status quo needs to be challenged.

BIBLIOGRAPHY

IMO Policies

MO, *Concept of a Sustainable Maritime Transport System* (Symposium on Sustainable Maritime Transportation System, World Maritime Day on 26 September 2013).

UK Policies and Documents

FCA consultation CP21/17: Enhancing climate-related disclosures by asset managers, life insurers and FCA-regulated pension providers (opened 22 June 2021).

FCA consultation CP21/18: Enhancing climate-related disclosures by standard listed companies (opened 22 June 2021).

FCA, Sustainability Disclosure Requirements (SDR) and investment labels (CP22/20), www.fca.org.uk/publication/consultation/cp22-20.pdf.

Green Technical Advisory Group (GTAG) Meeting Notes, Meeting 1: 23 June 2021, www.greenfinanceinstitute.co.uk/wp-content/uploads/2021/08/GTAG-Meeting-1_Public-minutes_23rd-June-2021.pdf.

HM Government, *Green Finance Strategy Transforming Finance for a Greener Future* (July 2019).

HM Treasury, *Budget 2021* (March 2021).

—— *UK Government Green Financing Framework* (June 2021).

EU Policies and Documents

Commission Documents

COM/2018/097 final, Communication From the Commission to The European Parliament, The European Council, The Council, The European Central Bank, The European Economic and Social Committee and The Committee of the Regions Action Plan: Financing Sustainable Growth, 8 March 2018.

COM/2018/353 final, Proposal for a Regulation of the European Parliament and of the Council on the establishment of a framework to facilitate sustainable investment, 24 May 2018.

COM/2019/38 final Proposal for a Regulation of the European Parliament and of the Council amending Regulation (EU) 2015/757 in order to take appropriate account of the global data collection system for ship fuel oil consumption data, 4 February 2019.

COM/2021/550 final, Communication from the Commission to the European Parliament, the Council, the European Economic and Social Committee And The Committee Of The Regions 'Fit for 55': delivering the EU's 2030 Climate Target on the way to climate neutrality, 14 July 2021.

COM/2021/551 final, Proposal for a Directive of The European Parliament and of The Council amending Directive 2003/87/EC establishing a system for greenhouse gas emission allowance trading within the Union, Decision (EU) 2015/1814 concerning the establishment and operation of a market stability reserve for the Union greenhouse gas emission trading scheme and Regulation (EU) 2015/757 EU Proposal, 14 July 2021.

COM/2021/559 final, Proposal for a Regulation of the European Parliament and of the Council on the deployment of alternative fuels infrastructure, and repealing Directive 2014/94/EU, 14 July 2021.
COM/2021/562 final, Proposal for a Regulation of the European Parliament and of the Council on the use of renewable and low-carbon fuels in maritime transport and amending Directive 2009/16/EC, 14 July 2021.
COM/2021/812 final, Proposal for a Regulation of The European Parliament And of the Council on Union guidelines for the development of the trans-European transport network, amending Regulation (EU) 2021/1153 and Regulation (EU) No 913/2010 and repealing Regulation (EU) 1315/2013, 14 December 2021.
COM/2023/3850 final, amending Delegated Regulation (EU) 2021/2139 establishing additional technical screening criteria for determining the conditions under which certain economic activities qualify as contributing substantially to climate change mitigation or climate change adaptation and for determining whether those activities cause no significant harm to any of the other environmental objectives, 27 June 2023.

EU Policy Documents

EIB, *EIB Transport Lending Policy* (13 December 2011), www.eib.org/attachments/strategies/transport_lending_policy_en.pdf.
European Banking Authority, EBA Progress Report on Greenwashing Monitoring and Supervision (31 May 2023) EBA/REP/2023/16.
European Commission, *Motorways of the Sea*, ec.europa.eu/transport/themes/infrastructure/motorways-sea_en.
—— *The TEN-T project*, ec.europa.eu/inea/en/ten-t/ten-t-projects.
European Securities and Markets Authority, 'Sustainable Finance Roadmap 2022–2024', www.esma.europa.eu/sites/default/files/library/esma30-379-1051_sustainable_finance_roadmap.pdf.
Translation of Circular 34/2002 (BA) to all credit institutions in the Federal Republic of Germany.

Authors

Abas AEP et al, 'Techno-Economic Analysis and Environmental Impact of Electric Vehicle' (2019) 7 IEEE 98565–98578.
Adăscăliței, O, 'An Overview on the Implied Obligations in a Contract of Affreightment' (2013) 92 *Procedia – Social and Behavioural Sciences* 7.
Adland, R, Cariou, P and Wolff, FC, 'Does energy efficiency affect ship values in the second-hand market?' (2018) ffhalshs-01706627f, halshs.archives-ouvertes.fr/halshs-01706627/document.
Agostini, F, 'From "Green Bond Principles" to "Green Bond Clauses": Mitigating Greenwashing Through Contract Law' in M Andenas and M Heidemann (eds), *Quo vadis Commercial Contract? Reflections on Sustainability, Ethics and Technology in the Emerging Lawand Practice of Global Commerce* (Springer Nature Switzerland AG, 2023).
Agreements (2020) 26 *International Trade Law and Regulation* 260.
Allen, M, 'DNV supports Hapag-Lloyd's milestone green financing' (Maritime Direct, 4 March 2021), maritime.direct/en/2021/03/04/dnv-supports-hapag-lloyds-milestone-green-financing/?utm_source=rss&utm_medium=rss&utm_campaign=dnv-supports-hapag-lloyds-milestone-green-financing.
Alqarni, MA et al, 'Use of Blockchain-Based Smart Contracts in Logistics and Supply Chains' (2023) 12 *Electronics* 1340.

Amnesty International and the Initiative for Good Governance and Human Rights, *Powering Change or Business as Usual? Forced evictions at industrial cobalt and copper mines in the Democratic Republic of the Congo* (AFR 62/7009/2023) joint report.
Athanassiou, LI, 'Shipping Operators' Obligations and Liabilities Under the International and EU Emission Reduction Strategy' in B Soyer (ed), *Damages Recoveries and Remedies in Shipping Law*, 1st edn (Informa Law, 2023).
Atiyah, PS, 'Form and substance in contract law' in *Essays on Contract* (Oxford University Press, 1988).
Baatz, Y, 'Charterparties' in *Maritime Law* (Informa, 2017).
—— 'Clauses Paramount' in B Soyer and A Tettenborn (eds), *Charterparties: Law, Practice and Emerging Legal Issues* (Informa Law from Routledge, 2017) ch 13.
Bai, J, 'The IMO Polar Code: The Emerging Rules of Arctic Shipping Governance' (2015) 30 *The International Journal of Marine and Coastal Law* 674.
Bai, J and Chircop, A, 'The Regulation of Heavy Fuel Oil in Arctic Shipping: Interests, Measures, and Impacts' in A Chircop et al (eds), *Governance of Arctic Shipping: Rethinking Risk, Human Impacts and Regulation* (Springer Polar, 2020).
Baughen, S, *Contracts for the Carriage of Goods by See and Multimodal Transport: Key issues arising from the Covid-19 Pandemic* UNCTAD/DTL/TLB/INF/2022/1.
Baughen, S, *Shipping Law*, 4th edn (Routledge Cavendish, 2009).
Baughen, S, 'Voyage Charterparties – Payment of Freight' in *Shipping Law*, 8th edn (Routledge, 2023).
Beheshti, R, 'Anticipatory breach of contract and the necessity of adequate assurance under English law and the Uniform Commercial Code' (2018) 2 *Lloyd's Maritime and Commercial Law Quarterly* (0306-2945).
Bekhechi, MA, 'Some observations regarding environmental covenants and conditionalities in World Bank lending activities' in A Bogdandy and R Wolfrum (eds), *Max Planck earbook of United Nations Law* (Kluwer Law International Ltd, 1991).
Benjamin, L and Andreadakis, S, 'Corporate Governance and Climate Change: Smoothing Temporal Dissonance to a Phased Approach' (2019) 40 *Business Law Review* 146.
Bennett, H, Dias, J, Girvin, S, Hofmeyr, S, Kerr, S, MacDonald, A, MacDonald Eggers, P and Sarll, R (eds), *Carver on Charterparties*, 2nd edn (Sweet & Maxwell, 2020).
Bernitz, U, 'Commercial Norms and Soft Law' (2013) 58 *Scandinavian Studies in Law* 29.
BIMCO, 2020 Fuel Oil Quality and Safety Survey (2020).
—— 2020 Fuel Transition Clause for Time Charter Parties (2020).
—— 2020 Marine Fuel Sulphur Content Clause for Time Charter Parties (2020).
—— BARECON (2017).
—— Bunker Terms (2018).
—— DEMOLISHCON (2001).
—— EEXI Transition Clause for Time Charter Parties (2021).
—— Emission Scheme Surcharge Clause for Voyage Charter Parties (2023).
—— Emission Trading Scheme Allowances Clause For Time Charter Parties (2022).
—— ETS – Emission Scheme Freight Clause for Voyage Charter Parties 2023 (2023).
—— ETS – Emission Scheme Transfer of Allowances Clause for Voyage Charter Parties (2023).
—— NEWBUILDCON (2007).
—— SHIPLEASE (2020).
—— Slow Steaming Clause for Time Charter Parties (2011).
—— Slow Steaming Clause for Voyage Charter Parties (2012).
—— Virtual Arrival Clause for Voyage Charter Parties (2013).
Bisogno, M, 'Tax In History: Twenty Years After the Adoption of the Energy Taxation Directive, Is Its Reform in a Greener Sense Just an Illusion?' (2023) 51 *Intertax* 679.
Borg, J and von Knorring, H, 'Inter-organizational collaboration for energy efficiency in the maritime sector: the case of a database project' (2019) 12 *Energy Efficiency* 2201–2213.
Braithwaite, J, 'Standard Form Contracts as Transnational Law: Evidence from the Derivatives Markets Standard Form Contracts as Transnational Law' (2012) 75 *Modern Law Review* 779.
Braucher, J, 'Contract versus contractarianism: The regulatory role of contract law' (1990) 47 *Washington and Lee Law Review* 697.

—— 'Contract versus contractarianism: The regulatory role of contract law' (1990) 47 *Washington and Lee Law Review* 697.
Brown, G, 'Sustainability-linked loans: how "greenwashing" risk is mitigated in documentation' (Allen & Overy LLP Publications, 2023), www.allenovery.com/en-gb/global/news-and-insights/publications/sustainability-linked-loans-how-greenwashing-risk-is-mitigated-in-documentation.
Bruce, G, 'Shipbuilding Company Strategy' in *Shipbuilding Management*, 1st edn (Springer, 2021).
Cafaggi, F and Iamiceli, P, 'Private Regulation and Industrial Organization: Contractual Governance and the Network Approach in S Grundmann, F Möslei and K Riesenhuber (eds), *Contract Governance: Dimensions in Law and Interdisciplinary Research* (Oxford, 2015).
Cafaggi, F and Muir-Watt, H, *Making European Private Law, Governance Design* (Edward Elgar Publishing Ltd, 2008).
Carter, J, 'Suspending Contract Performance for Breach' in *Good Faith and Fault in Contract Law* (Oxford University Press;, 1997).
Case, P, *Environmental risk management and corporate lending: a global perspective* (Woodhead Publishing Limited, 1999).
Casino, F, Dasaklis, TK and Patsakis C, 'A systematic literature review of blockchain-based applications: Current status, classification and open issues' (2019) 36 *Telematics Informatics* 55.
CBI, CBI Climate Bonds Taxonomy (October 2021), www.climatebonds.net.
—— *Shipping* (2020), www.climatebonds.net/standard/shipping.
—— 'Shipping Criteria Document', www.climatebonds.net/standard/shipping.
Cevik, S, 'Waiting for Godot? The case for climate change adaptation and mitigation in small island states (2022) 11 *Journal of Environmental Economics and Policy* 420.
Chambers, S, '"Vague and non-committal": MEPC green targets text comes in for fierce criticism' (Splash247.com, 7 July 2023), splash247.com/vague-and-non-committal-mepc-green-targets-text-comes-in-for-fierce-criticism.
Chemical Industry Digest, 'Maersk Signs Landmark Green Methanol Offtake Agreement' (November 2023), www.proquest.com/docview/2894002691?accountid=14510&forcedol=true&pq-origsite=summon&sourcetype=Magazines.
Cheng, M, Chong, HY and Xu, Y, 'Blockchain-smart contracts for sustainable project performance: bibliometric and content analyses' (2023) 2 *Environment, Development and Sustainability* 1.
Cherednychenko, OO, 'Contract Governance in the EU: Conceptualising the Relationship between Investor Protection Regulation and Private Law' (2015) 21 *European Law Journal* 500.
—— 'EU Financial Regulation, Contract Law and Sustainable Consumer Finance' (2019) University of Groningen Faculty of Law Research Paper Series No 4/2020.
Chester, MV and Horvath, A, 'Environmental assessment of passenger transportation should include infrastructure and supply chains' (2009) 4 *Environmental Research Letters* 024008.
Chircop, A, 'Canada and the Polar Code: Balancing Unilateralism and Multilateralism in the Regulation of Arctic Shipping' (2018) 51 *Revue Belge de Droit International* 380.
Chircop, A et al (eds), *Governance of Arctic Shipping: Rethinking Risk, Human Impacts and Regulation* (Springer Polar, 2020).
Chuah, J, 'Contents' in M Furmsto (ed), *Butterworths Common Law Series: Law of Contract* (LexisNexis, 2015) ch 3.
—— 'International Conventions on Carriage of Goods by Sea' in *Law of international trade: cross-border commercial transactions*, 6th edn (Sweet & Maxwell, 2019) ch 8.
—— 'Legal Aspects of Green Shipping Finance – Insights from the European Investment Bank's Schemes' in P Mukherjee et al (eds), *Maritime Law in Motion. WMU Studies in Maritime Affairs, vol 8* (Springer, 2020).
—— 'Pragmatism and Principle in Supply Chain Governance: Some emerging financing themes' (2020) 26 *International Trade Law Review* 203.
Clegg, J, 'The Ship Mortgage – Introduction' in S Harwood, *Shipping Finance: A Practical Handbook* (Globe and Law Business, 2018).
Climate Case Chart, 'Misleading Advertising', climatecasechart.com/non-us-case-category/misleading-advertising.

Clyde & Co, 'Bunker Quality Claims in 2020 – Issues to Consider' (2 January 2020), www.clydeco.com/en/insights/2020/01/bunker-quality-claims-in-2020-issues-to-consider.

Cofer The Nordic Association of Marine Insurers, The Nordic Marine Insurance Plan of 2013, Version 2023, www.nordicplan.org/The-Plan.

Cooper, G and Brimmer-Landy, J, 'Alternative Financing in the Shipping Industry' (Conveyers, September 2021), www.conyers.com/publications/view/alternative-financing-in-the-shipping-industry.

Cross, ID and Congreve, A, 'Teaching (super) wicked problems: authentic learning about climate change' (2021) 45 *Journal of Geography in Higher Education* 491.

Crowe, J and Agnew, L, 'Legal Obligation and Social Norms' (2020) 41 *Adelaide Law Review* 217.

Curtis, S, Gaunt, I and Cecil, W, *The Law of Shipbuilding Contracts*, 5th edn (Informa Group Ltd, 2020).

Dadush, S, 'Prosocial Contracts: Making Relational Contracts More Relational' (2022) 85 *Law and contemporary problems* (0023-9186) 153.

Dagan, H, 'The Limited Autonomy of Private Law' (2008) 56 *The American Journal of Comparative Law* 809.

Daisy, S, 'Choosing Words Wisely: Climate Agreements Viewed Through a Legal Contractual Framework' (2022) 48 *Columbia Journal of Environmental Law* 41

Davies, M, 'When Was the Last Time You Were Restrained by a Prince? Conservatism and the Development of Maritime Law' in Mukherjee P et al (eds), *Maritime Law in Motion. WMU Studies in Maritime Affairs*, vol 8 (Springer, 2020).

Davies, PS, *JC Smith's The Law of Contract* (Oxford University Press, 2016).

Dedek, H, 'Art 6:102: Implied Terms' in N Jansen and R Zimmermann (eds), *Commentaries on European Contract Laws* (Oxford University Press, 2017).

Deloitte, *ESG in the Shipping sector: The role of ESG in the evaluation of shipping companies* (2021), www2.deloitte.com/content/dam/Deloitte/gr/Documents/consumer-business/gr_esg_in_the_shipping_sector_noexp.pdf.

Diab, K, 'International shipping's new climate plan provokes storm of protest' (Carbon Market Watch, 7 July 2023), carbonmarketwatch.org/2023/07/07/international-shippings-new-climate-plan-provokes-storm-of-protest.

Du Plessis, H, 'Legal Pluralism, uBuntuand the Use of Open Norms in the South African Common Law of Contract' (2019) 22 *Potchefstroom Electronic Law Journal*.

Echebarria Fernández, J, 'Paramount Clause and Codification of International Shipping Law' (2019) 50 *Journal of Maritime Law and Commerce* 45.

EESC, Opinion of the European Economic and Social Committee on 'An industrial strategy for the maritime technology sector' (Own-initiative opinion) (2023/C 100/05).

Eftestøl-Wilhelmsson, E, 'European Sustainable Carriage of Freight – The Role of Contract Law' in *Environmental Liabilities in Ports and Coastal Areas – Focus on Public Authorities and Other Actors* (Åbo Akademi University, Institute of Maritime and Commercial Law, 2011).

—— *European Sustainable Carriage of Goods: The Role of Contract Law*, 1st edn (Routledge, 2015).

Eftestøl-Wilhelmsson, E and Sankari, S, 'Nudging a behavioural change in maritime carriage of goods – the role of information' in J Chuah (ed), *Research Handbook on Maritime Law and Regulation* (Edward Elgar Publishing, 2019) ch 7.

Eftestøl, E and Yliheljo, E, 'International Shipping: Who Levels the Playing Field?' in A Basu Bal et al (eds), *Regulation of Risk Transport, Trade and Environment in Perspective* (Brill | Nijhoff, 2022) 282–314.

EIB, Green Shipping Guarantee Programme, www.eib.org/en/projects/all/20150334.

EIB GSG, 'Environmental and Social Data Sheet' (11 May 2018), www.eib.org/attachments/registers/67288970.pdf.

EMSA, 'The EU Maritime Profile – the maritime cluster in the EU' (2023), www.emsa.europa.eu/eumaritimeprofile/section-2-the-eu-maritime-cluster.html.

Equator Principles, Guidance For EPFIs On Incorporating Environmental And Social Considerations Into Loan Documentation (December 2020), https://equator-principles.com/app/uploads/Loan_documentation_EP_Dec2020.pdf.

European Banking Authority, EBA Progress Report on Greenwashing Monitoring and Supervision (31 May 2023) EBA/REP/2023/16.

European Commission, 'Questions and Answers – Emissions Trading – Putting a Price on carbon' (Press Release 14 July 2021), ec.europa.eu/commission/presscorner/api/files/document/print/en/qanda_21_3542/QANDA_21_3542_EN.pdf.

Evans, M, 'Meeting the challenge of impact investing: how can contracting practices secure social impact without sacrificing performance?' (2013) 3 *Journal of Sustainable Finance & Investment*, 138.

Færden, AW, Saue, H, Otterstrøm, O, 'Insurers prevail in landmark – Nordic Plan CTL judgment' (Wikborg Rein, newsletter 31 May 2023), www.wr.no/en/news/insurers-prevail-in-landmark-nordic-plan-ctl-judgment.

Fedi, L, Faury, O and Gritsenko, D, 'The impact of the Polar Code on risk mitigation in Arctic waters: a "toolbox" for underwriters?' (2018) 45 *Maritime Policy & Management* 478.

Financial Conduct Authority, 'Review of the Sustainability-Linked Loans (SLL) Market' (29 June 2023), www.fca.org.uk/publication/correspondence/sll-letter-june-2023.pdf.

Foxton, D et al, *Scrutton on Charterparties and Bills of Lading*, 24th edn (Sweet & Maxwell, 2021).

French, L, 'Introduction' in S Harwood (ed), *Shipping Finance*, 3rd edn (Euromoney, 2006).

Frey, BS and Cueni, R, 'Moral Hazard and Herd Behaviour in the Financial Crisis' in S Grundmann, F Möslein and K Riesenhuber (eds) *Contract Governance: Dimensions in Law and Interdisciplinary Research* (Oxford University Press, 2015).

Frydlinger, D et al, 'Welcome to the Contracting Paradox' in *Contracting in the New Economy* (Palgrave Macmillan, 2021).

G20 Green Finance Study Group, G20 Green Finance Synthesis Report (5 September 2016).

Ganguly, G, Setzer, J and Heyvaert, V, 'If at First you don't Succeed: Suing Corporations for Climate Change' (2018) 38 *Oxford Journal of Legal Studies* 841.

Gard, 'Gard signs Poseidon Principles for Marine Insurance' (12 January 2022), www.gard.no/web/news/article?p_document_id=32803930.

Geels, FW et al, 'The Socio-Technical Dynamics of Low-Carbon Transitions' (2017) 1 *Joule* 463.

GEF-UNDP-IMO GloMEEP Project and members of the GIA, 'Just In Time Arrival Guide – Barriers and Potential Solutions', greenvoyage2050.imo.org/wp-content/uploads/2021/01/GIA-just-in-time-hires.pdf.

Generation Foundation, *Stranded Carbon Assets: Why and How Carbon Risks Should Be Incorporated in Investment Analysis* (2013), www.genfound.org/media/1374/pdf-generation-foundation-stranded-carbon-assets-v1.pdf.

Getting to Zero Coalition, 'Appendix 1: Guidelines on Competition Law' (2022), www.globalmaritime-forum.org/content/2022/08/Guidelines-on-Competition-Law.pdf.

—— 'Call to Action for Shipping Decarbonisation' (2021), www.globalmaritimeforum.org/content/2021/09/Call-to-Action-for-Shipping-Decarbonization.pdf.

—— 'Industry Roadmap' (2019), www.globalmaritimeforum.org/content/2019/09/Getting-to-Zero-Coalition_Industry-Roadmap.pdf.

—— 'Role of Companies in Getting to Zero Coalition' (2022), www.globalmaritimeforum.org/content/2022/08/Getting-to-Zero-Coalition-role-of-companies-July-2022.pdf.

Giannakoulis, F, 'Overview of ship finance' in M Kavussanos and ID Visvikis, *The International Handbook of Shipping Finance* (Palgrave Macmillan, 2016) 71–94.

Gibbs-Kneller, D, 'Corporate Strategy on Climate Risk in the Courtroom: Not Worth Powder in Shot' (2023) 25 *Sage Journals* 326.

Giesen, I, de Jong, E and Overheul, M, 'How Dutch Law responds to Risks' in M Dyson (ed), *Regulating Risks through Private Law* (Intersentia, 2018) ch 7.

Gilbert, P et al, 'Assessment of full life-cycle air emissions of alternative shipping fuels' (2018) 172 *Journal of Cleaner Production* 855.

Gilson, R, Sabel, C and Scott, R, 'Contract, Uncertainty, and Innovation' in S Grundmann, F Möslein and K Riesenhuber (eds), *Contract Governance: Dimensions in Law and Interdisciplinary Research* (Oxford University Press, 2015).

Global Maritime Forum, 'Getting to Zero Coalition', www.globalmaritimeforum.org/getting-to-zero-coalition.

Goerlandt, F and Pelot, R, 'An Exploratory Application of the International Risk Governance Council's Risk Governance Framework to Shipping Risks in the Canadian Arctic' in A Chircop et al (eds), *Governance of Arctic Shipping: Rethinking Risk, Human Impacts and Regulation* (Springer Polar, 2020).

Green, A, 'Drake Insurance Plc v. Provident Insurance Plc' (British Insurance Law Association), bila.org.uk/wp-content/uploads/old/4ff4163e752fd1.62779926.pdf.

Green Marine, Certification Policy: Green Marine Environmental Program (2021), green-marine.org/certification/ accessed 2 September 2021.

Green Technical Advisory Group (GTAG) Meeting Notes, Meeting 1: 23 June 2021, www.greenfinanceinstitute.co.uk/wp-content/uploads/2021/08/GTAG-Meeting-1_Public-minutes_23rd-June-2021.pdf.

Groschopf, W et al, 'Smart Contracts for Sustainable Supply Chain Management: Conceptual Frameworks for Supply Chain Maturity Evaluation and Smart Contract Sustainability Assessment' (2021) *Frontiers in Blockchain.*

Grundmann, S, Möslein, F and Riesenhuber, K, 'Contract Governance: Dimensions in Law and Interdisciplinary Research' in *Contract Governance: Dimensions in Law and Interdisciplinary Research* (Oxford University Press, 2015).

Hackmann, B, 'Analysis of the Governance Architecture to Regulate GHG Emissions from International Shipping' (2012) 12 *International Environmental Agreements: Politics, Law and Economics* 85.

Hardin, R, 'The New Social Contract: An Inquiry into Modern Contractual Relations, Ian R. Macneil' (1982) 93 *Ethics* 168.

Hassellöv, IM et al, 'Effects of seawater scrubbing on a microplanktonic community during a summer-bloom in the Baltic Sea' (2021) 291 *Environmental Pollution* 118251.

Hebbar, AA et al, 'The IMO Regulatory Framework for Arctic Shipping: Risk Perspectives and Goal-Based Pathways' in A Chircop et al (eds), *Governance of Arctic Shipping: Rethinking Risk, Human Impacts and Regulation* (Springer Polar, 2021).

Hellenic Shipping News, 'Contaminated bunkers: "the Houston problem"' (26 September 2018), www.hellenicshippingnews.com/contaminated-bunkers-the-houston-problem-2.

Henderson, N, 'Keeping a hand on the tiller: the Poseidon Principles for Marine Insurance' (23 May 2023) *Maritime Risk International* (© Maritime Insights & Intelligence Limited).

Herberg, M, 'Private authority, global governance, and the law' in G Winter (ed), *Multilevel Governance of Global Environmental Change: Perspectives from Science, Sociology and the Law* (Cambridge University Press, 2006) 149–78.

Hill, J, *Environmental, Social, and Governance (ESG) Investing* (Academic Press, 2020).

HM Treasury, 'Chancellor sets out ambition for future of UK financial services' (9 November 2020), www.gov.uk/government/news/chancellor-sets-out-ambition-for-future-of-uk-financial-services.

—— 'Mobilising green investment: 2023 green finance strategy' (updated 11 April 2023), www.gov.uk/government/publications/green-finance-strategy/mobilising-green-investment-2023-green-finance-strategy-annexes.

—— 'New independent group to help tackle "greenwashing"' (9 June 2021), www.gov.uk/government/news/new-independent-group-to-help-tackle-greenwashing.

Hong Kong Monetary Authority, Project Genesis 2.0: Smart Contract-based Carbon Credits attached to Green Bonds (October 2022), www.bis.org/publ/othp58.pdf.

Huntington, H et al, 'Effects of Arctic commercial shipping on environments and communities: context, governance, priorities' (2023) 118 *Transportation Research Part D: Transport and Environment* 103731.

ICMA, *Green Bond Principles: Voluntary Process Guidelines for Issuing Green Bonds* (June 2021), www.icmagroup.org/assets/documents/Sustainable-finance/2022-updates/Green-Bond-Principles-June-2022-060623.pdf.

—— Guidance Handbook (January 2022), www.icmagroup.org/assets/GreenSocialSustainabilityDb/The-GBP-Guidance-Handbook-January-2022.pdf.

—— Handbook: Harmonised Framework for Impact Reporting (June 2022), www.icmagroup.org/assets/documents/Sustainable-finance/2022-updates/Harmonised-Framework-for-Impact-Reporting-Green-Bonds_June-2022-280622.pdf.

InfluenceMap, 'Corporate Capture of the IMO: How shipping lobbies to stay out of the Paris Agreement on climate' (October 2017), influencemap.org/site/data/000/302/Shipping_Report_October_2017.pdf.

INTERTANKO, '2020 Bunker Clauses INTERTANKO Bunker Compliance Clause for Time Charterparties' (2018), www.intertanko.com/images/topics-issues/documentary/2018/Bunkers_Compliance_web_10_12.pdf.

—— 'Ballast Water Management Clauses' (2012), www.intertanko.com/info-centre/model-clauses-library/templateclausearticle/ballast-water-management-clauses.

ISO, ISO standards, www.iso.org/standards.html.

ITC, 'What is Green Finance?', www.intracen.org/What-is-green-finance.

Jacquet, J and Jamieson, D, 'Soft but Significant Power in the Paris Agreement' (2016) 6 *Nature Climate Change* 643, 645.

Jakobsen, IU and Johansen, E, 'Efforts of the Arctic Council to Protect Sensitive Arctic High Sea Areas from the Impact of Shipping' (2016) *Scandinavian Institute of Maritime Law* MarIus number 471.

Johnson, H and Andersson, K, 'Barriers to energy efficiency in shipping' (2016) 15 *World Maritime University Journal of Maritime Affairs* 79.

Joseph, L et al, 'A techno-economic environmental cost model for Arctic shipping' (2021) 151 *Transportation Research Part A* 28.

Kahn, Z, 'It's time we faced the fact that banks and shipping don't mix' (*TradeWinds*, 20 September 2019), www.tradewindsnews.com/opinion/it-s-time-we-faced-the-fact-that-banks-and-shipping-don-t-mix/2-1-670495.

Karim, MS, *Prevention of Pollution of the Marine Environment from Vessels: The Potential and Limits of the International Maritime Organisation* (Springer, 2015).

Kavussanos, MG and Tsouknidis, DA, 'Green Shipping Finance: Existing Initiatives and the Road Ahead' in B-W Ko and D-W Song (eds), *New Maritime Business. WMU Studies in Maritime Affairs* Vol 10 (Springer, 2021).

Keating, B, Quazi, A, Kriz, A, Coltman, T et al, 'In pursuit of a sustainable supply chain: insights from Westpac Banking Corporation' (2008) 13 *Supply Chain Management* 182.

Kingston, C, 'Marine Insurance in Britain and America, 1720–1844: A Comparative Institutional Analysis' (2007) 67 *The Journal of Economic History* 379.

Kwok, R, 'Arctic sea ice thickness, volume, and multiyear ice coverage: losses and coupled variability (1958–2018)' (2018) 13 *Environmental Research Letters* 105005.

Lasserre, F et al, 'Polar seaways? Maritime transport in the Arctic: An analysis of shipowners' intentions' (2016) 57 *Journal of Transport Geography* 105.

Lerch, A, Zadkovich, L and Floyd, E, 'International Uniformity and Maritime Liens over Cargo: An Ocean Not Easily Navigated', (2020) 44 *Tulane Maritime Law Journal* (1048-3748) 251.

LexisNexis® Practical Guidance, 'Contract interpretation – conditions, warranties and intermediate terms', Practice Note: Commercial, Dispute Resolution (LexisNexis, UK, 2020).

LexisPSL 'Offtake contracts – key issues for project finance lenders' (Practice Note, Lexis+ UK, 2023).

Lipson, JC, 'Promising Justice: Contract (As) Social Responsibility' (2019) *Wisconsin Law Review* 1109.

Lister, J, Poulsen, RT and Ponte, S, 'Orchestrating Transnational Environmental Governance in Maritime Shipping' (2015) 34 *Global Environmental Change* 185.

Llewellyn, K, 'Some Realism about Realism-Responding to Dean Pound' (1931) 44 *Harvard Law Review* 1222.

Lloyds, Lloyd's Standard Form Of Salvage Agreement (2020).

Lloyd's List, Lloyd's Maritime Law Newsletter (London 7/14 October 2014).

LMA, Model Provisions for Sustainability-Linked Loans (May 2023).

—— Sustainable Lending Glossary (August 2021) https://www.lsta.org/content/sustainable-lending-glossary-of-terms/ accessed 10 August 2023.

Loan Market Association, 'Green Loan Principles' (February 2023), www.lma.eu.com/application/files/8916/9755/2443/Green_Loan_Principles_23_February_2023.pdf
—— 'Social Loan Principles' (February 2023), https://www.lma.eu.com/application/files/3716/7715/0338/Social_Loan_Principles_23_February_2023.pdf.
—— 'Sustainability-Linked Loan Principles' (February 2023), www.lma.eu.com/application/files/9216/9755/2878/Sustainability_Linked_Loan_Principles_23_February_2023_v.2.pdf.
Lundgren, K, 'Arctic Oil drilling plans revived in Norway as priorities change' (Bloomberg, May 2023) www.bloomberg.com/news/articles/2023-05-03/arctic-oil-drilling-plans-revived-in-norway-as-priorities-change?leadSource=uverify%20wall.
Mace-Kokota, D and Hosek-Ugolini, D, 'The Financing of Second-Hand Vessels' in S Harwood, *Shipping Finance: A Practical Handbook* (Globe and Law Business, 2018).
Mainstreaming Climate Action within Financial Institutions Emerging Practices, www.mainstreamingclimate.org/wp-content/uploads/2017/03/fi_mainstreaming_epp_en-1.pdf.
Marcelline, T et al, 'Impact of Green Construction Procurement on Achieving Sustainable Economic Growth Influencing Green Logistic Services Management and Innovation Practices' (2022) 9 *Frontiers in Environmental Sciences* 815928, 12.
McKendrick, E, *Contract Law*, 13th edn (Macmillan Law Masters, 2019).
Messner, S, 'Future arctic shipping, black carbon emissions, and climate change' in AKY Ng, J Monios and C Jiang (eds), *Maritime Transport and Regional Sustainability* (Elsevier Inc, 2020).
Micklitz, HW, 'Herd Behaviour and Third Party Impact as a Legal Concept: On Tulips, Pyramid Games, and Asset-backed Securities' in S Grundmann, F Möslein and K Riesenhuber (eds), *Contract Governance: Dimensions in Law and Interdisciplinary Research* (Oxford University Press, 2015.
Mission Possible Partnership, *The Next Wave Green Corridors: A special report for the Getting to Zero Coalition*, www.globalmaritimeforum.org/content/2021/11/The-Next-Wave-Green-Corridors.pdf.
Mitchell, C, 'Vanishing Contract Law' in *Vanishing Contract Law: Common Law in the Age of Contracts* (Law in Context, Cambridge University Press, 2022).
Mitkidis, KP, 'Using Private Contracts for Climate Change Mitigation' (2018) 2 *Groningen Journal of International* Law 54.
—— 'Sustainability Clauses in International Supply Chain Contracts: Regulation, Enforceability and Effects of Ethical Requirements' (2014) 1 *Nordic Journal of Commercial Law* 3.
Monitor Deloitte, *EU Shipping Competitiveness Study: International benchmark analysis*, (study commissioned by the European Community Shipowners' Associations, February 2017).
Morgan, J, 'Against regulation through contract law' in *Contract Law Minimalism: A Formalist Restatement of Commercial Contract Law* (Law in Context, Cambridge University Press, 2013) 114–57.
Mukherjee, PK and Liu, H, 'Legal Regime of Marine Insurance in Arctic Shipping: Safety and Environmental Implications' in LP Hildebrand et al (eds), *Sustainable Shipping in a Changing Arctic* (Springer, 2018) 192.
Nagle, MK, 'Tracing the Origins of Fairly Traceable: The Black Hole of Private Climate Change Litigation' (2010) 85 *Tulsa Law Review* 477.
Nikaki, T, 'The fundamental duties of the carrier under the Rotterdam Rules' (2008) 14 *Journal of International Maritime Law* 512.
Noordewier, TG, John, G and Nevin, JR, 'Performance Outcomes of Purchasing Arrangements in Industrial Buyer-Vendor Relationships' (1990) 54 *Journal of Marketing* 80.
Norton Rose Fulbright, 'What do you need to know about the new LMA drafting for sustainability-linked loans?' (May 2023), www.nortonrosefulbright.com/en/knowledge/publications/15ccc56b/what-do-you-need-to-know-about-the-new-lma-drafting-for-sustainability-linked-loans.
Nuttal, P, 'Small islands with a strong voice: Why Pacific Islands are playing a critical role in the current shipping decarbonization debate', Article No 46 [UNCTAD Transport and Trade Facilitation Newsletter No 85 – First Quarter 2020].
OECD, Environmental and Social Due Diligence (The 'Common Approaches', OECD/LEGAL/0393.
—— *Green Bonds: Mobilising the debt capital markets for a low-carbon transition* (Bloomberg Philanthropies, 2015).

—— OECD Guidelines for Multinational Enterprises on Responsible Business Conduct, (OECD Publishing, Paris, 2023), doi.org/10.1787/81f92357-en.
—— Recommendation of the Council on Sustainable Lending Practices and Officially Supported Export Credits, OECD/LEGAL/0442.
—— Recommendation of the Council on Bribery and Officially Supported Export Credits, OECD/LEGAL/0447.
OECD et al, *Green Bonds: Country Experiences, Barriers And Options* (in support of the G20 Green Finance Study Group, 2016), unepinquiry.org/wp-content/uploads/2016/09/6_Green_Bonds_Country_Experiences_Barriers_and_Options.pdf.
Opportunity Green, 'Shipping ETS – Charterer Liability' (Analysis carried out for Transport & Environment, December 2021), www.transportenvironment.org/wp-content/uploads/2022/01/OG-Analysis-ETS-Responsible-Entity_FINAL.pdf.
Ørsted, 'Ørsted and Maersk sign landmark green fuels agreement, as Ørsted enters the US Power-to-X market' (22 March 2022), orsted.com/en/media/newsroom/news/2022/03/20220310491311.
Osborne, D, Bowtle, G and Buss, C, *The Law of Ship Mortgages* (Informa law from Routledge, Milton Park, 2017) 221.
Ostrom E, 'A Long Polycentric Journey' (2010) 13 *Annual Review of Political Science* 1.
Ostrom, E and Cox, M, 'Moving beyond panaceas: A multi-tiered diagnostic approach for social-ecological analysis' (2010) 37 *Environmental Conservation* 451.
Ostrom, E, Janssen, M and Anderies J, 'Going beyond Panaceas' (2007) 104 *Proceedings of the National Academy of Sciences of the United States of America* 15176.
Otto, S and Scholl, T, 'Legal Treatment of Ship Finance Loans: Analysis of the Ship Loan Contract' in O Schinas, C Grau and M Johns (eds), *HSBA Handbook on Ship Finance* (Springer, 2015).
Ozdel, M, 'Enforcement of arbitration clauses in bills of lading: where are we now?' (2016) 33 *Journal of international arbitration* (0255-8106) 151.
Papapostolou, NC, Pouliasis, PK and Kyriakou, I, 'Herd behavior in the drybulk market: An empirical analysis of the decision to invest in new and retire existing fleet capacity' (2017) 104 *Transportation Research Part E: Logistics and Transportation Review* 36.
Pargendler, M, 'The Role of the State in Contract Law: The Common-Civil Law Divide' (2018) 43 *Yale Journal of International Law* 143 (NYU Law and Economics Research Paper No 17-01).
Parker, B, 'The Poseidon Principles and a "green transformation" of shipping' (*Seatrade Maritime Review*, 20 June 2019), www.seatrade-maritime.com/americas/poseidon-principles-and-green-transformation-shipping.
Paterson, S and Zakrzewski, R (eds), *McKnight, Paterson and Zakrzewski on The Law of International Finance*, 2nd edn (Oxford University Press, 2017).
Pinto-Bazurco, JF, *Brief #4: The Precautionary Principle* (International Institute for Sustainable Development, October 2020).
Pizzetti, M, Gatti, L and Seele, P, 'Firms Talk, Suppliers Walk: Analyzing the Locus of Greenwashing in the Blame Game and Introducing "Vicarious Greenwashing"' (2021) 170 *Journal of Business Ethics* 21.
Plomaritou E, 'A Review of Shipowner's & Charterer's Obligations in Types of Charter' (2014) 4 *Journal of Shipping and Ocean Engineering* 307.
Plomaritou, E and Papadopoulos, A, *Shipbroking and Chartering Practice*, 8th edn (Informa Law, 2017).
Południak-Gierz, K, 'Eco-Reasonableness. Possibilities of Incorporating Green Principles Into General Private Law Clauses' in M Andenas and M Heidemann (eds), *Quo Vadis Commercial Contract?* vol 1 (LCF Studies in Commercial and Financial Law, Springer, 2023) 107–27.
Poncibò, C, 'The Contractualisation of Environmental Sustainability' (2016) 12 *European Review of Contract Law* 339.
Poseidon Principles, www.poseidonprinciples.org/#about.
—— Standard Covenant Clause (January 2020), www.poseidonprinciples.org/finance/wp-content/uploads/2020/01/PP-Standard-Covenant-Clause.17.1.20.pdf.
—— *Technical Guidance* (Version 4.2, April 2023), www.poseidonprinciples.org/finance/wp-content/uploads/2019/07/Poseidon_Principles.pdf.

Poseidon Principles for Marine Insurance (PPMI), www.poseidonprinciples.org/insurance/#about.
—— PPMI Annual Disclosure Report 2022 (January 2023), www.poseidonprinciples.org/insurance/wp-content/uploads/2023/01/Poseidon-Principles-for-Marine-Insurance-Annual-Disclosure-Report-2022.pdf.
—— Standard Covenant Clause (updated October 2023), www.poseidonprinciples.org/insurance/wp-content/uploads/2023/10/PPMI-Standard-clause_October-23_v2.pdf.
—— Technical Guidance (Version 1.1, May 2023), www.poseidonprinciples.org/insurance/wp-content/uploads/2021/12/Poseidon-Principles-for-Marine-Insurance-Technical-Guidance.pdf.
Principale, S, 'Corporate Governance and Strategic Management' in *Fostering Sustainability in Corporate Governance* (SIDREA Series in Accounting and Business Administration, Springer, 2023) 1–17.
Psaraftis, HN, 'Shipping decarbonization in the aftermath of MEPC 76' (2021) 1 *Cleaner Logistics and Supply Chain* 100008.
Psaraftis, HN and Kontovas, CA, 'Influence and transparency at the IMO: the name of the game' (2020) 22 *Maritime Economics and Logistics* 151.
Psaraftis, HN, Zis, T, and Lagouvardou, S, 'A comparative evaluation of market-based measures for shipping decarbonization' (2021) 2 *Maritime Transport Research* 100019.
Psarros, GA, *Energy Efficiency Clauses in Charter Party Agreements: Legal and Economic Perspectives and Their Application to Ocean Grain Transport* (Springer, ProQuest, 2016).
Qin, B and Shogren, JF, 'Social norms, regulation, and environmental risk' (2015) 129 *Economic Letters* 22.
Rahman, A and Karim, M, 'Green Shipbuilding and Recycling: Issues and Challenges' (2015) 6 *International Journal of Environmental Science and Development* 838.
Rainey, S, '"Interrupting the lifeblood": The Owner's remedies for non-payment of hire after Spar Shipping' in B Soyer and A Tettenborn, *Charterparties: law, practice, and emerging legal issues*, 1st edn (Informa Law, 2018).
Rebelo P, 'BIMCO's Carbon Intensity Indicator Clause (CII) for time charters: towards a new era of climate drafting' (2022) 28(4) Journal of International Maritime Law 240.
—— 'Green Finance for a Sustainable Maritime Transport System: Developing a Universal Vernacular for Green Shipping' (2020) 34 (1) Australian and New Zealand Maritime Law Journal 15.
—— 'Legal Tools for Overcoming Perceived Risks' in Green Shipping in Regulation of Risk (Leiden, The Netherlands: Brill | Nijhoff 2022).
—— 'Sustainable Supply Chain Finance: The Incorporation of Green Principles into SCF Agreements (2020) 26 *International Trade Law and Regulation* 260.
Rebelo, P and Rebelo, X, 'Rights-Based Climate Change Litigation Against Private Actors' in K Bouwer et al (eds), *Climate Litigation and Justice in Africa* (Bristol University Press, 2024) 187–219.
Rehmatulla, N and Smith, T, 'The impact of split incentives on energy efficiency technology investments in maritime transport' (2020) 147 *Energy Policy* 111721.
Reich, N, *General Principles of EU Civil Law*, 1st edn (Intersentia, 2014).
Roe, M 'Maritime Governance and Policy-Making: The Need for Process Rather than Form' (2013) 29 *The Asian Journal of Shipping and Logistics* 167.
Rogers, A, Chuah, J and Dockray, M, *Cases and Materials on the Carriage of Goods by Sea* (Taylor & Francis Group, 2019).
Rosaeg, E, 'The Aviation and Shipping Exemptions in the Paris Agreement on Climate Change' (2021) 27 *Journal of International Maritime Law* 55.
Rowan, S, *Remedies For Breach Of Contract: A Comparative Analysis Of The Protection Of Performance* (Oxford University Press, 2012).
Ruggie, J, 'Protect, Respect & Remedy: A Framework for Business and Human Rights' (2008) 3 *Innovations: Technology, Governance, Globalization* 189.
Schinas, O and Kewitsch, S, 'Loans and Risk Management Considerations' in O Schinas, C Grau and M Johns (eds), *HSBA Handbook on Ship Finance* (Springer, 2015).
Schwarzschild, M, 'Keeping it private' (2006) 25 *University of Queensland Law Journal* 215.
Sea Cargo Charter, www.seacargocharter.org.

—— 'How did we get here', www.seacargocharter.org/about/how-did-we-get-there.
—— 'Publication of the first Sea Cargo Charter Annual Disclosure Report' (15 June 2022), www.seacargocharter.org/wp-content/uploads/2022/06/Sea-Cargo-Charter-Annual-Disclosure-Report-2022.pdf.
—— Sea Cargo Charter Technical Guidance Version 2.2 (August 2022), www.seacargocharter.org/wp-content/uploads/2020/10/SCC-Brochure-V09.pdf.
—— *The Sea Cargo Charter Association Membership Agreement* (updated 10 March 2022), www.seacargocharter.org/wp-content/uploads/2021/01/The-Sea-Cargo-Charter-Association-%E2%80%93-Membership-Agreement.pdf.
Setzer, J and Byrnes, R, Global trends in climate change litigation: 2023 snapshot (Grantham Research Institute on Climate Change and the Environment and Centre for Climate Change Economics and Policy, London School of Economics and Political Science, 2023).
Share Action, 'Changing Course: Bank Financing of the Shipping Industry' (May 2019 Investor Briefing).
Simon Kucher & Partners, *Global Sustainability Study 2021*, www.simon-kucher.com/sites/default/files/studies/Simon-Kucher_Global_Sustainability_Study_2021.pdf.
Slaughter and May, *A Borrower's Guide To Sustainability-Linked Loan Terms* (The Association of Corporate Treasurers, August 2023).
—— *The ACT Borrower's Guide to the LMA Facilities Agreement for Leveraged Transactions* (The Association of Corporate Treasurers, October 2008).
—— *The ACT Borrower's Guide to LMA Loan Documentation for Investment Grade Borrowers* (The Association of Corporate Treasurers, April 2013).
Smith, KT, Smith, M and Wang, K, 'Does brand management of corporate reputation translate into higher market value?' (2010) 18 *Journal of Strategic Marketing* 201.
Smith, SA, 'The Normativity of Private Law' (2011) 31 *Oxford Journal of Legal Studies* 215.
Spoullos, K, 'Key Clauses of a Shipping Loan Agreement' in MG Kavussanos and ID Visvikis (eds), *The International Handbook of Shipping Finance: Theory and Practice* (Palgrave Macmillan, 2016).
State of New York Law Revision Committee Report, Hearing on the Uniform Commercial Code (1954).
Stulgis V et al, *Hidden treasure: Financial models for retrofits* (The Carbon War Room / UCL Energy Institute, 2014).
Sustainable Shipping Initiative, *Save As You Sail*, www.ssi2040.org/news/call-for-ship-owners-to-join-pilot-of-innovative-save-as-you-sail-technology-financing-model.
Taghizadeh-Hesary, F and Yoshino, N, 'Sustainable Solutions for Green Financing and Investment in Renewable Energy Projects' (2020) 13 *Energies* 788.
Tasić Z, 'The prevention principle and the extension of time clauses in English law shipbuilding contracts' (2020) 59 *Poredbeno Pomorsko Pravo* 121.
Taylor I, 'MEPC 80: IMO "Detached" From The "Urgent Reality" Of Climate Change, Says Environmental NGO' (Bunkerspot, 6 July 2023), www.bunkerspot.com/global/59454-mepc-80-imo-detached-from-the-urgent-reality-of-climate-change-says-environmental-ngo.
TCDF, *Final Report on the Recommendations of the Task Force on Climate-related Financial Disclosures* (15 June 2017), www.fsb-tcfd.org/wp-content/uploads/2017/06/FINAL-2017-TCFD-Report-11052018.pdf.
TCLP, *Aiden's Clause – Essential notes and guidance* (5 November 2021), chancerylaneproject.org/climate-clauses/fuel-reporting-clause-for-shipping-charterparties-new.
—— *Aiden's Clause – Fuel Reporting Clause for Shipping Charterparties* (5 November 2021).
—— *Ariel's Clause – Incentivising Fuel Efficiency Investments In Time Chartered Vessels* (8 November 2021).
—— *Bradleigh's Clause – Maximising the Laden Ratio of Vessels in Shipping Charterparties* (8 November 2021).
—— *Climate Clauses: Transport*, chancerylaneproject.org/climate-action-pathways/transport.
—— *Eddie's Recital* (updated 29 September 2021).
—— *Harrison's Clause – 'Green Loan Starter Pack'* (updated 19 October 2022).

—— *Laith & Irsa's Clause – Essential notes and guidance* (2022).
—— *Laith & Irsa's Clause – Interest Ratchet Clause for Carbon Saving* (14 October 2022)
—— *Levi's Clause – Green Fuel Requirement and Termination for Greener Carrier or Shipper (Maritime)* (15 August 2022).
—— *Mary's Clause – JCT Energy Efficiency and Environmental Obligations* (updated 30 November 2022).
—— *Matilda's Annex – The Net Zero Standard for Suppliers* (10 November 2021).
—— *Nozomi's Clause – Net Zero Convertible Loan Note* (updated 1 November 2021).
—— *Otto's Clause – Otto's Clause* (updated 3 November 2021).
—— *Otto's Clause – Essential Notes and Guidance* (2021).
—— *Robyn's Questionnaire – Subcontractor/Supplier Self-Assessment Climate Questionnaire (Construction)* (29 September 2021).
—— *Willow's Clause – Construction Materials: Procurement* (updated 20 October 2023).
Tettenborn, A, 'Contracting by numbers: the different characteristics of the main shipbuilding contracts' in B Soyer and A Tettenborn (eds), *Ship Building, Sale and Finance* (Informa Law, 2015).
Teubner, G, 'Coincidentia Oppositorum: Hybrid Networks Beyond Contract and Organisation' in M Amstutz and G Teubner (eds), *Networks. Legal Issues of Multilateral Cooperation* (Hart Publishing, 2009).
The Chancery Lane Project, Green Loan 'Starter Pack' (19 October 2022), chancerylaneproject.org/climate-clauses/green-loan-starter-pack.
The Law Commission, *Privity Of Contract: Contracts For The Benefit Of Third Parties Item 1 of the Sixth Programme of Law Reform* (LAW COM No 242, July 1996).
The Swedish Club, 'The Risk of Ship Arrest for unpaid Bunkers arising from the OW Bunker group collapse' (Member Alert, 23 February 2016), www.swedishclub.com/news/member-alert/ow-bunker-2?query=RISK+OF+SHIP+ARREST.
Theocharis, D et al, 'Arctic shipping: A systematic literature review of comparative studies' (2018) 69 *Journal of Transport Geography* 112.
Todd, P, 'NYPE 2015: Wholesale Reform or an Invitation to Cherry-Pick?' (2016) *Lloyd's Maritime & Commercial Law Quarterly* 306.
Torrens, DL, 'Marine Insurance for the Northern Sea Route: Pilot Study' INSROP Working Paper IV.3.3, No 1-1994, 133.
Treasury Select Committee, 'Committee launch inquiry into decarbonisation of the UK economy', old.parliament.uk/business/committees/committees-a-z/commons-select/treasury-committee/news-parliament-2017/decarbonisation-uk-economy-launch-17-19.
—— 'Decarbonisation of the UK economy and Green Finance terms of reference', old.parliament.uk/business/committees/committees-a-z/commons-select/treasury-committee/inquiries1/parliament-2017/decarbonisation-of-uk-economy-and-green-finance-17-19.
Tsimplis, M, 'Environmental norms in maritime contracts' in Environmental Norms in Maritime Law (Edward Elgar Publishing, 2021) 220.
Treiblmaier, H, 'The impact of the blockchain on the supply chain: a theory-based research framework and a call for action' (2018) 23 *Supply Chain Management* 545.
UK Defence Club, 'Bunker contamination claims in the US Gulf' (August 2018), www.ukdefence.com/fileadmin/uploads/uk-defence/Documents/Soundings/2018/1111-UKDC-Soundings-Bunker-contamination-claims-v7.pdf.
UK Department of Transport, 'The Clean Maritime Demonstration Competition' (2019) apply-for-innovation-funding.service.gov.uk/competition/888/overview?_ga=2.61428395.627485050.1699718893-646967318.1698333333.
UK Export Finance, 'Guidance: What UKEF considers in your application form' (updated 26 November 2021), www.gov.uk/government/publications/processes-and-factors-in-uk-export-finance-consideration-of-applicants/what-ukef-considers-in-your-application-form.
UK Government, 'Shipbuilding Credit Guarantee Scheme', www.gov.uk/guidance/shipbuilding-credit-guarantee-scheme#eligibility-criteria.

Ulfbeck, V, Hansen, O and Andhov, A, 'Contractual enforcement of CSR clauses and the protection of weak parties in the chain' in V Ulfbeck, A Andhov and K Mitkidis, *Law and Responsible Supply Chain Management* (Routledge, 2019) 46–52.

UMAS, *Navigating Decarbonisation: An approach to evaluate shipping's risks and opportunities associated with climate change mitigation policy* (2017), rmi.org/wp-content/uploads/2017/03/Shipping_Navigating_Decarbonization_Report_2017.pdf.

UN Global Compact Office and Business for Social Responsibility, *Supply Chain Sustainability: A Practical Guide for Continuous Improvement* (2010).

UN Global Compact, *Scaling SDG Finance for the Sustainable Development Goals: Foreign Direct Investment, financial intermediation and public-private partnerships* (Report 2019), www.unglobalcompact.org/library/5721.

UN Human Rights Office of the High Commissioner, *Guiding Principles on Business and Human Rights: Implementing the United Nations "Protect, Respect and Remedy" Framework* (2011), www.ohchr.org/sites/default/files/Documents/Publications/GuidingPrinciplesBusinessHR_EN.pdf.

UNCTAD, *Charterparties*, Report from the Secretariat of the UNCTAD (United Nations 1974).

UNFCCC, 'Summary of Global Climate Action at COP 28' (2023), unfccc.int/sites/default/files/resource/Summary_GCA_COP28.pdf.

United Nations Environment Programme, The Emissions Gap Report (2018).

Vakili, S et al, 'A Conceptual Transdisciplinary Framework to Overcome Energy Efficiency Barriers in Ship Operation Cycles to Meet IMO's Initial Green House Gas Strategy Goals: Case Study for an Iranian Shipping Company' (2022) 15 *Energies* 2098.

—— 'Energy-related clean and green framework for shipbuilding community towards zero-emissions: A strategic analysis from concept to case study' (2022) 46 *Int J Energy Res* 20624.

—— 'The road to zero emission shipbuilding Industry: A systematic and transdisciplinary approach to modern multi-energy shipyards' (2023) X *Energy Conversion and Management* 100365.

Vandenbergh, M and Gilligan, J, 'The Governance Challenge' in *In Beyond Politics: The Private Governance Response to Climate Change* (Business and Public Policy, Cambridge University Press, 2017) 64–116.

Vandenbergh, MP, 'Private Environmental Governance' (2013) 99 *Cornell Law Review* 129.

Varellas, J, 'Contract law, securitization and the pre-crisis transformation of banking' (2016) in B Lomfeld, A Somma and P Zumbansen (eds), *Reshaping Markets: Economic Governance, the Global Financial Crisis and Liberal Utopia* (Cambridge University Press, 2016).

Vasani, A, *Shipbuilding disputes: influence of industry norms on law and contracts* (Unpublished Doctoral thesis, City, University of London, 2018) 146.

Vranken, JBM, 'Methodology of legal doctrinal research: A comment on Westerman' in M Van Hoecke (ed), *Methodologies of legal research: Which kind of method for what kind of discipline?* (Hart, 2011).

Walenta, J, The Limits to Private-sector Climate Change Action: The Geographies of Corporate Climate Governance (2018) 94 *Economic Geography* 461.

Walker, K and Wan, F, 'The harm of symbolic actions and green-washing: Corporate actions and communications on environmental performance and their financial implications' (2012) 109 *Journal of Business Ethics* 227.

Watson Farley & Williams, *The Sustainability Imperative – Part 2* (2023) 11, www.wfw.com/reports/the-sustainability-imperative-part-2-report/?intIaContactId=nXBhr5xyjz7BTXN2noycig%3d%3d&intExternalSystemId=1.

Watt R, 'The fantasy of carbon offsetting' (2021) 30 *Environmental Politics* 1069.

Westerman, P, 'Open or autonomous? The debate on legal methodology as a reflection of the debate on law' (2011) in M Van Hoecke (ed), *Methodologies of legal research: Which kind of method for what kind of discipline?* (Hart, 2011).

Wettestad, J and Gulbrandsen, LH, 'On the Process of Including Shipping in EU Emissions Trading: Multi-Level Reinforcement Revisited' (2022) 10 *Politics and Governance* 246.

Wilson, JF, 'Implied obligations in a contract of affreightment' in *Carriage of Goods by Sea*, 7th edn (Pearson Education Ltd, 2010).

Winans, KS et al, 'The history and current applications of the circular economy concept' (2017) 68 *Renewable and Sustainable Energy Reviews* 825.

Xu, Y et al, 'The Impacts of Environmental Risks on Bank Loan Covenants and the Cost of Bank Loans: an Australian Case Study and the Implications for China' in *Proceedings of the 2018 International Conference on E-Business and Applications* (ICEBA, 2018).

Young, HP, 'The Evolution of Social Norms' (2015) 7 *Annual Review of Economics* 359.

Zografakis, H, 'The third pillar: a contractual architecture for maritime decarbonisation' (Gard Insight, 2021), www.gard.no/web/updates/content/32513672/the-third-pillar-a-contractual-architecture-for-maritime-decarbonisation.

Zumbansen, P, 'Law, Economics, and More: The Genius of Contract Governance: Comment on T. Kameda, K. Inukai, T. Wisdom, and W. Toyokawa, "The Concept of Herd Behavior: Its Psychological and Neural Underpinnings"' in S Grundmann, F Möslein and K Riesenhuber (eds), *Contract Governance: Dimensions in Law and Interdisciplinary Research* (Oxford University Press, 2015).

INDEX

www.ingramcontent.com/pod-product-compliance
Ingram Content Group UK Ltd.
Pitfield, Milton Keynes, MK11 3LW, UK
UKHW020814290926
15470UKWH00003B/1147

9 781509 967926